Remembering Partition
Violence, Nationalism and History in India

Through an investigation of the violence that marked the partition of British India in 1947, this book analyses questions of history and memory, the nationalisation of populations and their pasts, and the ways in which violent events are remembered (or forgotten) in order to ensure the unity of the collective subject – community or nation. Stressing the continuous entanglement of 'event' and 'interpretation', the author emphasises both the enormity of the violence of 1947 and its shifting meanings and contours. The book provides a sustained critique of the procedures of history-writing and nationalist myth-making on the question of violence, and examines how local forms of sociality are constituted and reconstituted by the experience and representation of violent events. It concludes with a comment on the different kinds of political community that may still be imagined even in the wake of Partition and events like it.

GYANENDRA PANDEY is Professor of Anthropology and History at Johns Hopkins University. He was a founder member of the Subaltern Studies group and is the author of many publications including *The Construction of Communalism in Colonial North India* (1990) and, as editor, *Hindus and Others: the Question of Identity in India Today* (1993).

Contemporary South Asia 7

Editorial board
Jan Breman, G.P. Hawthorn, Ayesha Jalal, Patricia Jeffery, Atul Kohli

Contemporary South Asia has been established to publish books on the politics, society and culture of South Asia since 1947. In accessible and comprehensive studies, authors who are already engaged in researching specific aspects of South Asian society explore a wide variety of broad-ranging and topical themes. The series will be of interest to anyone who is concerned with the study of South Asia and with the legacy of its colonial past.

Remembering Partition

Violence, Nationalism and History in India

Gyanendra Pandey

Johns Hopkins University

CAMBRIDGE
UNIVERSITY PRESS

PUBLISHED BY THE PRESS SYNDICATE OF THE UNIVERSITY OF CAMBRIDGE
The Pitt Building, Trumpington Street, Cambridge, United Kingdom

CAMBRIDGE UNIVERSITY PRESS
The Edinburgh Building, Cambridge CB2 2RU, UK
40 West 20th Street, New York, NY 10011-4211, USA
477 Williamstown Road, Oakleigh, VIC 3207, Australia
Ruiz de Alarcón 13, 28014 Madrid, Spain
Dock House, The Waterfront, Cape Town 8001, South Africa

http://www.cambridge.org

© Gyanendra Pandey 2001

First published 2001

Printed in the United Kingdom at the University Press, Cambridge

Typeface Plantin 10/12 pt.   *System* LATEX 2$_\varepsilon$ [TB]

A catalogue record for this book is available from the British Library.

Library of Congress Cataloguing in Publication Data
Pandey, Gyanendra.
  Remembering Partition: violence, nationalism and history in India /
Gyanendra Pandey.
    p.   cm.
  Includes bibliographical references and index.
  ISBN 0 521 80759 X – ISBN 0 521 00250 8 (pbk)
  1. India – History – Partition, 1947. 2. Nationalism – India.
3. Communalism – India. I. Title.
  DS480.842 .P363   2001
  954.03′5 – dc21   2001025600

ISBN 0 521 80759 X hardback
ISBN 0 521 00250 8 paperback

To Nishad (once more)
and
to Ruby – for being there.

Contents

Acknowledgements   page x
List of abbreviations   xiii

1 By way of introduction   1

2 The three partitions of 1947   21

3 Historians' history   45

4 The evidence of the historian   67

5 Folding the local into the national:
   Garhmukhteshwar, November 1946   92

6 Folding the national into the local: Delhi 1947–1948   121

7 Disciplining difference   152

8 Constructing community   175

Select bibliography   206
Index   212

Acknowledgements

I owe a deep debt of gratitude to colleagues, friends and the many other people who have helped in innumerable ways in the making of this book.

First, to those who raised many of the questions considered in this book as they watched Colombo 1983, Delhi 1984 and Ayodhya 1992, with tears in their eyes.

Secondly, to those who lived through 1947 and have given so generously of their time and energy in talking to me, and to many other researchers, about it. For invaluable assistance and kindness in aiding my search for oral accounts of Partition, I especially thank Sant Harnam Singh Gandhi, our eighty-year-old 'newspaper man' who introduced me to the vibrant community of Kahuta Sikhs settled in Bhogal; and Mr S. S. Dhanoa in Chandigarh for his personal recollections and for taking me to Gharuan and facilitating my numerous conversations there and in Mohali. Also, for their camaraderie and exceptional support: Anuradha Kapur, Mrs M. N. Kapur and Syeda Saiyidain Hameed in Delhi; Anil Joshi in Chandigarh; Mohammad Aslam in Allahabad; and David Page, Viqar Ahmed and Sayeed Hasan Khan saheb in London.

Thirdly, to the academic and research institutions that made this work possible. To the librarians and staff of the National Archives of India and the Nehru Memorial Museum and Library, New Delhi; the UP State Archives, Lucknow; the Haryana Secretariat Library, Chandigarh; the India Office Library, London; the Indian Institute Library, Oxford; the Southampton University Library; and the Regenstein Library, University of Chicago. To colleagues, students and staff in the history department, University of Delhi, where I taught from 1986 to 1998; and in the anthropology and history departments at the Johns Hopkins University where I am currently teaching. Also to the history departments, University of Chicago and University of Michigan at Ann Arbor; the politics department, La Trobe University, Melbourne; and the South Asia Research Unit, School of Social Sciences, Curtin University of Technology, Perth, which have invited me periodically over the last decade and given me the benefit of responses and questions in numerous seminars and classes: and especially to Bernard Cohn, Nicholas Dirks, Peter Reeves, John McGuire and Robin Jeffrey for making these visits possible. To Peter Reeves at Curtin, and Ravinder Kumar, then Director of the Nehru Memorial Museum and Library and Chairman of the Indian Council of Historical Research, I am also grateful for grants that enabled me to carry out a good part of the oral history research that underlies many of the questions raised in this study. Also to Dr Mohinder Singh in Delhi, and to Dr Paramjit Singh Judge and Professor Harish Puri in Amritsar, for help in research on Punjab and in translation from the Punjabi.

Then, there are intellectual debts that are less easily pinpointed. My colleagues in the Subaltern Studies editorial group have seen this book grow from very small beginnings. Shahid Amin, Gautam Bhadra, Dipesh Chakrabarty, Partha Chatterjee and David Hardiman are intellectual comrades of three decades' standing. As on earlier occasions, they have been subjected to multiple versions of the various parts of this book and have given freely of their advice and criticism. My heartfelt thanks to them. Also to a more recent set of comrades, critics and friends – Talal Asad, Veena Das, Nicholas Dirks, M. Ali Khan, Ruby Lal, Deepak Mehta, Gabrielle Spiegel – who read the manuscript, insisted on further reflection and clarification and saved me from many errors.

Javeed Alam, Alok Bhalla, Sudhir Chandra, Mamadou Diouf, Peter Geschiere, Anjan Ghosh, Nayanjot Lahiri, Chowdhury Mohammad Naim, David Page and Peter Reeves have been important interlocutors. Sudhir, David and Peter (Reeves), Barbara and Tom Metcalf and two anonymous readers of Cambridge University Press took on the additional burden of reading through and commenting on the entire manuscript. Christopher Bayly did the same and made several helpful suggestions regarding publishers. My deep gratitude to all of them.

Qadri Ismail, Pradeep Jeganathan, Vijay Prashad, Ram Narayan Singh Rawat, Nilanjan Sarkar and Ravikant Sharma have helped with many questions over the years. The last three, along with Shahina Arslan, Pragati Mahapatra and Sanjay Sharma also provided valuable research assistance. Again, I could not have done without the technical assistance given by Reena Tandon, Deepak Verma and Liz Torres in the final stages of preparation of the manuscript. To them all, and to Marigold Acland and Sara Adhikari, my vigilant editors at Cambridge University Press, I am greatly indebted for their part in the making of this book.

Parts of chapters 6 and 8 have appeared in a different form, in papers I published in *Economic and Political Weekly* (9 August and 6 September 1997); part of chapter 7 in *Comparative Studies in Society and History*, 41, 4 (1999); and parts of chapters 3 and 8 in my Deuskar lectures, published by the Centre for Studies in Social Sciences, Calcutta, under the title *Memory, History and the Question of Violence*, in 1999. I am indebted to the editors and publishers of all these for permission to use this material once again in this book.

Finally, and briefly, a few essential personal acknowledgements: to Bhupen Khakhar who so readily and generously allowed the use of his untitled painting for the cover; to my parents, my sisters and their significant others, for their interest and support; and to Nishad, and to Ruby, for all they have meant to me.

Abbreviations

IOR   India Office Library and Records, now part of the British Library, London.
NAI   National Archives of India, New Delhi.
NMML   Nehru Memorial Museum and Library, New Delhi.

1 By way of introduction

Questions of violence, nationhood and history

This book focuses on a moment of rupture and genocidal violence, marking the termination of one regime and the inauguration of two new ones. It seeks to investigate what that moment of rupture, and the violent founding of new states claiming the legitimacy of nation-statehood, tells us about the procedures of nationhood, history and particular forms of sociality. More specifically, it attempts to analyse the moves that are made to nationalise populations, culture and history in the context of this claim to nation-statehood and the establishment of the nation-state. In the process, it reflects also on how the local comes to be folded into the national in new kinds of ways – and the national into the local – at critical junctures of this kind.

The moment of rupture that I am concerned with has been described as a partition, although it is more adequately designated the Partition and Independence of the Indian subcontinent in 1947.[1] As a partition, it shares something with the political outcomes that accompanied decolonisation in a number of other countries in the twentieth century: Ireland, Cyprus, Palestine, Korea, Vietnam and so on. Orientalist constructions, and ruling-class interests and calculations, through the era of formal colonialism and that of the Cold War, contributed fundamentally to all of these. In addition, it may be that the liberal state has never been comfortable with plural societies where communities of various kinds continue to have a robust presence in public life alongside the post-Smithian economic individual: perhaps that is why the combination of such mixed societies with the demands of colonialism – and of decolonisation – has often been lethal.[2] Yet the specifics of different partitions, and of the

---

[1] I discuss this question of nomenclature more fully in the next section.
[2] Note, however, that the process of migration and 'mixing' was greatly increased – in the New World as well as the Old – with the growth of world capitalism and colonialism. Also, most African territories suffered a process of Balkanisation with the end of colonial rule: here, the retention of the unity of a colonial territory – as in the case of Nigeria or Kenya – was the exception rather than the rule. (I am grateful to Mahmood Mamdani for stressing this last point to me.)

discourses surrounding each of these, require careful attention if we are to make more than a very superficial statement regarding the procedures of nationhood, history and local forms of sociality.

The next chapter outlines the particularities of the Indian partition of 1947. A few of its striking features may, however, be noted immediately. The singularly violent character of the event stands out. Several hundred thousand people were estimated to have been killed; unaccountable numbers raped and converted; and many millions uprooted and transformed into official 'refugees' as a result of what have been called the partition riots.[3] Notably, it was not a once-subject, now about-to-be-liberated population that was pitted against departing colonial rulers in these riots, but Hindus, Muslims and Sikhs ranged against one another – even if, as Indian nationalists were quick to point out, a century and more of colonial politics had something to do with this denouement.

The partition of the subcontinent, and the establishment of the two independent states of India and Pakistan, occurred with remarkable suddenness and in a manner that belied most anticipations of the immediate future. There was a very short time – a mere seven years – between the first formal articulation of the demand for a separate state for the Muslims of the subcontinent and the establishment of Pakistan. The boundaries between the two new states were not officially known until two days *after* they had formally become independent. And, astonishingly, few had foreseen that this division of territories and power would be accompanied by anything like the bloodbath that actually eventuated.

The character of the violence – the killing, rape and arson – that followed was also unprecedented, both in scale and method, as we shall see below. Surprisingly, again, what all this has left behind is an extraordinary love–hate relationship: on the one hand, deep resentment and animosity, and the most militant of nationalisms – Pakistani against Indian, and Indian against Pakistani, now backed up by nuclear weapons; on the other, a considerable sense of nostalgia, frequently articulated in the view that this was a partition of siblings that should never have occurred – or, again, in the call to imagine what a united Indian–Pakistani cricket team might have achieved!

---

[3] '... Two events, the Calcutta killing [of August 1946], and the setting up of Mr. Nehru's first Government... [in September]... signalled the start of a sixteen-months' civil war; a conflict in which the estimated total death-roll, about 500,000 people, was roughly comparable to that of the entire British Commonwealth during the six years of World War II', wrote Ian Stephens, in his *Pakistan* (New York, 1963), p. 107. I discuss this and other estimates more fully in ch. 4.

From the 1940s to today, a great deal has been written about 'the partition of India' and the violence that – as we are told – 'accompanied' it.[4] Given the specificities of subcontinental history, however, the ideological function of 'partition' historiography has been very different, say, from that of Holocaust literature. The investigation has not, in this instance, been primarily concerned with apportioning guilt on the opposing sides. In my view, its chief object has not even been to consolidate different ethnic/national identities in South Asia, though there is certainly an element of this, especially in right-wing writings. It has been aimed rather at justifying, or eliding, what is seen in the main as being an illegitimate outbreak of violence, and at making a case about how this goes against the fundamentals of Indian (or Pakistani) tradition and history: how it is, to that extent, not *our* history at all. The context has made for a somewhat unusual account of violence and of the relation between violence and community – one that is not readily available in literature on other events of this sort. This provides the opportunity for an unusual exploration of the representation and language of violence.

It is one of the central arguments of this book that – in India and Pakistan, as elsewhere – violence and community constitute one another,

---

[4] See, for example, B. R. Ambedkar, *Pakistan, or the Partition of India* (Bombay, 1946); I. H. Qureshi, *The Muslim Community of the Indo-Pakistan Subcontinent, 610–1947: a Brief Historical Analysis* (The Hague, 1962); Satya M. Rai, *Partition of the Punjab* (London, 1965); Chowdhury Muhammad Ali, *The Emergence of Pakistan* (New York, 1967); Khalid bin Sayeed, *Pakistan: the Formative Phase, 1857–1948* (2nd edn, London, 1968); H. V. Hodson, *The Great Divide: Britain, India and Pakistan* (London, 1969); K. K. Aziz, *The Historical Background of Pakistan, 1857–1947: an Annotated Digest of Source Material* (Karachi, 1970); C. H. Philips and M. D. Wainright, eds., *The Partition of India. Policies and Perspectives, 1935–1947* (London, 1970). More recent works include David Page, *Prelude to Partition. Indian Muslims and the Imperial System of Control, 1920–1932* (Delhi, 1982); Ayesha Jalal, *The Sole Spokesman: Jinnah, the Muslim League and the Demand for Pakistan* (Cambridge, 1985); Anita Inder Singh, *The Origins of the Partition of India* (Delhi, 1987); David Gilmartin, *Empire and Islam: Punjab and the Making of Pakistan* (London, 1988); Ian Talbot, *Provincial Politics and the Pakistan Movement: the Growth of the Muslim League in North-West and North-East India, 1937–47* (Karachi, 1988); Farzana Shaikh, *Community and Consensus in Islam: Muslim Representation in Colonial India, 1860–1947* (Cambridge, 1989); Asim Roy, 'The High Politics of India's Partition', review article, *Modern Asian Studies*, 24, 2 (1990); Sarah F. D. Ansari, *Sufi Saints and State Power: the Pirs of Sind, 1843–1947* (Cambridge, 1992); Mushirul Hasan, ed., *India's Partition. Process, Strategy and Mobilization* (Delhi, 1993); Joya Chatterji, *Bengal Divided. Hindu Communalism and Partition, 1932–1947* (Cambridge, 1995); and Tazeen M. Murshid, *The Sacred and the Secular: Bengal Muslim Discourses, 1871–1977* (Calcutta, 1995). Some of the more recent of these studies are rich in their accounts of the social and economic context of political mobilisation on the ground: yet they remain concerned primarily with the question of political/constitutional outcomes at the national level. An exception is Suranjan Das, *Communal Riots in Bengal, 1905–1947* (Delhi, 1991), which investigates the details of the crowds and the context of violent outbreaks in Bengal from 1905 to 1947.

but also that they do so in many different ways. It is my argument that in the history of any society, narratives of particular experiences of violence go towards making the 'community' – and the subject of history. The discipline of history still proceeds on the assumption of a fixed subject – society, nation, state, community, locality, whatever it might be – and a largely pre-determined course of human development or transformation. However, the agent and locus of history is hardly pre-designated. Rather, accounts of history, of shared experiences in the past, serve to constitute these, their extent and their boundaries.

In the instance at hand, I shall suggest, violence too becomes a language that constitutes – and reconstitutes – the subject. It is a language shared by Pakistanis and Indians (as by other nations and communities): one that cuts right across those two legal entities, and that, in so doing, cuts across not only the 'historical' but also the 'non-historical' subject.

'Official' history and its other

Official claims and denials – often supported by wider nationalist claims and denials – lie at the heart of what one scholar has described as the 'aestheticising impulse' of the nation-state.[5] These claims and denials provide the setting for a large part of the investigation in the following pages. In this respect, the present study is animated by two apparently contradictory questions. First: how does 'history' work to produce the 'truth' – say, the truth of the violence of 1947 – and to deny its force at the same time; to name an event – say, the 'partition' – and yet deny its eventfulness?

Secondly: how can we write the moment of struggle back into history? I have in mind here Gramsci's critique of Croce's histories of Europe and of Italy.[6] What I wish to derive from this, however, is not merely the historian's exclusion of the *time*, but of the very *moment* (or aspect) of struggle. I am arguing that even when history is written as a history of struggle, it tends to exclude the dimensions of force, uncertainty, domination and disdain, loss and confusion, by normalising the struggle, evacuating

---

[5] E. Valentine Daniel, *Charred Lullabies. Chapters in an Anthropography of Violence* (Princeton, N.J., 1996), p. 154. Shahid Amin describes the same process when he speaks of the drive to produce the 'uncluttered national past'; 'Writing Alternative Histories: a View from South Asia' (unpublished paper).

[6] 'Is it possible to write (conceive of) a history of Europe in the nineteenth century without an organic treatment of the French Revolution and the Napoleonic Wars? And is it possible to write a history of Italy in modern times without a treatment of the struggles of the Risorgimento? . . . Is it fortuitous, or is it for a tendentious motive, that Croce begins his narratives from 1815 and 1871? That is, that he excludes the moment of struggle . . .'; Antonio Gramsci, 'Notes on Italian History', in Quintin Hoare and Geoffrey Nowell Smith, eds., *Selections from the Prison Notebooks* (London, 1971), pp. 118–19.

it of its messiness and making it part of a narrative of assured advance towards specified (or specifiable) resolutions. I wish to ask how one might write a history of an event involving genocidal violence, following all the rules and procedures of disciplinary, 'objective' history, and yet convey something of the impossibility of the enterprise.

It is this latter concern that has led me, throughout this book, to provide a closely detailed account of what the contemporary and later records tell us about what transpired in and around 1947. Part of my purpose is to underscore the point about how different the history of Partition appears from different perspectives. More crucially, however, I hope that what sometimes looks like a blitz of quotations, and the simply overwhelming character of many of the reports, will help to convey something of the enormity of the event.

The gravity, uncertainty and jagged edges of the violence that was Partition has, over the last few years, received the attention of a growing number of scholars and become the subject of some debate.[7] This marks an important advance in the process of rethinking the history of Partition, of nationhood and of national politics in the subcontinent. It has been enabled in part by the passage of time, for it is now more than fifty years since the end of British colonial rule and the establishment of the new nation-states of India and Pakistan (the latter splitting up into Pakistan

---

[7] Ritu Menon and Kamla Bhasin, 'Recovery, Rupture, Resistance. Indian State and Abduction of Women During Partition', and Urvashi Butalia, 'Community, State and Gender: on Women's Agency During Partition', *Economic and Political Weekly*, 'Review of Women's Studies' (24 April 1993); Gyanendra Pandey, 'The Prose of Otherness', in *Subaltern Studies*, VIII (Delhi, 1994); Nighat Said Khan, *et al*, eds., *Locating the Self. Perspectives on Women and Multiple Identities* (Lahore, 1994); Mushirul Hasan, ed., *India Partitioned. The Other Face of Freedom*, 2 vols. (Delhi, 1995); Veena Das, *Critical Events: an Anthropological Perspective on Contemporary India* (Delhi, 1995); Gyanendra Pandey, 'Community and Violence', *Economic and Political Weekly* (9 August 1997) and 'Partition and Independence in Delhi, 1947–48', *ibid.* (6 September 1997); Shail Mayaram, *Resisting Regimes. Myth, Memory and the Shaping of a Muslim Identity* (Delhi, 1997); Urvashi Butalia, *The Other Side of Silence: Voices From the Partition of India* (Delhi, 1998); Ritu Menon and Kamla Bhasin, *Borders and Boundaries: Women in India's Partition* (Delhi, 1998); Ayesha Jalal, 'Nation, Reason and Religion. Punjab's Role in the Partition of India', *Economic and Political Weekly* (8 August 1998); *Seminar*, 'Partition' number (August 1994); and *South Asia*, 18, Special Issue on 'North India: Partition and Independence' (1995). For literature, Alok Bhalla, *Stories on the Partition of India*, 3 vols. (New Delhi, 1994); and Muhammad Umar Memon, ed., *An Epic Unwritten. The Penguin Book of Partition Stories* (Delhi, 1998). For some reflection of the animated debate, see Jason Francisco, 'In the Heat of the Fratricide: the Literature of India's Partition Burning Freshly', review article, *Annual of Urdu Studies* (1997), pp. 227–57; Ayesha Jalal, 'Secularists, Subalterns and the Stigma of "Communalism": Partition Historiography Revisited', *Indian Economic and Social History Review*, 33, 1 (January–March 1996), pp. 93–104; 'Remembering Partition', a dialogue between Javeed Alam and Suresh Sharma, *Seminar*, 461 (January 1998); David Gilmartin, 'Partition, Pakistan, and South Asian History: in Search of a Narrative', *Journal of Asian Studies*, 57, 4 (November 1998).

and Bangladesh in 1971). But the passage of time does not, of its own accord, unconsciously produce a set of new perspectives and questions. On the contrary, a set of far-reaching political and historiographical considerations lies behind the renewed thinking in this area.

In India the 1970s already saw the beginning of the end of the Nehruvian vision of a modern, secular, welfare state – leading a developing society to socialism and secularism through the gentle arts of persuasion, education and democracy. It was clear that the privileged and propertied classes were not going to be readily persuaded of the need to share the fruits of development; that the oppressed and downtrodden, but now enfranchised, were threatening more and more to take matters into their own hands and to meet upper-class violence with violence; in a word, that secularism, democracy, welfare and the right to continued rule (and re-election) were not so easily secured. One result of this was a new consolidation of a right-wing, religious-community based politics – which was in the eyes of many of India's secular intellectuals not unlike the politics of the Pakistan movement of the 1940s. This was one reason to return to a study of the history of those earlier times.

The 1980s saw the emergence of exceptionally strong Hindu (and Sikh) right-wing movements – very much in line with the rise of fundamentalist and absolutist forces all over the world. Above all, that decade saw the naked parade – and astounding acceptance – of horrifying forms of violence in our own 'civilised' suburbs. The massacre of Sikhs on the streets of Delhi and other cities and towns of northern India in 1984 was only the most widely reported example of this:[8] and a shocked radical intelligentsia greeted this, as it greeted other instances of the kind, with the cry that it was 'like Partition all over again'. The spate of new studies of Partition and Partition-like violence is one consequence of this entry of barbarity – or should one say 'history'? – into our secure middle-class lives.

There is a historiographical imperative at work here too. For too long the violence of 1947 (and, likewise, I wish to suggest, of 1984, 1992–3 and so on) has been treated as someone else's history – or even, *not* history at all. I shall have more to say about this in the chapters that follow. But it is necessary, at this stage, to state the broad outlines of a problem that, especially after the 1980s and 1990s, Indian historiography simply has to face. Stated baldly, there is a wide chasm between the historians' apprehension of 1947 and what we might call a more popular, survivors' account of it – between history and memory, as it were. Nationalism

---

[8] There was, in addition, the massacre of Muslims in a spate of so-called 'riots' (better described as pogroms) throughout the 1980s, which peaked in 1992–3. More recently there has been a series of attacks against Christians scattered in isolated communities. All this, apart from the continuing attacks against Dalits (earlier, and sometimes still, called 'Untouchables') and women of all castes and classes.

and nationalist historiography, I shall argue, have made an all too facile separation between 'Partition' and 'violence'. This is one that survivors seldom make: for in their view, Partition *was* violence, a cataclysm, a world (or worlds) torn apart. Whereas historians' history seems to suggest that what Partition amounted to was, in the main, a new constitutional/ political arrangement, which did not deeply affect the central structures of Indian society or the broad contours of its history, the survivors' account would appear to say that it amounted to a sundering, a whole new beginning and, thus, a radical reconstitution of community and history.

How shall we write this other history? To attempt an answer to this question, it will help to step back and consider the history of 'history'.

The history of 'history'

Once upon a time, as we all know, China, India and the Arab lands had civilisation and Europe did not. But that was long ago. Then came a time when Europe claimed 'civilisation' from the rest of the world: and things have never been the same since. Ever after that, Europe is supposed to have possessed many attributes that the rest of the world never had.

Europe had 'civilisation' – which meant capitalism, the industrial revolution and a new military and political power; the rest of the world did not.

Europe had 'feudalism' – now seen as a prerequisite for development to 'civilisation'; the rest of the world (with the possible exception of Japan) did not.

Europe had 'history' – the sign of self-consciousness; the rest of the world (with the possible exception of China) had only memories, myths and legends. Today, by a curious turn of events, and in the shadow of the Holocaust, that 'extremest of extreme' events as it has been characterised,[9] Europe (now, of course, including – even being led by – the United States) has memories; the rest of the world apparently has only history.

What does all this indicate about the larger question of civilisation and the place in it of nationhood and history? First, that the plot has never been simple; and, secondly, that it has rarely seemed to work quite as it was planned. The current debate on the vexed question of memory and history, in fact, tells us more than a little about the relationship between nation and history, and history and state power. Let us stay with it for a moment.

---

[9] See Dan Diner, 'Historical Understanding and Counterrationality: the Judenrat as Epistemological Vantage', in Saul Friedlander, ed., *Probing the Limits of Representation. Nazism and the 'Final Solution'* (Cambridge, Mass., 1992), p. 128.

The debate has, of course, served to put both concepts, memory and history, under the sign of a question mark. To understand something historically, a historian of Holocaust memories and histories tells us, 'is to be aware of its complexity, . . . to see it from multiple perspectives, to accept the ambiguities, including moral ambiguities, of protagonists, motives and behavior'.[10] Even with qualifications, this is in line with the old, established view of the objectivity and scientificity of history. By contrast, Novick goes on to say 'collective memory simplifies; sees events from a single, committed perspective; is impatient with ambiguities of any kind; reduces events to mythic archetypes': typically, it would be understood as expressing some eternal or essential truth about the group whose memory it is. For collective memory is, as the same author puts it in a paraphrase of Halbwachs, 'in crucial senses ahistorical, and even anti-historical'.[11]

Yet it is necessary to stress that the relationship between memory and history has always been an unstable one – more so perhaps than historians have acknowledged. Today, according to Pierre Nora, the leading French scholar of the subject, history has 'conquered' memory. 'Modern memory is, above all, archival'; and 'We speak so much of memory because there is so little of it left.' Nora speaks, indeed, of a new 'historical memory', based upon increasingly institutionalised sites of memory.[12]

There is some force in the argument. There is no such thing as 'spontaneous memory' now – if there ever was. However, the historian perhaps proclaims the triumph of 'history' – and with it of historical societies, the modern nation-state, democratisation and mass culture – too quickly. The ascendancy of capital and its concomitant forms of modern statehood and culture has not been quite so absolute. The face-to-face communities of peasant society may be in decline, although they have hardly disappeared everywhere. But other communities of shared, inherited cultures – bonded by common memories and 'irrational' rituals, themselves contested and variously interpreted – continue to have a real existence even in the most advanced capitalist societies, living in an often tense relationship with the omnipresent state, yet autonomous and even resistant to its rules in many ways.

---

[10] Peter Novick, *The Holocaust in American Life* (Boston and New York, 1999), pp. 3–4. Cf. Gabrielle Spiegel's characterisation of history as 'a discourse drafted from other discourses'; 'Memory and History: Liturgical Time and Historical Time' (unpublished paper).

[11] Novick, *Holocaust*, pp. 3–4. See also Maurice Halbwachs, *The Collective Memory* (New York, 1980), pp. 78–87 and *passim*.

[12] Pierre Nora, 'Between Memory and History: Les Lieux de Memoire', *Representations*, 26 (Spring 1989), pp. 7, 8, 13, 21; cf. his *Rethinking the French Past. Realms of Memory. Volume I: Conflicts and Divisions*, English edn (New York, 1996), 'General Introduction', *passim*.

If, as Halbwachs suggests, there are as many memories as there are groups (or communities),[13] then it is not to be wondered at that collective memories continue to have a vigorous existence – even if they do so in altered, and more historicised forms. Where the ruling classes and their instruments have failed to establish their hegemony through persuasion, or where historiography has failed (or refused) to address serious moments of dislocation in the history of particular societies in all their complexity and painfulness – which I believe has often been the case – it has perhaps given an additional lease of life to 'memory'. Furthermore, the triumph of the nation-state, the long arm of the major publishing houses and modern media and the homogenisation of culture, have not only produced more history: they have also produced more archetypal myths.

Indeed, with the new reach of nationalism and of the modern state, and the new sites of memory that they have established, it is not fantastic to suggest that history itself appears in the form of memory – a national memory as it were. In other words, the world today is populated not only by the 'historical memory' of various groups, dependent upon museums, flags and publicly funded celebrations. It is also flooded with the mythical histories of nations and states, histories that are themselves an institutional 'site of memory', locked in a circular, and somewhat parasitical, relationship with other, more obvious *lieux de mémoire*. This hybrid 'memory-history', whose presence Nora again notes, is surely one of the distinguishing marks of our age. Pronouncements about the worldwide progress – or decline – of 'history' do not, however, sit very well with this complexity, one that challenges the stark separation that is sometimes made between 'memory' and 'history'.

On the question of disciplinary history, one might note, parenthetically, that a slippage frequently occurs between the conception of history as an objective statement of all that is significant in the human past, and as a statement of purposive movement. For Hegel, the leading philosopher of the practice, the state is the condition of history: for the state symbolises self-consciousness and overall purpose, and thus makes for the possibility of progress – and regress. 'We must hold that the narration of history *and* historical deeds and events appear at the same time . . . It is the State which first presents subject matter that is not only appropriate for the prose of history but creates it together with itself.'

Only in the State with the consciousness of laws are there clear actions, and is the consciousness of them clear enough to make the keeping of records possible and desired. It is striking to everyone who becomes acquainted with the treasures of Indian literature that that country, so rich in spiritual products of greatest

---

[13] Cf. Nora, *Rethinking the French Past*, p. 3.

profundity, has no history. In this it contrasts strikingly with China, which possesses such an excellent history going back to the oldest times.[14]

Within the academy, however, history is sometimes presented as a scientific description of anything in the human past; at other times, as an account of anticipated advance, of known directionality and accumulating progress. In order to avoid any confusion in this regard, I want to underscore Hegel's proposition about the latter aspect of the discipline, and to say that even when history becomes rather more reflexive – and adds historiography, the history of history, to its concerns – it continues to work within a context defined by modern (or shall we say, nineteenth-century) science and state. It continues to be based on the belief in the past as past, in the privilege of large and centralised socio-political formations, in objective facts and predictable futures: and it relies heavily on the power of those beliefs.

It is my argument that the writing of history – in each and every case – is implicated in a political project, whether consciously or unselfconsciously. There is a crucial need to explicate the politics of available histories. 'At one time', writes Nora, 'the Third Republic [in France] seemed to draw together and crystallize, through history and around the concept of "the nation".' 'History was holy because the nation was holy.' 'The memory-nation was . . . the incarnation of memory-history.' The crisis of the 1930s changed all that. The 'old couple', state and nation, was replaced by a new one, state and society. History was 'transformed into social self-understanding'. 'We no longer celebrate the nation, . . . we study the nation's celebrations.'[15] French history, he tells us, was once 'the very model of national history in general'. Now, it seems we are being told, it is the very model of a non-national, open-ended, many-centred history. But model nonetheless.

'We live in a fragmented universe . . . We used to know whose children we were; now we are the children of no one and everyone.' 'Since the past can now be constructed out of virtually anything, and no one knows what tomorrow's past will hold, our anxious uncertainty turns everything into a trace . . .' 'With the disintegration of memory-history, . . . a new kind of historian has emerged, a historian prepared, unlike his predecessors, to avow his close, intimate, and personal ties to his subject . . . [and] entirely dependent on his subjectivity, creativity, and capacity to re-create.' 'The demise of memory-history has multiplied the number of private memories demanding their own individual histories'; everything we touch or use is

[14] G. W. F. Hegel, *Reason in History. A General Introduction to the Philosophy of History*, tr. by Robert S. Hartman (Indianapolis, 1953), pp. 75–7.
[15] Nora, *Rethinking the French Past*, pp. 5–7.

preserved as an archival document, and of course (historical) memory is everywhere. There has been 'a decisive shift from the historical to the psychological, from the social to the individual, from the concrete message to its subjective representation . . .'[16] 'Memory has become the discourse that replaces history', as another commentator on memory has it.[17]

I have to say, in response to this, that this is not the only world I recognise. Who is it, in fact, who lives in a 'fragmented' universe, and turns every 'trace' into a historical document? This is not my history and – probably – not the history of the majority of people across the globe. Where I come from, and I daresay in many other parts of what was once called the Third World, an incredible range of old and abandoned objects gets recycled, including discarded official documents and forms – the staple of historians for a long time now – which are often found being used as wrapping for snack foods. At this point, our historian, with his feet planted firmly in Europe and little awareness of how the rest of the world thinks or feels, moves too quickly – and unreflexively.

When Nora and others dismiss the history–nation connection, as belonging to the past, they appear to me to be mistaken on two counts. To speak of history entering 'the epistemological age' is to confine history to the narrow space of academic production – precisely when the sites of historical production have expanded dramatically – and within that too, perhaps, to that of detailed research publications for a small circle of readers. What happens here to Hegel's self-conscious state and overall purpose? What happens, besides, to the 'histories' published in the *New Yorker*, the London *Times*, and *The Times of India*, not to mention the popular historical publications put out by a host of right-wing political parties, and nationalist and nativist movements, that flood streets and stalls the world over? Or are all these now to be classified as 'memory'?

Which leads to a second objection: don't 'private memories' and 'individual histories' continue to feed upon the 'memory-histories' of states, parties and pressure groups representing communities and nations? Is it not premature, just at present, to pronounce the death of memory-history – and with it the death of the 'nation' idea – especially when the self-assured nationalisms and nation-states of the West have been so naturalised as to be rendered invisible, at precisely the same time that the less disguised nationalisms of the rest are declared suspect? Are we really supposed to accept the argument, implicit in the periodic outpourings of Western governments and media alike, that *our* nationalisms – like *our*

---

[16] The above quotations are all from Nora's 'General Introduction' in *Rethinking the French Past*.

[17] Charles Maier, 'A Surfeit of Memory? Reflections on History, Melancholy and Denial', *History and Memory*, 5 (1993), p. 140.

religions – are fine: *theirs* are unfortunately troublesome, and need we tell you, dated?

It is notable that national identity has been one of the obsessions of French politics and history in these post-national times. Braudel was not the only distinguished historian of France to succumb to the temptation of returning to national history, with the publication of the first volume of his *L'Identite de la France* in 1986. As one commentator has noted, 'the 1980s saw a huge outpouring of multi-volume collective histories of France, mostly in traditional narrative mode, which would not have looked out of place at the end of the nineteenth century'.[18] In the ambitious project that he guided on *Les Lieux de Memoire*, a project self-consciously designed to break down narrative history, Nora's own contributions appear to be suffused with nostalgia for an earlier history. Interestingly, while repeatedly announcing the demise of the nation and of its attendant national history, he speaks at the same time of 'the permanence of a . . . [French] identity even now in the throes of fundamental change'.[19]

Perhaps what lies behind this ambivalence is the still refractory question of what constitutes the domain of 'history'. The long enduring colonial distinction between the historical continent called Europe and the continents (and peoples) without history has, one imagines, been finally laid to rest. Quite apart from the story of world capitalism, that is, the history of the dominant world order within which diverse societies have been compelled to live for some time now, as Talal Asad notes in a review of Eric Wolf's *Europe and the People without History*, 'there are also histories (some written, some yet to be written) of the diverse traditions and practices that once shaped people's lives and that cannot be reduced to ways of generating surplus or of conquering and ruling others'.[20]

While Asad's statement may seem to apply only to a time past, before the advance of capitalism and its attendant political and ideological structures, it is possible to suggest that these other histories, other traditions and practices, continue to have a significant life – sometimes robust, sometimes fitful and fugitive – even under the sway of capitalism and the new globalisation, and even in the heartlands of capitalism. Indeed one

---

[18] Julian Jackson, 'Historians and the Nation in Contemporary France', in Stefan Berger, Mark Donovan and Kevin Passmore, eds., *Writing National Histories. Western Europe since 1800* (London, 1999), p. 242. On Braudel he writes: 'That the leading representative of the Annales school should in his twilight years renounce the Annaliste contempt for purely national history and produce a massive exploration of France's past is itself significant; so is the enthusiasm with which the book was greeted; so, even more, is the self-consciously elegiac tone which pervades it; so, most of all, is the mystically nationalist tone, reminiscent of Michelet', p. 241.

[19] Nora, *Rethinking the French Past*, p. 23.

[20] Talal Asad, 'Are there Histories of Peoples without Europe? A Review Article', *Comparative Studies in Society and History*, 29, 3 (1987), p. 604.

might argue, with Partha Chatterjee, that 'community' remains the insufficiently acknowledged shadow, the alter ego, the underside of capital, very much a part of the here-and-now of the modern world order. The contradiction between the two narratives of capital and of community, writes Chatterjee, lies at the very heart of the history and progress of modernity.[21]

The point relates to our practice of history writing. Dipesh Chakrabarty and Ranajit Guha have demonstrated how 'Europe' – which may also be called capitalism or modernity – tends to become the subject of all history.[22] Could one say, more specifically, that it is in the unrecorded history of the contradiction between 'community' and 'capital', between the 'particular' and the 'universal' – in the unrecorded or, at least, unintegrated histories of other traditions and other practices – that we shall find much of the specificity, and diversity, of our lives and times, of our nation-states, of our capitalist economies and our modern institutions? Perhaps it is precisely in the ambivalences that we shall find the particular valence of our histories. Consider this question in terms of the naming of the object of investigation in this book.

A note on the term 'Partition'

The 'partition of India', which is how the division of the subcontinent in 1947 is universally referred to in Indian historiography, is also (for Pakistanis) the 'independence of Pakistan'. Within India, the 'partition' of the historians, and of the official pronouncements of the nation-state, lives side by side with the 'partition'/'uproar'/'migration' that survivors of 1947 speak of. What lies behind these alternative names, I suggest, are diverse claims regarding nationalism and the nation-state: the claims of the Indian state against the Pakistani, on the one hand; and, on the other, the claims of the Indian and Pakistani states against non-statist reconstructions of the past, which sometimes deny the claims of nationalism and the nation-state altogether.

In spite of occasional objections, however, historians belonging to both India and Pakistan continue to write of the partition of India, or of British India, in 1947. Indeed, the proper noun, 'Partition', has passed untranslated into several South Asian languages (including languages spoken in Pakistan and Bangladesh) as the name of a significant break that occurred

[21] Partha Chatterjee, *The Nation and its Fragments. Colonial and Postcolonial Histories* (Princeton, N.J., 1994), p. 237.
[22] See Dipesh Chakrabarty, 'Postcoloniality and the Artifice of History: Who Speaks for "Indian" Pasts', *Representations*, 37 (Winter 1992); and Ranajit Guha, *Dominance without Hegemony. History and Power in Colonial India* (Cambridge, Mass., 1997), esp. ch. 1.

in, or about, 1947. Along with vernacular equivalents like *batwara*, *vibhajan* and *taqseem*, and other local terms for the violence of the time that I shall have occasion to discuss below, the English word 'Partition' has come to be used in the region of Punjab and Delhi, UP (Uttar Pradesh) and Bihar, Bengal and beyond, for the events (or some of the events) that marked the establishment of India and Pakistan, the Hindu–Muslim discord of that moment and the fratricide (or 'civil war') that occurred in 1947. In Bangladesh, many ordinary peasants and labourers, speaking in the common Musalmani Bengali of the rural poor, refer to 1947 as '*partitioner bacchar*' (the year of Partition), as they refer to 1971 as '*svadhintar* [or *mukti-juddher*] *bacchar*' (the year of Independence, or 'of the liberation war' – referring to the massacres and widespread resistance and fighting that came with the Pakistani army's actions of that year).[23]

I shall therefore refer to the object of the present inquiry as Partition. As chapter 2 will indicate, however, there are several different conceptions of 'partition' that went into the making of the Partition of 1947. There was the partition signalled in the Lahore Resolution of March 1940, the demand of an important section of the Muslim political leadership for a state of their own – which was articulated more and more widely by Muslims across the subcontinent over the next seven years. There was, secondly, the demand put forward in early 1947 by sections of the Sikh, Hindu and Congress leadership, for the partition of Punjab and Bengal – linguistic regions which had a great deal of cultural uniformity. There was, yet again, the feared, and then dreadfully realised, partition of families and local communities, whereby millions of people were torn from ancestral homes, fields and fortunes, life-long friends and childhood memories, relatives and loved ones, the knowledge of the familiar and the comfort of the known – a third partition, shall we say, that so many survivors speak of, in words that we hear but do not always listen to, as 'migration', '*maashal-la*' (martial law), '*mara-mari*' (killings),

---

[23] I derive this information from conversations with a number of Bangladeshi colleagues and students, among them Ahmed Kamal, Aminul Faraizi, Dina Siddiqi and Tehmima Anam. Within the wider rubric of Partition, it is possible to refer to several different 'partitions'. The provinces of Punjab and Bengal, for example, were divided as part of the breakup of British India, and establishment of India and Pakistan, in 1947. In the case of Bengal again, observers have spoken of earlier and later 'partitions'. The province was partitioned in 1905, when the British made an abortive attempt to carry through an administrative division of east from west Bengal, to spike the growing militancy of the nationalist movement in that region and to win for the British the support of the Muslim aristocratic and professional elite of East Bengal; in 1947 when the partition we are here discussing took place; and in 1971, when Pakistan was 'partitioned' and the erstwhile East Bengal or East Pakistan became the independent nation-state of Bangladesh. However, it is '1947' that is usually described as the year of Partition, with a capital 'P' – not only in the written, but also in oral accounts of the subcontinent's recent past.

'*raula*', '*hullar*' (disturbance, tumult, uproar), or negatively in the rhetorical question, '*Beta, is neem ke ped ko chhorkar kahan jaate?*' ('Where could we have gone leaving this [old] neem tree behind?').

I raise the question of nomenclature at the outset in order to stress the fact that our very choice of terms determines not only the images we construct but also the questions we ask about historical (and contemporary) events.[24] Shall we continue to think of 1947 as a constitutional division, an agreed-upon partition of territories and assets? Or shall we face up to the enormity of the violence and the incredible acts of rape, torture and humiliation? Shall we call it 'civil war', recognising the fact that there were well organised local forces on both sides and a concerted attempt to wipe out entire populations as enemies? Some have used the expression holocaust as well.[25] In the lower case, for which the *Random House Dictionary* (1987) gives as the primary meaning of the term, 'a great or complete devastation or destruction, esp. by fire', this is entirely appropriate. Surely, 1947 was all of that. It may, indeed, be seen as having elements of a sacrificial offering rendered up at the birth of two new nations – which is perhaps more in line with the original meaning of holocaust than many other events for which the name has been applied. More to the point, the term captures something of the gravity of what happened in the subcontinent at this time that is not usually conveyed in the somewhat mild and, in the Indian context, hackneyed term, 'partition'. Posing the question of the adequacy of the latter description may, therefore, lead us to rethink the meaning of that history.

New nations, new histories

What the violence of 1947 did was to create new subjects and subject positions: a fact that in itself necessitates a reconsideration of the standard view of history as a process with an always already given subject. After

---

[24] James Young makes the point about the importance of naming very well in his discussion of narratives of the German Holocaust. 'That events of this time [could] be contained under the rubric of [different] names like "Patriotic War" (in Russia), "Hitler-time" (in Germany), or "World War II" (in America) tells us as much about the particular understanding of this period by the namers as it does about the events themselves.' Precisely so, 'the terms sho'ah and churban figure these events in uniquely Jewish ways, which simultaneously preserve and create specifically Jewish understanding and memory of this period'; James E. Young, *Writing and Rewriting the Holocaust. Narrative and the Consequences of Interpretation* (Bloomington, 1988), p. 87.

[25] For an early example, see Sardar Bhupinder Singh Man's speech in the Constituent Assembly of India, 19 December 1948, *Constituent Assembly of India (Legislative). Official Report*. vol. VII, no. 1 (1949), pp. 798–9; for a very recent one, Tapan Raychaudhuri, 'Re-reading Divide and Quit' in the new edition of Penderel Moon's *Divide and Quit. An Eyewitness Account of the Partition of India* (Delhi, 1998), pp. 297 and 306.

Partition, individuals, families and communities in the subcontinent re-
made themselves in radically altered settings. They had to struggle to
overcome new fears, to gradually rebuild faith and trust and hope and
to conceive new histories – and new 'memories' that are, in some reck-
onings, 'best forgotten'. 'What is the point of telling today's children about
these things?' Partition survivors sometimes say. 'All that has nothing to
do with their lives and their problems.'

And yet, while individuals and families recreate themselves in changed
times and changed conditions, sometimes by forgetting, they – and the
communities and nations in which they live – are not able to set aside
the memory of the violence quite so easily. For there are numerous
ways in which the life and conditions of India and Pakistan, and perhaps Bangladesh too, have been obviously re-made by that violence and
the curious memory-history we have of it. In saying this, I refer not only
to the immediate problems of rehabilitation and resettlement, and the
reordering of industries, armed forces, administrative apparatuses and
supply lines that were divided and disrupted, but also to the fashioning
of longer term policies, mentalities and prejudices.

Sikhs, Muslims and Hindus were all redefined by the process of
Partition: as butchers, or as devious others; as untrustworthy and anti-
national; but perhaps most fundamentally, as Sikhs and Muslims and
Hindus alone. All over the subcontinent, for extended periods, at many
times since 1947, men, women and children belonging to these communities – yet belonging to different castes, classes, occupations, linguistic
and cultural backgrounds – have been seen in terms of little but their
Sikh-ness, their Muslim-ness or their Hindu-ness.[26] And periodically,
Christians have been treated in a similar way. Journalists and other commentators in India invoke Partition whenever there is a major instance of
inter-community strife; and local administrators have been known to describe predominantly Muslim localities as 'little Pakistans', even at other,
'normal', times.

The 'Sikh problem' arose in 1947 and has remained a major factor
in Indian politics ever since. Their homeland, Punjab, split down the
middle, with a large part of their property and pilgrim-sites left in West
Pakistan, the Sikhs as a political community have never been allowed to
forget what they suffered at Partition. This is summed up in the commonly encountered statement that while the Hindus got their Hindustan
and the Muslims got their Pakistan, the Sikhs were like orphans, left with

---

[26] Today a Muslim shopkeeper in the southern Indian state of Kerala easily exclaims, on
learning that his middle-class customer from northern India is also a Muslim, 'Oh!
You should have told me you were one of us.' (I am indebted to Javeed Alam for this
information.)

nothing. The Punjabi Suba movement of the 1950s and 1960s and the
Khalistani movement of the 1970s and 1980s both derived a considerable part of their strength from such sentiments.[27] On the state's side,
the question of 'minorities' in India – Sikh, Muslim and at times even
Christian – has continued to be handled in the light of the 'lessons' of
Partition. Military coups in Pakistan are still justified on the grounds of
the unfinished work of Partition.

What this book is (not) about

'Nations' – modern political communities, products of history that are
forged in struggle – are made, to a large extent, through the actions of
emergent nation-states, or their ruling classes, which seek to nationalise
different elements of the social and intellectual body of the putative national community. This procedure may be seen in its most concentrated
form, perhaps, at the moment of the establishment of the new national
state: Partition and Independence in the case of India and Pakistan. A primary object of this book is to trace this process of nationalising the nation
through a close study of the experiences and struggles of several different
sections of the population, and the disputes over other elements (history,
collective memory) that were crucial to the making of a particular kind
of – modern, democratic, progressive – nation.

A small clarification is in order. It is obviously not my argument that
modern states (or ruling classes) make nations at will. Instead, I seek to
recover the moment of Partition and Independence in India as a moment
of nationalisation, and a moment of contest regarding the different conditions of such nationalisation. On what terms would Muslims, Dalits
('Untouchables') and women be granted the rights of citizenship? Could
they become citizens at all?

I wish to try and recover the history of Partition, therefore, as a renego-
tiation and a re-ordering, as the resolution of some old oppositions and
the construction of new ones. I wish to see it as a history not of large,
historical processes alone; nor yet of victimhood, plain and simple (which
may amount to something very similar); nor yet of madness or natural
calamities that swept all before them (though madness is surely one way

---

[27] For one example of the connections made, see 'Stupid Sikhs', a speech on Sikhs and
Sikhism by Sirdar Kapur Singh on 7 October 1974 (published by the All Canada Sikh
Federation, Vancouver, 1975); and for more critical academic assessments, Mohinder
Singh, 'Reconstruction of Recent Sikh Past and the Diaspora' (unpublished MS); Rajiv
A. Kapur, *Sikh Separatism: the Politics of Faith* (London, 1986); and Robin Jeffrey, 'Grap-
pling with History: Sikh Politicians and the Past', *Pacific Affairs*, 60, 1 (Spring 1987),
and his *What's Happening to India? Punjab, Ethnic Conflict, Mrs. Gandhi's Death, and the
Test of Federalism* (Basingstoke, 1986).

of making sense of the violence of the time, and natural calamities do come to mind); but also as a history of struggle – of people fighting to cope, to survive and to build anew; as a history of the everyday in the extraordinary. I wish to see it, in a word, as a history of contending politics and contending subject positions.

Is it necessary to add that this book, and perhaps the entire corpus of powerful new writing on Indian nationalism and on Partition, does no more than to signal new questions? Much of the detailed research, analysis and reflection required for a more effective response to the political and intellectual challenges of our times still remains to be done.

To that obvious qualification, let me add two more about the present study. Ideally this book would have dealt with the nationalisation of society, politics, culture and history in two nation-states, India and Pakistan. Owing to the exigencies of international relations, and the consequent difficulty of obtaining visas for travel (not to mention research) between India and Pakistan, however, it has to be restricted to one of those countries, present-day India. I can only hope that in spite of this limitation, the questions raised and the propositions advanced here have a wider application.

In the matter of coverage, this book is wanting in several other respects too, including one that will be immediately noticed. The Partition of 1947, and the establishment of the new states of India and Pakistan, directly and drastically altered the constitutional, political and social condition of both north-western and north-eastern India: Punjab in the north-west and Bengal in the north-east were both split up and divided between India and Pakistan. However, owing to the limited extent of my linguistic abilities, and because the subject is large and calls for far more detailed research on the different provinces and regions of the subcontinent, the material for this book comes in the main from Punjab, Delhi and UP, or northern and north-western India more broadly. This bears noting, but does not in my view call for extended apology. The area I have studied would cover a large part of western Europe, in geographical spread as well as in the strength of its population; it is rich in history, and accommodates a great variety of social and cultural practices; and in its evidence, from and about 1947, it raises many of the most important questions that must arise when it comes to the question of nationalising richly layered and culturally varied societies and peoples.

A final disclaimer: this critique of nationalism in India does not imply that national movements have not played an outstanding part in liberating people far and wide, in ex-colonial Africa and Asia as elsewhere, from the clutches of imperialism – political, economic and intellectual. On the contrary, what it does seek to show is that nationalism is the expression of a particular historical conjuncture, albeit one that was fairly extended in time and played out very differently in different parts of the world between the eighteenth and the twentieth centuries. Nationalism everywhere has been the product of particular, distinctive histories. It has been as strong as its leading class or classes: visionaries as well as practical men and women, devoted to commerce and industry, education and culture, aspiring to rule, to unify peoples, mobilise resources and transform economic, social and political conditions in a new, progressive spirit. And – like every other major development in history – it has been shot through with its own contradictory impulses. Given the particularity (and partiality) of its claims and achievements, and the necessarily contradictory quality of its conditions of existence, we can scarcely accept at face value the self-representation of a particular nationalism or of nationalist ideology in general (however short-lived or long term its triumph) any more than we would accept the claims of a self-contented imperialism or of a grander 'modern civilisation'.[28]

The point is obvious, but perhaps in need of reiteration. Liberation is not a cut-and-dried object, obtained once and for all in some seamless form. Progress and justice are not notions of crystal-clear content and unmistakable indices, which may be easily measured. Every liberation in history has come at the cost of the establishment of new hierarchies and new kinds of bondage, not to mention the reinvention of old ones. To what extent have the concerns and struggles of the lower castes, of millions of ordinary workers, peasants and artisans, of peripheral nationalities struggling for democratic rights (for example, in the north-eastern states of India and in Kashmir), of women now working in new locations, under new pressures, related to the nationalist elite's (and the nationalist historian's) lasting concern with the representation (and hence maintenance?) of homogenised and uniform nations, and homogenised and uniform national cultures and histories?

Recognition of the severity, the broken edges, and the uncertain boundaries of Partition allows us a standpoint that was perhaps unavailable to an earlier generation of writers of a nationalist Indian history. How much violence and intolerance has it taken to produce the 'successful' nation-states of the twentieth century? How many partitions did it take to make the Partition of 1947? How different is the history of those citizens, on the one hand, whose position is so 'natural' that they are not even aware of their privilege as citizens; and that, on the other, of people whose

---

[28] On this last, Gandhi's response to the question what he thought of 'western civilisation' remains apposite in many ways: 'It would be a good thing.' Cf. the important reflections of Aime Cesaire in his *Discourse on Colonialism* (1955; English edn, New York, 1972), p. 14 and *passim*.

livelihood and security in their assigned nation-states is so uncertain that the phrase 'privileges of citizenship' might sound somewhat ironical? Among the latter are many faceless 'victims' of Partition: Muslim artisans, peasants and labourers in India; Dalit sweepers; 'recovered' women, Chakmas and Anglo-Indians; people who stayed or fled at Partition, to face new circumstances and build new lives and communities, in India, Pakistan and Bangladesh.

This book is about the making of the Partitioned subject in the subcontinent, the nationalising of nations and the selection of particular pasts. As part of the context, the next chapter seeks to provide a dense, summary account of the major lines of argument and confrontation that developed between the self-appointed or acclaimed representatives of 'Hindus', 'Muslims' and 'Sikhs' in the mid-1940s – insofar as any such dense but 'summary' account is possible.[29]

---

[29] This 'summary' is intended for the reader who feels handicapped because of unfamiliarity with the subcontinent and subcontinental politics in the last years of British rule. Those familiar with the main lines of that history may wish to move directly to ch. 3.

2   The three partitions of 1947

Elections, commissions, protest and strife

The years 1945 to 1947 were marked by intense struggle in the sub-continent. What the Second World War established, and the end of the war only underlined, was the changed military, political and economic position of Britain in the world and the radical transformation of the political temper in India. All this lent unprecedented urgency to the question of the transfer of power and the establishment of national government(s) in the subcontinent. It was in this situation that the Indian National Congress leadership was released from jail, efforts at mobilisation of different sections of the society were actively renewed, large-scale urban demonstrations and rural uprisings occurred, new elections were held and sustained high-level constitutional negotiations took place after 1945.

Much of the politics of the previous three or four decades had been about national liberation. It was a serious complication that the call for Indian self-government was now joined by the call for Muslim self-government in a new country to be named Pakistan. Talk of independence was rife. However, while the Congress and those in sympathy with it expected the independence of a united India, the Muslim League slogan became 'Pakistan for Independence'. There were two nations in India, it was argued, and the acceptance of the Pakistan demand was the only road to the genuine independence of all Indians, the Muslims in a free Pakistan and the Hindus in a free Hindustan.

Yet the idea of Pakistan itself, the proposal for a partition of British India between its Muslim-majority and its Hindu-majority provinces, had not had a long history. It was in March 1940 that the Muslim League formally proposed the establishment of separate states for the Muslim-majority regions of north-western and north-eastern India; and as late as September 1944, in his correspondence with Gandhi, and April 1946, in a meeting of all Muslim League legislators of the centre and the provinces, Jinnah and the Muslim League were still having to clarify that the proposal was for *one* sovereign, independent state called Pakistan (with its separate, eastern and western, wings). Elections in early 1946 were widely represented as being a plebiscite on the question of Pakistan. The Muslim League performed very well in the majority of Muslim constituencies across the subcontinent and quickly laid claim to being the sole representative of the Muslims of India (although, as Indian nationalist commentators and other scholars too have pointed out, no more than 10–12 per cent of the adult population was enfranchised at this time; and the League was unable to form a ministry in the Muslim-majority provinces of Punjab and the North West Frontier Province (NWFP), and managed to do so only by the skin of its teeth in Sind).

The summer of 1946 brought momentary agreement between the Congress and the Muslim League on the Cabinet Mission Plan to establish a loose federation in India, with the Muslim-majority provinces and states of north-western and north-eastern India being grouped initially into two of the federating units, and the rest of India into a third: there was provision for a constitutional review after ten years. The agreement was welcomed widely and with the most visible relief in nationalist (i.e. pro-Congress) Muslim circles. It collapsed, however, owing to continued suspicions and reservations in both Congress and League camps. Congress leaders, in particular, were agitated over the compulsory grouping of provinces and states into regional units (with the Muslims holding a majority in two regions), and extremely concerned to preserve the sovereign authority of the proposed Constituent Assembly.

Following the breakdown of this Congress–League agreement, the Congress leadership – heading by far the most powerful and well-organised strand of the anti-colonial movement in the country – was still able to press on the British the need to move quickly towards an Interim Government (controlled by representative Indians) and a Constituent Assembly (elected by the legislators returned in the 1946 elections), in line with the 16 May Cabinet Mission proposals. Congress leaders believed that this was the most urgent need of the day, with or without the participation of the Muslim League: once power was transferred to Indian hands, the people of India would themselves resolve all remaining issues.

In August 1946, the Muslim League decided on 'Direct Action' – the first extra-constitutional action in a wholly constitutionalist movement, as Jinnah said – against the direction that constitutional negotiations seemed to be taking. This followed the Congress president Jawaharlal Nehru's apparent retraction of commitments made by his party in accepting the 16 May Cabinet Mission Plan, and the threat of the installation of a

Congress-controlled Interim Government at the centre. On 'Direct Action Day', 16 August 1946, violence broke out between Hindus and Muslims in Calcutta. Several thousand people were killed in four days. From here, the violence spread, one way and then the other, to engulf many parts of northern India by March 1947.

After Calcutta, the violence and killings were reported to have been at their worst in Bombay in early September (with over 300 reported killed), East Bengal in early October (several hundreds killed), Bihar in late October (several thousands killed), Garhmukteshwar in UP in November (several hundreds killed). The fire spread to the North West Frontier Province in January 1947 and to Punjab in March (where the casualties were again very high). In the last two instances, the violence coincided with civil disobedience campaigns launched by the Muslim League to dislodge the provincial ministries (a move that occurred in Assam as well).

At the beginning of March 1947, the League agitation succeeded in bringing down the Khizr Hayat Khan-led coalition ministry in Punjab comprising Muslim, Sikh and Hindu ministers from the Unionist, Congress and Panthic parties. The League renewed its claim to form the government in the province that was now seen as the cornerstone of the Pakistan proposal. The fall of the coalition government was seen as a turning point. The demand for Pakistan had reached fever pitch and reports spoke of how 'communal frenzy' had gripped the population at large. The imminence – as it seemed – of a new and far more militant Muslim League government was widely apprehended and reported as the achievement of Pakistan.[1] It led at once to demonstrations, counter-demonstrations, threats of a fight to the finish, and the outbreak of violence on a large scale. It was not only cities like Lahore and Amritsar that were affected this time. The violence was likened to a tidal wave that engulfed Sikh and Hindu 'minorities' scattered in the rural areas of Rawalpindi and Multan divisions.

A British general wrote of the fierceness of the attacks and the rapidity with which they spread from the cities to the countryside. In the cities of Rawalpindi and Multan, 'attacks were fiercer, more sudden, and more savage than ever. In the rural areas attacks were launched by large mobs of Muslim peasants who banded together from several hamlets and villages to destroy and loot Sikh and Hindu shops and houses in their area. In some areas . . . savagery was carried to an extreme degree and men, women and children were hacked or beaten to death, if not burned in

---

[1] In the event, a Muslim League ministry was not installed. The governor imposed governor's rule because of the outbreak of serious disturbances and this, of course, served to provoke Muslim League supporters even further.

their houses. There were also quite a number of cases of forcible conversion of males and abduction of females . . . ' Casualties were heavy, especially in Rawalpindi division, and there was a considerable exodus towards central and East Punjab, and indeed Delhi and UP: by the end of April 1947, official estimates of refugees in Punjab put the figure at 80,000.[2]

Some of the most haunting images of Partition violence come from this period. Many people took their own lives, or those of their family members, rather than surrendering to bondage and dishonour. The collective suicide of ninety or more women and children in the village of Thoa Khalsa is now the best known of these incidents.[3] Accounts of huge numbers of refugees, and refugee camps, had already become common at the time of the massacre of Muslims in Bihar several months before. But, perhaps because of the altered political context at the all-India level, the Punjab events outdid even Calcutta and Bihar in the all-round hatred that they generated and the polarisation that they produced in Punjab and beyond.

Hindus and Sikhs in far-flung districts of Punjab, and elsewhere, united in an intensified hatred of all Muslims – as contemporary accounts now commonly had it – and began, in the words of a colonial official, actively 'organising for strife'.[4] Sikh leaders called on every living Sikh to emulate 'the spirit of sacrifice, chivalry and bravery as exhibited and demonstrated by the tenth Guru Gobind Singh Ji', and to 'give his [*sic*] best in the cause of the Panth which is covered in courageous glory by the numerous sacrifices of our martyrs'.[5]

The pride of Jat Sikhs, whose militaristic traditions had been pumped up by their favoured recruitment into the British Indian army and the rise of the Singh Sabha movement in the nineteenth century, was especially wounded. In West Punjab, stories spread of how the Sikhs' 'much vaunted

---

[2] (IOR) T. W. Rees coll., Punjab Boundary Force (PBF) bundles, General Messervy, 'Some Remarks on the Disturbances in the Northern Punjab' (May 1947?), paras. 2 and 8; also 'Events leading up to the Present Situation in Punjab', precis of address by G II Intelligence, Northern Command (25 May 1947). (The Rees papers were uncatalogued at the time that I consulted them: hence I give no reference to volume numbers. I am deeply grateful to Robin Jeffrey for drawing my attention to the existence of these papers, photocopies of many of which he had obtained earlier for the Sussex University Library, and to the archivist and staff at the India Office Library and Records, London, for permission to consult them so soon after they had been acquired.) The question of estimates (of casualties and refugees), which appear almost always in round figures, is discussed more fully in ch. 4.

[3] See Butalia, 'Community, State and Gender', and Menon and Bhasin, 'Recovery, Rupture, Resistance'.

[4] Rees coll., PBF bundles, Lt Col W. J. Young, 'Note on the Political Situation in the Punjab' (May 1947), para. 7C.

[5] (IOR) Mss Eur. F200/192, Tara Singh and others to the raja of Faridkot (19 March 1947).

militancy' had been 'exploded'. Sections of the Muslim press declared that the community had been 'mauled . . . and the Muslims need not fear them any more'. The London *Times* correspondent in India, betraying his own public school manners and a more general colonial account of manliness, told an English acquaintance that the Muslims had 'thrashed hell out of the Sikhs and Hindus' in the Punjab.[6]

In early September 1947 Nehru, the beleaguered prime minister of newly independent India, distressed and bewildered by all that had gone so wrong, summed up the Punjab events as follows. After Rawalpindi and Multan, he wrote, 'The Sikhs felt exceedingly bitter and angry. Certain subsequent happenings added to this bitterness, more especially the open taunts thrown out to them that they were cowards . . . They took all this very much to heart and prepared for revenge . . . Every kind of weapon was eagerly seized and preserved.'[7]

Several historians, and contemporary observers, have spoken of the 'Great Calcutta Killing' of August 1946 as marking the point of no return in the history of Partition. Others might wish to shift that moment to Punjab in March 1947. Yet it remains unclear how deeply all of this affected Bombay or Madras, or other parts of southern, western or central India, none of which was hit by Partition violence in quite the same shattering way as the north. In the winter of 1946–7, moreover, many people still had faith in the miraculous power of the Mahatma. Freedom was in the air, and Gandhi's wanderings in Noakhali meant that the temporary setback represented by Calcutta or Noakhali would soon be overcome, recalls a Gujarati academic (a leftist student at the time) as having been the general feeling among secular, nationalist youth in Bombay.[8] Even after Calcutta and Noakhali, and Bihar and Rawalpindi, there were other partitions still to come before Partition became a settled fact.

The first 'partition'

It is my contention that there were at least three different conceptions of 'partition' that went into the making of the Partition of 1947. The first of these may be discerned in the Muslim League demand for 'Pakistan' from 1940 onwards.[9] In its clearest expositions, and for most of the period 1940–7, what this envisaged was the autonomy, or independence,

---

[6] (IOR) R/3/1/174, Sardar Baldev Singh's statement 'Who is guilty?'(16 typed pp.) put up to the governor general and his staff on 3 October 1947; and Mss. Eur. D621, Wilfrid Russell diaries, vol. 14, entry for 27 March 1947.

[7] Rees coll., PBF bundles, Nehru–Rees (camp Lahore, 3 September 1947).

[8] Interview with Rashmi Desai (Melbourne, July 1997).

[9] 'Pakistan' was not named in the Lahore Resolution, as Sikandar Hayat Khan and others pointed out at several points over the next few years; but, as Jinnah noted, the press reports and the public response made this into the 'Pakistan' resolution.

of Muslim-majority regions in the north-west and north-east of India – a land (or lands?) where Muslims, and therefore the ideals of Islam, would hold sway.

Two aspects of this demand for a 'Muslim' state need to be noted. First, this was to be a Muslim-majority state. The Muslim-majority provinces of north-western and north-eastern India would be constituted into separate blocks, with minor adjustments, if necessary, in existing provincial boundaries. The plan entailed a minimal disturbance in the demographic distribution of Hindus and Muslims, the communities they lived in and local, social and economic arrangements.

'The Pakistan movement, as envisaged by Mr Jinnah, [does not] require any uprooting of associations and ties of homeland which have existed for generations by an interchange of populations from the Hindu majority Provinces to the Muslim majority Provinces', declared Hassan Suhrawardy in November 1942.[10] Or, as a Muslim student of Lucknow University in 1946–7 recalled, 'Nobody thought in terms of migration in those days: [the Muslims] all thought that everything would remain the same, Punjab would remain Punjab, Sindh would remain Sindh, there won't be any demographic changes – no drastic changes anyway – the Hindus and Sikhs would continue to live in Pakistan . . . and we would continue to live in India.'[11]

'Pakistan' was to be a Muslim-dominated state to balance a Hindu-dominated 'Hindustan'. This is why Jinnah and the Muslim League were ready to accept the Cabinet Mission Plan. In the words of a leading supporter of Jinnah, 'The Muslim League accepted the cabinet mission's plan, as it met the *substance of the demand for Pakistan* and kept the way open for the emergence of a sovereign Pakistan in case the union centre functioned to the detriment of the Muslim provinces.'[12] A group of Punjabi Muslims put the point even more strongly on the Muslim League's withdrawal of its earlier acceptance of the Mission's scheme. 'The most important part of the Scheme is complete provincial autonomy', they noted; '. . . this is, for all practical purposes, *real Pakistan*. One wonders what more the Pakistan of our Leaders' conception can give us.'[13]

However, the goal of separation and autonomy (or independence) for the Muslim-majority regions of north-western and north-eastern India

---

[10] Latif Ahmed Sherwani, ed., *Pakistan Resolution to Pakistan, 1940–1947. A Selection of Documents Presenting the Case for Pakistan* (Karachi, 1969; reprinted Delhi, 1985), p. 36.

[11] Interview with Viqar Ahmed (London, 15 October 1995).

[12] M. A. H. Ispahani, 'Factors Leading to the Partition of British India', in Philips and Wainright, eds., *Partition*, p. 350 (emphasis added).

[13] Cited in Ayesha Jalal, *Sole Spokesman*, p. 263 (emphasis added).

might not have galvanised the dreams of Muslims across the country. What appears to have moved large numbers of younger, urban Muslims, and enabled them to draw into the movement an even broader mass of Muslims, was the possibility of a Muslim state, at a time when Muslim power was at a low ebb the world over and when few people had considered the possibility of establishing such a modern, Muslim state in the subcontinent.

The growing belief in this possibility – of a state where Islam, and with it equality and justice, would reign – generated great enthusiasm among the Muslim middle classes, especially the youth. University students from Aligarh and elsewhere provided some of the most dedicated and important workers of the Muslim League. As the Raja of Mahmudabad, himself one of the closer younger lieutenants of Jinnah in the period before Partition, recalled twenty years after the event, 'the idea of a separate Muslim state in India [*sic*] stirred the imagination of the Muslims as nothing else had done before'.[14]

Leading intellectuals of the earlier generation in Pakistan have made the same point, saying that progressive historians should not run away with the idea that Pakistan came to be established 'in a fit of absent-mindedness'. The younger generation of Muslim students, teachers and professionals of the 1940s supported the idea of Pakistan without exception. One of them said to me: 'We believed in every word of Mr Jinnah, and we went there [to Pakistan, from territories that remained in India] because we had great hopes for the future.'[15] 'Jinnah and the Muslim League and Pakistan are realities', noted a British ICS official posted in Banaras in 1946. 'All my Muslim officers are Muslim Leaguers.'[16]

The goal of Pakistan (the 'Pure Land') was seen as the 'Muslim' answer to 'Hindu oppression' and 'Hindu capitalism'. In the climactic years of 1946 and 1947, the League campaigned energetically against the '*bania*' (trading, money lending, interest-gathering and, in that sense, fundamentally un-Islamic) Congress and its '*bania*' leader (Gandhi); against a Congress which was under the thumb of Hindu capitalists and – for

---

[14] See Raja of Mahmudabad, 'Some Memories', in Philips and Wainright, eds., *Partition*, p. 388. Cf. Mahmud Husain, 'Dacca University and the Pakistan Movement', in *ibid.*, pp. 371–2; A. B. A. Haleem, 'The Aligarh Muslim University' and M. N. Safa, 'Dacca University – Its Role in the Freedom Movement' in *History of the Freedom Movement in Pakistan* (Pakistan Historical Society, 1970; reprinted, Delhi, 1984); and Ahmed Kamal, 'A Land of Eternal Eid – Independence, People, and Politics in East Bengal', *Dhaka University Studies*, Part A, 46, 1 (June 1989).

[15] Interview with Mubashir Hasan (Delhi, 27 February 1995); and Gitanjali Shree and Sudhir Chandra's conversation with Intizar Husain (Dhulikhel, Kathmandu, March 1994).

[16] (IOR) Mss. Eur. D724/101, papers of Andrew Parke Hume, ms. entitled 'To Anyone Interested' [impressions of the situation in India] (13 January 1946).

all its protestations to the contrary – working hand-in-glove with British imperialism; against 'Hindu capitalism and fascism' which oppressed not only the Muslims, but also 'Untouchables' and other 'minorities'.[17]

By contrast, the Muslim League demand for Pakistan was presented as aiming at true freedom – the freedom of both the Hindus and the Muslims, the 'fairest deal' for minorities and justice for all who were oppressed and poor. 'Divide to unite' was the League's paradoxical battle cry.[18] Once the Muslims were free and secure in Pakistan, and the Hindus in Hindustan, the two could come together in many areas: communications, defence, foreign affairs, civil rights.

The votaries of Pakistan promised a great deal. As Islam is by nature egalitarian, it was argued, the Muslim state would provide the best conditions for genuine democracy and socialism. Hence Jinnah said in March 1946: 'I am an old man. God has given me enough to live comfortably at this age. Why would I turn my blood into water, run about and take so much trouble? Not for the capitalists surely, but for you, the poor people... In Pakistan, we will do all in our power to see that everybody can get a decent living.'[19]

Headlines in *Dawn* in November 1946 made the same point: 'Qaed-e-Azam and Muslim League Have Always Befriended the Downtrodden.' The accompanying report was run alongside an advertisement in Urdu, printed around Jinnah's photograph, citing the results of Jinnah's talks with a number of leaders of the depressed classes in Lucknow in 1937: '*Muslim League tamam kamzor jama'aton ke huquq chahti hai! Government ya kisi taaqat se samjhauta karte vaqt musalman, aadinivasi, acchuton ko insaf ke saath har qism ke huquq dilane mein har qism ki qurbani karenge!*' ('The Muslim League stands for the rights of all weak [oppressed] communities! In reaching an agreement with the Government or any other power, we will make every sacrifice necessary to obtain... every right for the Muslims, the Adivasis and the Untouchables!').[20]

The Punjab Muslim League Manifesto of 8 November 1944 was read in several quarters as a charter of rights for the working classes and

[17] See K. K. Aziz, *Muslims Under Congress Rule, 1937–39. A Documentary Record*, vols. I and II (1978; reprinted Delhi, 1986); Mushirul Hasan, 'The Mass Contacts Campaign', in Hasan, ed., *India's Partition*; and *Dawn* for 1946 and 1947.
[18] See Sarat Chandra Bose, *I Warned My Countrymen. Being the Collected Works 1945–50 of Sarat Chandra Bose* (Calcutta, 1968), p. 136. See also Indian Communist Sajjad Zaheer's comment asking the Congress 'to welcome this awakening national consciousness of brother nationalities, to recognize their just democratic demand, and to end once and for all the present unhappy epoch of disunity, discord and deadlock'; cited in Shafiq Ali Khan, *The Demand for Pakistan and the CPI* (Karachi, 1986), pp. 64–5.
[19] *Dawn* (1 March 1946), see the rest of the speech too.
[20] The advertisement is repeated in many issues of November and December 1946.

the peasantry. A Communist Party report spoke of the Punjab League's 'proud record of service in the *kisan* [peasant] movement . . . These workers of Punjab's new Muslim League have taken the message of Pakistan deep among the peasant masses. But the message they teach is not one which separates the Muslim *kisan* from his Sikh and Hindu brothers [*sic*], but on the contrary, unites him with them.'[21]

In the age of nationalism, however, the strongest argument in favour of Pakistan was probably the claim that the Muslims of India constituted a nation of their own. Jinnah declared: 'The problem [between the Hindus and Muslims of India] is not of an inter-communal character, but manifestly of an international one . . . Mussalmans are a nation according to any definition of a nation.'[22] The argument was repeated down the line, and elaborated into the kind of requirement that nationalism has unashamedly demanded in the twentieth century. To be a true Muslim in India at this time was to be prepared to lay down one's life for Pakistan. Anyone who was unable to contemplate such sacrifice for religion and nation was no Muslim at all, but a 'renegade', a 'quisling' and a *'kafir'* (non-believer).[23]

Indeed, as the struggle for Pakistan reached its high point and the lines came to be drawn more and more sharply between 'us' and 'them', the wrath of God was called down upon all those who stood in the way of the achievement of Pakistan. It was 'traitors' within the community who became the targets of the most virulent and continuous attacks. 'Mahatma' Gandhi was a 'celestial quack', 'Pandit' Nehru a 'hypocrite', 'Sardar' Patel a Hindu Mahasabhite, but it was Abul Kalam Azad, long-term president of the Congress (until mid-1946), renowned for his Islamic learning, so-called 'Maulana' Azad – in reality, as League propagandists had it, no 'Maulana' at all – 'renegade' Azad who was guiltiest of all. He was taunted when the Bihar massacres occurred, reviled for his preaching of Indian unity, prevented from entering various mosques at prayer-time, and insulted and spat upon by students of Aligarh Muslim University when his train stopped at Aligarh railway station.[24] Other nationalist Muslims suffered in a similar way. As we know, the experience has not been uncommon in nationalist – or communist – movements elsewhere.

---

[21] See Sho Kuwajima, *Post-war Upsurge of Freedom Movement and 1946 Provincial Elections in India* (Osaka, 1992), p. 157; cf. p. 155. Muslim League activists made the same sort of argument during their election campaign in Sind: *haris* (farm labourers) and *mazdoors* (workers) would get their fair share in Pakistan and their children would be assured of education.

[22] Sherwani, *Pakistan Resolution*, pp. 23–4.

[23] Cf. David Gilmartin, 'Religious Leadership and the Pakistan Movement in the Punjab', *Modern Asian Studies*, 13, 3 (1979).

[24] See Syeda Saiyidain Hameed, *Islamic Seal on India's Independence. Abul Kalam Azad – a Fresh Look* (Karachi, 1998), p. 290; Jalil Abbasi, *Kya din the* (Delhi, 1987), p. 108; and numerous interviews.

In spite of all the militant propaganda, however, the idea of Pakistan remained remarkably vague. It was never clarified how Muslims spread out over the subcontinent, and divided by class, sect, gender, regional interests and language, would become part of *one* separate country; or indeed exactly where this new state called Pakistan would be. In any event, there was little desire to move from long-established homes – the *vatan*, homeland, country, native place. Indeed, for numerous supporters of Pakistan, for much of the period up to 1947, the object was to gain assured Muslim dominance in the Muslim-majority zones of north-western and north-eastern India, without any substantial change in existing provincial boundaries or any significant movement of populations.

Many in Punjab and Bengal, even among those who were supporters of the League and the Pakistan movement in the mid-1940s, had reservations about the theory that the Hindus and Muslims of the entire subcontinent formed two separate and homogenous nations. Abul Hashim, secretary of the Bengal Muslim League, declared: 'Liberated India must necessarily be, as God has made it, a subcontinent having complete independence for every nation inhabiting it . . .' While this could be seen, at a stretch, as a statement in favour of the two-nation theory, it reads more obviously as the advocacy of not two, but several nations: 'a subcontinent' with 'complete independence for every nation inhabiting it' – Bengal, Punjab, Sindh and so on.[25]

When Hindu, Sikh and Congress leaders proposed the partition of Bengal and Punjab, neither Jinnah nor the Punjab and Bengal Leaguers were pleased. In April 1947, Jinnah pleaded with Mountbatten not to play with the unity of Bengal and Punjab which have 'national characteristics in common: common history, common ways of life', and where 'the Hindus have stronger feelings as Bengalis or Punjabis than they have as members of the Congress'. Liaqat Ali Khan, the first prime minister of Pakistan, echoed the sentiment. The Bengal Muslim League leader, Husain Suhrawardy, asked the Viceroy to postpone a decision on Partition until November 1947 to give his 'united Bengal' scheme a little more time to succeed. Fazlul Haq, mover of the original 'Pakistan' resolution in Lahore in 1940, expressed the opinion even more strongly, declaring that the British should stay on, rather than partition the country.[26]

'The most striking fact about Pakistan is how it failed to satisfy the interests of the very Muslims who are supposed to have demanded its creation', Ayesha Jalal has written.[27] It was in the clash between different

---

[25] See Leonard A. Gordon, 'Divided Bengal: Problems of Nationalism and Identity in the 1947 Partition', in Mushirul Hasan, ed., *India's Partition*, pp. 297–8.

[26] *Ibid.*, p. 307; and Jalal, *Sole Spokesman*, pp. 252 and 265.

[27] Jalal, *Sole Spokesman*, p. 2.

notions of Pakistan – as the 'land of the Indian Muslims', and as a state which would protect all the subcontinent's Muslims, who could stay on wherever they were – that a second conception of 'partition' crept in.

The second 'partition'

This second 'partition' entailed the splitting up of the Muslim-majority provinces of Punjab and Bengal. By March 1947, an increasing number of Sikh and Congress leaders were persuaded that Partition was necessary – as the lesser evil. In that month, the Congress high command voted for a partition of Punjab into Muslim-majority and Hindu/Sikh-majority halves and asked that the same principle be applied to Bengal. It was as if a frustrated and angry Congress leadership had decided to thwart the League by offering it an overdose of its own medicine. If you must have your Partition, you'll have it with a vengeance.[28]

The Hindu Mahasabha had made the proposal for a division of Bengal even earlier. The Sikh leadership supported the Congress call for a division of Punjab even though it was clear that their community would face the severest difficulties from such a development. It was the short-sightedness and selfishness of Congress leaders that led to the Partition of 1947, argues Jalal. Jinnah himself never wanted Partition: the Congress and the Hindu Mahasabha insisted on it.[29] Joya Chatterji demonstrates this proposition for Bengal, suggesting that *bhadralok* Bengali Hindus, who thought of Bengal as *their* province, were unprepared to live under the 'permanent tutelage of Muslims' (as one of their leaders put it) and were persuaded by events that occurred in the period of the first Muslim League ministry in the province that Partition was necessary. 'In 1947,' she writes, '*bhadralok* Bengalis, once the pioneers of nationalism, used every available stratagem and device to demand that their province be divided.'[30]

History has often worked in just such curious ways. In spite of the Muslim League's espousal of the two-nation theory and the Congress–Sikh–Mahasabha rejection of it, it was the latter's initiatives that seemed

---

[28] Cf. Sarat Bose who speaks of a notion of 'self-determination all the way', *I Warned My Countrymen*, p. 133.

[29] Jalal, *Sole Spokesman*, pp. 262, 216 and *passim*.

[30] Joya Chatterji, *Bengal Divided*, pp. 230–1 and 253. 'The Sikhs were the main authors of the partition demand', wrote an Intelligence official in August 1947; Rees coll., PBF bundles, 'Secret Note' (a pencilled note at the top identifies the writer as 'Mr. Jenkins, C. I. D.', and gives the date, Lahore, 4 August 1947). Diwan Chaman Lal had earlier described the March 1947 violence in Punjab as 'Pakistan in action', adding: '. . . We are determined now to see that the Punjab is divided'; (Southampton University Library) Khizr Hayat Khan Tiwana papers, MS 210/4, 'Newspaper reports' (15 April 1947).

to call for a complete separation of the religious communities, and not the former's. The consequences were far reaching.

They led, first, to the demand for the establishment of separate states in many other parts of the subcontinent through a further extension of the same principle of the self-determination of religious communities. There were widespread calls for the establishment of Muslim states in the Muslim-majority districts or sub-districts of Malabar ('Mappillasthan'), west UP, Rampur, Bihar, Delhi, apart from the major princely states of Hyderabad, Bhopal and so on.

Secondly, they reinforced the opinion that the 'minority' (or 'other' community) did not belong in lands that had now been designated Muslim or non-Muslim. This was to lead, in the months following the establishment of India and Pakistan, to the eviction of virtually all Hindus and Sikhs from West Punjab and other north-western parts of erstwhile British India, as it did of Muslims from East Punjab. By a final irony, the deputy prime minister of India and, presumably on the government of India's instructions, the deputy High Commissioner for India in Pakistan were found calling for the withdrawal of all Hindus and Sikhs from Pakistani Punjab and the NWFP, while the government of Pakistan was urging Muslims of the territories lying beyond East Punjab *not* to migrate to Pakistan.[31]

No one knew in August 1947 what the long-term consequences of Partition would be; none could have predicted the devastation and bitterness it left behind. However, the signs were already ominous in the months when the proposals for the partition of Punjab and Bengal were still being discussed, and long before the mass movement of peoples from one side to the other had taken on its ultimate gigantic proportions. The bewildering variety of the Sikh leaders' responses on the issue of the division of Punjab – which they themselves had advanced as the 'best' solution under the circumstances – illustrates the point well.

In early April 1947, not long after Master Tara Singh and other Akali leaders had come out in support of the Congress plan to divide Punjab, a meeting called by non-Akali Sikh leaders declared it 'sheer tyranny and [a] moral betrayal' to leave the Sikhs of the western Punjab districts to fend for themselves, as it were. The migration of a few thousand Sikhs to Patiala or other Sikh states offered no solution to this problem, they noted. 'What will you do with the 20 lakhs that will be left behind?' asked Sardul Singh Caveeshar. 'The Punjab, I tell you, will never be divided', said Professor Mota Singh.[32]

---

[31] Mss. Eur. F200/53, emergency committee meeting (17 October 1947); and *ibid.*, vol. 128, Indian High Commission (camp Lahore) to India Foreign, telegram (27 August 1947). Cf. *ibid.*, vol. 149, R. F. Mudie to Liaqat Ali Khan (24 December 1948).
[32] *Dawn* (12 April 1947).

In keeping with the extraordinarily confused nature of this extraordinary time, Sikh leaders across the board seemed to backtrack as soon as the principle of the partition of British India (and, with it, of Punjab and Bengal) was accepted on 3 June 1947. In the second week of July 1947, when the Punjab and Bengal legislatures (each divided into an eastern and a western section) met to vote – and thus express the 'opinion of the people' – on whether their provinces should or should not be partitioned, each and every Sikh member of the eastern section of the Punjab Assembly voted for the division of the Punjab (just as the Hindu members of western Bengal did in the Bengal vote on Bengal's partition).

Yet, a short while afterwards, Giani Kartar Singh, president of the Shiromani Akali Dal, and one of the most prominent of the Sikh leaders at this time, declared that 'The Sikhs have not accepted the [3 June] Plan as such. The Sikh position is that they do not agree to a partition that does not maintain the solidarity of their population in the East Punjab and does not consolidate their shrines in the East Punjab.' What that meant in effect was that East Punjab had to be made so large as to include the vast majority of the Sikh people and the vast majority of Sikh shrines within its borders. The British had short-changed the Sikhs in the Cabinet Mission Plan, Kartar Singh went on, and again on 3 June 1947 when they 'gave' sovereign states to the Hindus and the Muslims, and left the Sikhs in the lurch. 'Now Sikhs ask for this only, that their integrity and solidarity should be maintained and the sacred shrines saved from Pakistan.'[33]

Several members of the Sikh intelligentsia declared that the Partition plan was 'grossly unjust' to the Sikhs. Sardar Baldev Singh, who had accepted the decision on behalf of the Sikhs, had been 'goaded by personal interests', they suggested, and had failed to properly represent the community. 'This has resulted in Sikhs being divided into two almost equal halves. A community numbering not more than 40 lacs [lakhs], if divided in this way, would be thoroughly incapacitated.'[34] Sikh organisations observed 8 July as a 'Protest Day' against the proposed partition and many Punjab Hindus joined them in the protest. 'After July 8,' commented the *Pakistan Times*, 'the justification for partitioning the Punjab, namely, appeasement of the Sikhs, no longer exists.'[35] By that time, Sikh newspapers were calling upon the Sikhs to foil the Partition scheme, this final attempt of the British to destroy the Sikhs and wipe them off the political map of India. 'With clear vision, determination, and vigour that is characteristic

[33] *Pakistan Times* (22 July 1947).
[34] *Dawn* (6 June 1947).
[35] *Pakistan Times* (11 July 1947). On intelligence reports regarding Master Tara Singh and other Sikh leaders' frame of mind at this juncture, and secret preparations for revenge against Muslims, see Mss. Eur. F200/141, minutes of meeting held after Provisional Joint Defense Council Meeting on 5 August 1947; and Rees coll., PBF bundles, intelligence summary no.1 (by Young), 6 August 1947.

of our virile race, we shall extricate ourselves out of this whirlpool of annihilation that is facing us. Our phoenix like rise shall signal the fall of our enemies.'[36]

Nor were the Sikhs alone in their call for 'manliness' and revenge. Stories of cruel attacks upon innocent Hindus, Muslims and Sikhs in different parts of the subcontinent generated calls for vengeance all round. A letter written by a Hindu resident of Peshawar to the general secretary of the All-India Hindu Mahasabha in March 1947 reflects both the effect of these widely relayed stories and the consolidation of warring positions. The 'age of Aurangzeb' had returned to haunt them, the writer says, and the Hindus and Sikhs of north-western India were living in terror – 'like rats in a hole'. The Jhelum, Rawalpindi and Campbellpur districts have been 'completely cleaned out' of Hindus and Sikhs. 'The Hindus and Sikhs in the villages have practically all been converted into Muslims . . . Vehicles are arriving laden with corpses.'

The inevitable prescription follows: 'You [your party] alone can put a stop to the unspeakable atrocities being perpetuated here on the Hindu community/nationality. The Hindu Mahasabha must now draw up its *programme of war*. It must go from *village to village, avenging this wrong* [*apmaan*: literally, insult] . . . Gandhi cannot be the protector of the Hindu community/nationality at this time: all his schemes have failed . . .'[37]

Muslim militants matched the rhetoric. A letter published in the *Al-Wahid*, a small-circulation Sindhi daily, on 9 April 1947, urged the writer's fellow Muslims to come out with the holy Quran in one hand and a sword in the other. Muslims in the provinces where they were a minority were 'straining their ears', this correspondent wrote, 'to hear the sound of the hoofs of galloping horses, the rattling of the swords and the sky-rending slogans of "Allah-ho-Akbar" of the Muslim crusaders'.[38] 'Unfair Partition Will Breed Civil War in India' declared a headline in the *Pakistan Times* on 17 July 1947. The Muslims would not tolerate any further appeasement of the Sikhs over their demand that Punjab be

---

[36] *The Liberator*, 'Spokesman of the Sikh people' (Delhi, 27 July 1947) in Rees coll., PBF bundles. See also *ibid.*, report of Central Intelligence officer, Lahore to I. B., H. D., government of India (28 July 1947), and intelligence report for Gujranwala city (9 August 1947). Cf. Tan Tai Yong, 'Prelude to Partition: Sikh Responses to the Demand for Pakistan, 1940–47', *International Journal of Punjab Studies*, 1, 2 (1994).

[37] (NMML) Hindu Mahasabha papers, file C-150, Dev Prakash Shastri, Peshawar Cantonement to Deshpande (n.d.; March 1947. The original letter in Hindi is filed along with this translation).

[38] (NAI) Home Poll (I), file 57/20/47, translated extracts from letter of Agha Badruddin Ahmad, member of the legislative assembly (MLA), deputy speaker of the Sindh legislative assembly, to Sukkur district Muslim League conference (forwarded to the chief secretary, government of Sindh, by Parasram V. Tahilramani, MLA, secretary, Sindh assembly Congress party).

divided in such a way that the sanctity of property ownership and religious shrines was preserved. Top-ranking Punjab Muslim League leaders warned that every man, woman and child in 'Muslim Punjab' 'will fight to the bitterest end, if a single man or a single acre of land, which rightly falls within Pakistan is taken away from us'.[39]

'We are determined not to leave any Hindu and Sikh,' a group of Muslim League National Guards of Lahore wrote to their compatriots in Delhi, in early July 1947.

We will treat them in the same manner as Muslims have been dealt with in Bihar...We are about to attack Gurdwara of Amritsar [the Golden Temple?]. If Amritsar is a holy place for Sikhs, Ajmer, Agra and Delhi are so for the Muslims where only yesterday Muslims were ruling...We ask you to hoist Muslim League flag on the Red Fort [in Delhi] on the 14th of August, otherwise all our efforts would go in vain. You should know that we would get either throne or earth [i.e., the grave]. Hindus are determined to wipe us out...[40]

The events of August provided the final, deadly push. The confusion and violence of that long-awaited month and the growing (and, for many, sudden) realisation that Pakistan was not going to be the panacea for all the ills of the Muslims – indeed, that those Muslims who lived far away from the new Muslim state were now in greater danger than before – led to something like a civil war. The third 'partition', in which hundreds of thousands were uprooted and slaughtered, raped and forcibly 'converted' in a display of almost unimaginable malevolence, was well under way.

The third 'partition'

Hundreds of thousands of people were on the road in Punjab within days of the official Partition and the massacres, the nightmares, those other partitions that people would have to live with for decades to come, had begun. Nehru, brought to Punjab by this outbreak of violence on the scale

---

[39] *Pakistan Times* (17 and 22 July 1947), and the following issues. A month later, the Hindu Mahasabha was calling for the observation of 30 August as martyrs' day, referring of course only to the Hindus and Sikhs who had been killed in Pakistan. Among the leaflets distributed by right-wing Sikhs and Hindus was one that reportedly read: 'The day should begin with mass murder of Muslim children and women alike. Forcible occupation of the Muslim buildings should be your objective. Set fire to Muslim mohallas...', and so on; see D. M. Malik, The Tragedy of Delhi (Through Neutral Eyes) in (IOR) Mss. Eur. F164/18.

[40] (NMML) Central Intelligence Directorate (CID) papers, 5th instalment, letter no. Mohd-75, from F. H. G. Bridgman, S. P., CID, Delhi, to G. R. Savage. S. P. (A), S. B., CID, Punjab, dated 10 July 1947, forwarding reply to the letter of Manzur-ul-Haq and Sadiq of the Muslim League National Guards, Delhi, from the Salar-i-Suba, Lahore. Cf. (IOR) R/3/1/173, copy of intercepted letter to Khan Faizullah Khan, district Muzaffargarh, 25 August 1947, enclosed with Patel to Mountbatten, 23 September 1947.

of a war, had the enormity of it all brought home to him by what he saw after the massacre of Sheikhupura (near Lahore). 'A very large number of persons was being done to death daily', he wrote. 'I do not mention the figure . . . as it is incredible.' Officials of the Indian High Commission in Pakistan telegraphed on the same date that '40,000 lives are in danger [in West Punjab] during the next 48 hours'.[41]

Towards the end of September 1947 the London *Times* reported: '4 million on the move in Northern India. Minorities in a state of panic.'[42] A month earlier, reports of the massacre of refugees fleeing by train were already common. Consider the *Daily Mail* correspondent, Ralph Izzard's account of his train journey from Karachi to Lahore on 22–3 August 1947. Luckily the passengers on this journey escaped massacre, but their terror was palpable. At Montgomery in Punjab, Izzard saw what he called the 'first signs of trouble'. The platforms were 'packed with Hindu and Sikh refugees waiting despairingly for transport to India. Those on the platform had been there three days, while on the siding a special train, packed to the doors and on all roofs with non-Moslems, had been waiting for five days.' The Muslim engine-driver of the special train had refused to cross the border to Ferozepur for fear that he would not return alive. At Okara, Izzard continued: 'My train was rushed by 5000 panic-stricken Hindu and Sikh workers from the local Birla textile mills. 40 crammed themselves into my compartment meant to hold 6 . . .' Beyond Raiwind, '. . . we met the vanguard of the Muslim refugees from India, each platform at Lahore being as crowded as previously they had been with non-Moslems, all as before with an utterly dazed . . . air'. A day or two earlier, the 15 Up from Delhi, a train with nine coaches and room enough, according to Izzard, for 'a thousand persons at least', had arrived in Lahore seven hours late with eight battered Muslim survivors on board.[43]

In the week ending 30 October 1947, over 570,000 Muslim refugees were said to have crossed into Pakistan via Amritsar and Ferozepur alone, while some 471,000 non-Muslims crossed the other way. By 1 October, there were 80,000 Muslim refugees in the Purana Qila in Delhi – and many more in other camps in the city. On 26 November, a British embassy official, motoring through Mewat, passed a ten-mile-long column – mostly Meos, he noted, but also other Muslims – being evacuated from a camp 'where they had been held for some time'.[44]

[41] (IOR) R/3/1/172, Nehru to Mountbatten (Delhi, 27 August 1947).
[42] *The Times* (25 September 1947).
[43] Ralph Izzard, 'Indian Massacres Grow. Every Station is Site for New Battle', *Daily Mail* (27 August 1947).
[44] (IOR) Mss. Eur. F200/190, weekly summary for week ending 30 October 1947; (IOR) L/P&J/7/12589, UK High Commission staff member, R. M. Hadow's report of his tour of Gurgaon and Alwar state from 17 November 1947 and of Ambala district between 24 and 26 November 1947.

The administrative problems of securing and co-ordinating the movement of great numbers of people in flight, of providing those who had
reached some sort of camp minimal support for food, shelter and clothing and of trying to ward off the outbreak of epidemic diseases, especially
in the rainy season (July–August), were early recognised. All this was
compounded by the political problem of the widening circle of terror
and violence and the calls for counter-attack and revenge that the very
flight of the refugees generated. Within two or three weeks of the official
Partition of India, the numbers that governments, political parties, relief
agencies and workers had to deal with had become both unthinkable and
unmanageable.

Thus on 7 September 1947, the government of India telegraphically
informed the premiers of Bombay, UP, Bihar, Central Provinces (CP,
today's Madhya Pradesh) and Madras – that is, all the provinces of the
new India barring East Punjab, West Bengal, Assam and the princely
states – of the great influx of refugees from Punjab, Sindh and the NWFP
into Delhi and asked for an immediate response as to the 'number of
refugees you can accommodate in your province and destination where
they should be sent by train or air'.[45] A week later, however, the most
urgent problem seemed to be one of preventing the spread of the 'troubles'
to UP.

It was noted on 15 September that four trainloads of refugees were
arriving in UP daily. The number of refugees in the province had already
swelled to 250,000. The small pilgrimage town of Hardwar, which had a
normal population of 25,000, now contained an additional 60,000 Hindu
and Sikh refugees. There were 20,000 Muslim refugees in the Dehradun–
Laksar area. Incidents of violence, it was reported, were moving from the
individual to the group stage; and the small police and military force
on duty in these areas was hardly adequate to the task of maintaining peace. Nehru now suggested that any further influx of refugees into
UP be stopped; that the 20,000 Muslim refugees in Dehradun–Laksar
and (all?) Muslim railway employees, including 1,500 Baluchis, be sent
to West Punjab; and that the barracks at Chakrata (near Dehradun),
where Muslim refugees had been housed, be made available to the Sikhs,
if possible.[46] Ten days later, the UP premier asked urgently for more
trains to move Muslims out. Meanwhile, the authorities in Meerut reported great panic in their district owing to the influx of Muslims from
Dehradun.[47]

[45] (IOR) R/3/1/172, telegram from the prime minister to premiers of Bombay, UP, Bihar,
CP, Madras (7 September 1947).
[46] (IOR) Mss. Eur. F200/168, minutes of meeting of emergency committee of the Cabinet
(15 September 1947).
[47] Ibid., emergency committee meeting (26 September 1947).

In mid-October, to take an example from elsewhere, Rajkumari Amrit Kaur, minister of health in the Indian government, reported that there were 10,000 Muslim refugees at Kalka, many of them Kashmiris from Shimla, living in particularly poor conditions. She asked that the authorities in Shimla be restrained from sending any more refugees to Kalka and urged that those already there be given priority in evacuation, while agreeing that this should not be allowed to affect the movement of Muslim refugees out of Delhi. At this very time, the prime minister of Pakistan was sending telegrams to his counterpart in India, asking that no more Muslim refugees should be sent to Pakistan from Delhi.[48]

In Shimla, the district authorities had been asked in mid-October 1947 not to send any more Muslim refugees to Kalka. It is difficult to establish how many Muslims were, at that stage, still left in the summer capital of the colonial government of India. But there is a report of 29 June 1948 which says that there was only one Muslim in Shimla on this date, a bearer who had been with Penderel Moon since 1929; and he was escorted 'back to Pakistan' by Moon that July.[49] Exaggerated or not, the report indicates the kind of search for 'enemy' nationals and the urge to drive out every sign of the 'other' from places far and wide in India and Pakistan.

In Delhi, already by September 1947, there were numerous elements that felt that there could no longer be any place in the city or its environs for Muslims: on occasion they suggested (hopefully?) that the vast majority of Muslims themselves preferred to leave.[50] Such proponents of a wholesale Muslim emigration were to be found at every level of society and government: from the deputy prime minister of India, Vallabhbhai Patel, to the deputy commissioner of Delhi, M. S. Randhawa, to the growing numbers of Sikh and Hindu refugees who had fled from Pakistan with, all too often, nothing but their clothes on their backs.

It is a feature of the records of the time that the terms, 'Hindus' and 'Hindu refugees', 'Muslims' and 'Muslim refugees', 'Sikhs' and 'Sikh refugees', are often used interchangeably. In many parts of northern, north-western and north-eastern India, the distinction was indeed difficult to maintain; and the question of choosing where they wished to stay, or which nation they would adopt as their own, hardly arose for very large numbers of Muslims, Sikhs and Hindus caught on the 'wrong side of the border'. In Delhi and Alwar, Ambala and Amritsar, Muslims were urged to leave – 'for their own good'; as were Hindus and Sikhs in

---

[48] (IOR) Mss. Eur. F200/53, emergency committee meeting (17 October 1947). See also *ibid.*, vol. 129, Suhrawardy to Gandhi (21 September 1947): 'In any event...Meo refugees ought not to be sent to Pakistan.'
[49] (IOR) Mss. Eur. F230/21, Penderel Moon to his sister (29 June 1948).
[50] (IOR) Mss. Eur. F200/53, emergency committee meeting (17 October 1947), for example.

Bahawalpur and Sindh, Lahore and Sialkot, and many other parts of the new Pakistan.

In Mewat, to take one final example, what was described as a war between a dominant, land-holding community of Hindu Jats and a cultivating community of Muslim Meos raged from May 1947 onwards and reached a climax in October–November of that year. This drove large numbers of Meo peasants out of their villages. Some of the worst outrages against the Meos occurred in the territories of the states of Alwar and Bharatpur, apparently with the tacit support of the state authorities; and in November, the maharaja of Alwar expressed himself against the return of any of the Meos who had earlier left the state in fear. On 17 November, a column of 80,000 Meo refugees was said to be on its way to Pakistan. Two days later, however, 10,000 Meos were found moving in the reverse direction, having decided that the risks entailed in remaining in Indian Mewat were smaller than those involved in trying to reach and settle down in Pakistan.[51]

The condition of the Meos does no more than underscore the extraordinary volatility of the moment. Proud inheritors of local traditions that they shared with Hindu neighbours, 'half Muslims' as they were sometimes described, a community which solemnised its marriages in both Muslim and Hindu ceremonies (the *nikaah* and the *phera*),[52] the Meos now became plain and simple 'Muslims', free-floating and faceless examples of the 'other', subject to attack like so many other north Indian 'Muslims', or 'Hindus' or 'Sikhs', at a time when the measure of a person's identity was the manner of her/his dress or the extent of his/her fear. They had suddenly become 'Indians' and 'Pakistanis' too. When this happened, and by whose choice, few could say.

The uncertainty of it all

The advent of Partition and Independence was marked by extraordinary uncertainty. A fact that is easily overlooked today, precisely because of the categorical establishment of India and Pakistan as separate, sovereign states on 15 August 1947, is that it was just ten weeks before that date, in early June 1947, that the formal, constitutional partition of British India was finally decided upon. A month before that, in early May, Mountbatten, widely described as the author of the plan to divide India surgically and quickly as the best way out of the existing political and constitutional

---

[51] (IOR) L/P&J/7/12589, R. M. Hadow's report of his tour of Gurgaon and Alwar state from 17 November 1947. Many Meos from the Bharatpur and Alwar territories shifted to the erstwhile British Indian parts of Mewat, sometimes occupying lands and houses evacuated by other Meos who had been driven out, killed or banished to Pakistan.

[52] On the Meos, see Mayaram, *Resisting Regimes*.

mess, was still discussing the repercussions (in Punjab and elsewhere) of a partition – 'if it comes to that'.[53] There was at the same time continued discussion of a possible agreement being reached among the major Indian political parties on some slightly modified version of the May 1946, Cabinet Mission Plan.

In late June, three weeks after the British announcement of their new plan to partition the subcontinent and withdraw from its government by August 1947, Congress workers and leaders in central India (today's Madhya Pradesh) were still talking of June 1948 – the deadline earlier announced by Attlee – as the date when the British would hand over power to Indians. There were many people in the country who were far from being persuaded that the British would actually leave.[54]

From early June 1947, within a few days of the announcement that the principle of Partition had been accepted, until July, Penderel Moon, concerned like many other Punjab civilians for the future well-being of 'his' province, made concerted efforts to get the Sikhs to 'throw in their lot with their Muslim brethren in the Punjab'.[55] In many parts of Punjab, relations between Muslims and Sikhs had already reached a nadir following the outbreak of mass violence and murder from March onwards. It speaks of the openness of so many questions even at this stage that, in spite of the extreme polarisation, the Sikh maharaja of Nabha and even Baldev Singh, perhaps the most prominent 'constitutional' representative of the Sikhs at this time, still responded to Moon's initiative and considered the possibility of establishing a Sikh-dominated East Punjab unit within the new state of Pakistan, provided this unit had the right to secede if necessary.[56] At the other end of the subcontinent, Abul Hashim, the secretary of the Bengal provincial Muslim League, joined H. S. Suhrawardy, the Muslim League chief minister of pre-Partition Bengal, and others in propagating the increasingly wishful scheme of a sovereign and united Bengal.[57]

The meaning of Partition was worked out step by step in 1947–8 and afterwards. The point is dramatically illustrated by some of the earliest

[53] (IOR) Mss. Eur. F200/168, Mountbatten to Wylie (4 May 1947).
[54] See *ibid.*, vol. 38, Mountbatten to Fred Bourne (25 June 1947); and vol. 28, Dow to Mountbatten (18 June 1947).
[55] (IOR) Mss. Eur. F230/31, Penderel Moon to Master Sujan Singh (Bahawalpur, 8 June 1947).
[56] *Ibid.*, Sant Singh, maharaja of Nabha, to Moon, letters of 18 June 1947, and 5 and 9 July 1947. See also Giani Kartar Singh's reported feeler to Jinnah regarding the possibility of a 'Sikh state' joining Pakistan after Partition; (IOR) Mss. Eur. F200/141, 'Refutation of Charges Regarding Sikhs', draft brief for Indian delegation to UN Security Council (24 February 1948).
[57] Cf. Ahmed Kamal, 'A Land of Eternal Eid'; and Gordon, 'Divided Bengal', in Hasan, *India's Partition*.

reported reactions of Muslim League leaders in UP after the announcement of the Partition plan of 3 June 1947. Muslim League members of the UP legislature had 'suddenly begun to coo like doves', wrote the British governor of the province. 'Seemingly the whole attitude now is that in UP we must forget the past and become all brothers together . . . The truth is that . . . Pakistan is of little use to the UP. It has to be got across that the Muslim League everywhere was in favour of Pakistan and that nothing less than a "national home" for the Muslims would meet the case. Now that the said home is *almost* certainly [*sic*] to be provided, our Leaguers quite obviously feel that they can drop out of the fight and look after their own local . . . interests.'[58]

Consider, again, the matter of the exchange of populations which transformed Partition into one of the greatest mass migrations in history. Although Jinnah had earlier expressed the view that such an exchange may well become necessary on the establishment of Pakistan, the realisation of that goal brought other hopes to the surface. In this respect, Jinnah's position was not unlike that of the League leaders in UP when they learnt that the principle of Partition had been conceded. Hence his address to the Pakistan Constituent Assembly: 'We are all . . . equal citizens of one state . . . Hindus would [soon] cease to be Hindus and Muslims would cease to be Muslims, not in the religious sense, because that is the personal faith of each individual, but in the political sense as citizens of the state.'[59]

Until almost the end of August 1947, Jinnah and Jawaharlal Nehru, along with a host of other leaders and officials on both sides, expressed their opposition to any large-scale transfer of populations.[60] Yet by the beginning of September, several lakhs of Punjabi refugees were on the move, under official 'coordination', in both directions. On 15 September, Nehru, making a reconnaissance flight over the area, saw two convoys of refugees on foot that stretched for forty miles.[61] Even at this stage, however, Jinnah and the governments of both East and West Punjab continued to express the hope that 'officials of the opposite community would at a later stage come back [or, where they had not left, stay on] and serve in their Provinces'.[62] And in 1948, while the struggle to keep Punjab as it once was had been abandoned, Suhrawardy was still

[58] (IOR) Mss. Eur. F200/168, Wylie to Mountbatten (9 June 1947), emphasis added.
[59] Shahid Javed Burki, *Pakistan. A Nation in the Making* (Boulder, Colo., 1986), p. 42.
[60] (IOR) Mss. Eur. F200/128, C. M. Trivedi, governor of East Punjab to Mountbatten (camp Jullunder, 28 August 1947).
[61] (IOR) Mss. Eur. F200/129, emergency committee meeting (15 September 1947).
[62] *Ibid.* See also (IOR) Mss. Eur. D621/14, Wilfrid Russell's diaries, entry for 28 September 1947, citing his meeting with the deputy commissioner of Gujranwala, 'Mahmud', who was 'insistent that Pakistan must try and attract [the] Hindus back sooner or later'.

urging the need to encourage the minorities to return to Sindh and East Bengal.[63]

It was in December 1947 that the government of India declared Pakistan to be 'foreign territory' for the purpose – and for this restricted purpose alone – of levying duties on raw jute and jute manufactures exported from India.[64] Exit permits, passports and visas for travel between the two countries – a special 'Pakistan passport' first, and only later the standard passport needed for international travel – were still some time in the future. On the Indian side, in 1947–8, there was persistent talk of possible re-unification, and many – even in the highest political circles – thought that Pakistan simply would not last.

An unusually telling example of contemporary uncertainties comes from September 1947. Pakistani army headquarters approached the authorities of Aligarh Muslim University, eighty miles east of Delhi and practically in the heart of the political and sectarian upheaval in India at the time, to provide appropriate candidates from the university for recruitment to regular commissions in the Pakistan army. That request, and the university authorities' innocent response – 'Those interested in the above [call for applications] should see me in the Geography Department with a written application giving full particulars'[65] – indicates how little the idea had sunk in, even for people in government, that these were now separate countries and that existing lines of communication and supply would therefore have to be reconsidered, if not cut off.[66]

There was not in August 1947, or for some time afterwards (in the case of Bengal, for many years afterwards), any way of knowing who would belong where when things finally settled down. While British India, and with it Punjab and Bengal, were officially partitioned on 15 August 1947, the precise boundary lines between the divided parts were not announced until 17 August. There was, even after that, considerable uncertainty on

[63] (IOR) Mss. Eur. F200/84, record of conversation between H. S. Suhrawardy and Alan Campbell-Johnson (30 May 1948, dictated by the latter on 31 May 1948).

[64] *The Hindustan Times*, 23 December 1947; see Ganda Singh's 'Diary of Partition Days', cited in Mushirul Hasan, ed., *India Partitioned*, vol. II, p. 87.

[65] Durga Das, ed., *Sardar Patel's Correspondence, 1945–50*, vol. IV (Ahmedabad, 1972), pp. 426–7.

[66] Another interesting illustration of this comes from the highest civil official of Lahore division, a Hindu member of the Indian Civil Service (ICS), living in the capital of the province and the headquarters of Muslim League politics at this time, who asked his mother and sister, as they prepared to journey to Delhi on 13 August 1947, to take clothes only for two or three weeks since they would be back in Lahore as soon as things settled down; interview with Romila Thapar about her uncle's experiences, Delhi, November 1996. See Nighat Said Khan, 'Identity, Violence and Women: a Reflection on the Partition of India, 1947', in Khan, *et al.*, eds., *Locating the Self*, p. 159, for a statement of how general this feeling was in provinces like Sindh.

the ground as to the exact arrangement of the dividing lines between India and Pakistan. Had Gurdaspur, or Malda, or particular *tahsils* and even villages in those districts, gone to India or Pakistan? Where would this – or that – village 'go'? The Chakmas are reported to have raised the Indian flag at Rangamati on 15 August 1947, when it was still unclear whether the Chittagong Hill Tracts (now part of Bangladesh, earlier of East Pakistan) had been 'awarded' to India or Pakistan; and the Marmas, the second largest non-Bengali group in the Chittagong Hill Tracts, raised the Burmese flag at Bandarban on the same day.[67]

Where would, or could, Toba Tek Singh 'go', in Manto's justly famous query?[68] And where was home, or nation, to be for that Muslim employee of Aligarh Muslim University who woke up a faculty member early on the morning of 15 August and said, in some consternation, 'I hear Pakistan has been established . . . , [but] Aligarh is not in Pakistan?'[69] Consider, again, the protagonist of Intizar Husain's 'An Unwritten Epic', who is 'flabbergasted' that Qadirpur, where he lives, could be outside of Pakistan.[70] This kind of uncertainty persisted in the case of several princely states, as we all know, for a considerable time. Where would Hyderabad or Kashmir, for instance, 'go'? In the case of the latter, the question is still being asked.

The 'three partitions' – or three different conceptions of Partition – to which I have alluded are not easily separated. They are perhaps better conceived of as three different moments (or aspects) of the same event, or at least an event that has become single – and singular – in our reconstruction of the past. They flow into one another, overlap and depend upon each other. It scarcely needs to be said that what is involved here is more than the drawing of new lines on a map, the unfurling of new national flags and the installation of new national governments. What we are dealing with is the tearing apart of individuals, families, homes, villages and linguistic and cultural communities that would once have been called nationalities; and the gradual realisation that this tearing apart was permanent – and that it necessitated new borders, communities, identities and histories.

---

[67] See Willem van Schendel, 'Who Speaks for the Nation? Nationalist Rhetoric and the Challenge of Cultural Pluralism in Bangladesh', in Eric-Jan Zurcher and Willem van Schendel, eds., *Opting Out of the Nation. Identity Politics in Central, South and West Asia* (London, 1999).

[68] The protagonist in Manto's famous story, the 'lunatic' Bishan Singh, asks repeatedly whether his native village of Toba Tek Singh has gone to India or Pakistan, without ever getting a satisfactory answer; see *Manto ke numaindah afsane* (comp. Atahar Parvez, Aligarh, 1981); and for an English translation, Khalid Hasan, *Kingdom's End and Other Stories* (London, 1987).

[69] Interview (Delhi, 7 February 1995).

[70] Intizar Husain, 'An Unwritten Epic', in Memon, ed., *An Epic Unwritten*, p. 162.

There are many different stories to be told about 1947, many different perspectives to be recovered. Stories and perspectives that tell of other histories and other political possibilities. I pursue the task of analysing other stories and thinking other histories and politics in the remaining chapters of this book. It may help, however, to begin with the historians' history of Partition – because it is the chief body of writing whose stated intention is to recount the 'truth' of that event, and because of its obvious influence.

3   Historians' history

Historians' history works, I suggest, to produce the 'truth' of the traumatic, genocidal violence of Partition and to elide it at the same time. Several different techniques are employed.

One is to declare such violence non-narratable: the 'limit case' of history, as it has been described in the instance of the Holocaust. The problem is that of the peculiar individuation of these 'uniquely unique' events, a leading philosopher has declared. 'Victimization is the other side of history that no cunning of reason can ever justify', writes Ricouer, reflecting on the theme of *tremendum horrendum* in our experience of the past. 'Every other form of individuation is the counterpart to a work of explanation that connects things together. But horror isolates events by making them incomparable, incomparably unique, uniquely unique.'[1]

It is possible to suggest that all societies have their own limit cases. The Nazi Holocaust occupies this place in a very wide range of European and American scholarship. For many Indian scholars, on the other hand, that unbelievable violence is still historicisable, organised as it is by the state – a factor that is said to allow for comparison and explanation. Partition is, in this perspective, even more 'unhistorical' and inexplicable than the Holocaust. For this was not industrialised slaughter, directed from a distance, but a hand-to-hand, face-to-face destruction, frequently involving neighbour against neighbour. Its sites were more random. Its archives are more dispersed and imprecise.

Another disciplinary device that is widely used to distance ourselves from such fearful moments of the past is that of transforming the history of the event into a history of its causes or origins – which, thus, themselves

---

[1] Paul Ricouer, *Time and Narrative*, vol. III, tr. by Kathleen Blamey and David Pellauer (Chicago, 1985), pp. 187, 188. Ricouer speaks in this context of the 'conflict between explanation that connects things together and horror that isolates . . .' Rather than allow this situation to lead to a ruinous dichotomy, he urges, we should seek 'to elevate, each by means of the other, historical explanation and individuation through horror'. Cf. Pradeep Jeganathan's critique of the trope of 'horror' in his 'After a Riot: Anthropological Locations of Violence in an Urban Sri Lankan Community' (Ph. D. dissertation, University of Chicago, 1997), p. 6 and *passim*.

become the event. Yet again, one may render the account null and void by representing the violence as a part not of this, but of some other history: an alien people or nation's doing.

One may also make the violence non-narratable in another way – by localising it: in time, as a freak occurrence, like a natural calamity, which requires no historical explanation ('these things happen'); or in space, as a characteristic happening in some unassimilated part of the society or the world ('these things happen there').[2]

The present chapter considers the effects of these common historiographical procedures in relation to some of the most significant Indian historical writings on Partition. We need to begin by situating this historiographical tradition in a wider perspective.

National traditions and national pasts

A feature of history writing that is not widely advertised in the profession or the wider reading public is that of the close inter-connection between state, nation and history in its modern incarnation. Another is that different nation-states and their histories have had rather different trajectories, careers and contexts. At the risk of considerable oversimplification, let me make the latter point quickly by reference to the specific conditions of a few well-known nationalisms and their different approaches to their pasts.

The example of Germany is widely seen as representing the culturalist/romantic moment in the theory of European nationalism. It was marked in the nineteenth century by an insistent search for unity and uniformity, inspired by visions of one language, one *volk*. In the decades since 1945, German historiography – and indeed all writing on Germany – appears to be transformed by the Holocaust. What we have thereafter is not a memory/history exclusively of the Holocaust, but certainly one that functions in its wake. Vigorous and long-lasting debates on the question of guilt or responsibility for the destruction of the Jews and other sections of Germany's population now become the means of shaping the boundaries of two nations or ethnicities (German and Jewish), even if the one begins to claim a history going back no further than 1945,[3] and the other, one that extends unbroken from pre-biblical times.

---

[2] This theme is elaborated in ch. 5.

[3] See Jurgen Habermas, 'The European Nation-State: on the Past and Future of Sovereignty and Citizenship', *Public Culture*, 10, 2 (1998); also his contributions in *Forever in the Shadow of Hitler? Original Documents of the* Historikerstreit, *the Controversy Concerning the Singularity of the Holocaust*, tr. by James Knowlton and Truett Cates (Atlantic Highlands, N.J. 1993); and Hans Mommsen, 'The Germans and the Holocaust: the Problem of Collective Responsibility' (lecture delivered in the history department, Johns Hopkins University, 2 March 2000). For the importance of the nation-state

France is said, by contrast, to provide the political/rational moment in the theory of nationalism, with its emphasis on the people of a territory, on freedom and equality, and on the future. The heritage of republicanism and socialism is of critical importance in the historical reconstruction of France after the Revolution, and even more so after the revolutions and counter-revolutions of the nineteenth century.

A recent analysis sums up the contrast between the French and the German case as follows. 'The French have defined themselves territorially in terms of a country created by a state and then productive of a nation; the Germans have defined themselves ethnocentrically in terms of a community of descent (in theory), of language (in practice), which is then productive of a state ... The one is inclusivist of everybody in a place, the other is inclusivist only of people who share certain ethnic or cultural characteristics.'[4]

In marking these distinctions, I am obviously not suggesting that the first (the culturalist, German moment) has nothing in it of the second (the political, rational), or vice versa. The point is rather to underscore what have been seen as primary elements in these different national traditions. In neither case, let me add, is there any acknowledgement of (French or German) conquests overseas and the fact that stability, prosperity, uniformity, culture and nationhood at home were built on the backs of colonial exploitation.[5] History – like the nation – is presented as a matter of natural, automatic and autonomous growth, an immaculate conception – uninfluenced, except in a contingent way, by the development of world capitalism, European dominance, scientific racism and other related phenomena.

The last point allows me to move straight on to the case of Indian nationalism and its historiography. What distinguishes this nationalism is its critical, oppositional character: scarcely surprising given its anti-colonial context. What is perhaps less obvious is that Indian historiography has shared this critical, oppositional stance from the beginning. This is evident in its openly political character, its recognition of the close and binding relationship between 'history' and politics, its awareness that the same history may be told from many perspectives and, implicitly (though

---

in Germany and the liberal-conservative proposition that the nation should be seen as the 'normal' form of organisation of societies, especially in the West, see also Stefan Berger, 'Historians and the Search for National Identity in the Reunified Germany', in Berger *et al.*, eds., *Writing National Histories*, pp. 252–64.

[4] Adrian Hastings, *The Construction of Nationhood. Ethnicity, Religion and Nationalism* (Cambridge, 1997), p. 13, drawing from Rogers Brubaker, *Citizenship and Nationhood in France and Germany* (Cambridge, Mass., 1992).

[5] See Habermas, 'The European Nation-State', and the critiques of his essay by Timothy Mitchell, Liisa Malkki and Arjun Appadurai in the same issue of *Public Culture*.

I know I exaggerate here), of the possibility of many histories – many kinds of histories – of the same event or object.

Two characteristics of nationalist history writing in India need to be underlined, even if they appear somewhat clichéd once set down. First, this writing developed directly in opposition to colonialism, yet in an ambivalent relationship with it: affinal, in the urge to write 'history', which must of course be a 'scientific', 'objective' history; and at the same time adversarial, in that this history challenges a great deal of the fundamental propositions of colonialist historiography. Secondly, this historiography was driven by a desire not only to show the antiquity, wisdom and 'manliness' of Indians in the past, but also to demonstrate the unity of India's diverse peoples and traditions – 'unity in diversity' as the nationalist slogan had it – which was in turn a proof of its singularity and greatness. This latter impulse was accentuated by the events of 1947, when decolonisation produced not only the division into India and Pakistan that actually occurred, but also the threat of a more far-reaching Balkanisation. Indian historical writing, it seems to me, has never escaped from the constraints of this obligation to demonstrate oneness. Writings on Partition bear the marks of it until today.

The acorn for the oak

The enduring concern with unity in Indian historiography is easier to comprehend if we see it in the context of nationalist histories produced in other countries that gained their independence in the twentieth century. The major organising principle in most of these has been, precisely, *the process leading to national independence*, which has then marked the end of history, as it were. History stops in textbooks of Indian history in 1947, after which Political Science and Economics supervene. Along with this, Indian historians have drawn an important dividing line between the history of nationalism in India leading to Independence in 1947, and the history of what is called 'communalism' (internal conflict and sectarian strife) leading to Partition.[6] Scholars of all persuasions have written forcefully, and often with considerable sophistication, of the new forces and contradictions that came with colonialism, and of the growth of an anti-colonial movement, leading inexorably – if slowly – to national independence. This is the *real* history of India, especially the India of the late nineteenth and twentieth centuries. By contrast, the history of Partition is seen as something of an intrusion – a dramatic and, as it was for some time represented, ephemeral deviation from

---

[6] For a fuller discussion of this theme, see my *Construction of Communalism in Colonial North India, passim.*

the 'natural' movement towards majority, independent rule in a united subcontinent.

Intrusion, imposition or whatever, Partition still required explanation. To ascribe it simply to the machinations of the colonial regime, or the fall-out of the misdeeds of anti-social elements and self-seeking politicians was, if rhetorically effective, historically unconvincing or at least inadequate. What Indian historians did in addition, therefore, was to move their case to another, less commonsensical plane: first, by drawing a distinction between 'cause' and 'event' and suggesting that the investigation of the former was the primary task of the historian; and secondly, by consigning violence, as historiography has often done, to a realm outside the domain of 'history'.

The disciplinary attachment to origins or causes has come in handy. Historians of Partition have departed even from the origins–outcomes arrangement that has been the trademark of history writing on many of the major events of recent centuries.[7] Research has focused on the years *preceding* Partition. Comparatively little attention has been paid by historians – as opposed to development experts, economists, political scientists and so on[8] – to the period *following* those years, let alone the period of Partition itself.

The event of Partition itself is supposedly implicit in its predisposing causes. Furet's important critique of the parallel procedures in the historiography of the French Revolution may be recalled here. Calling attention to the 'unvarying internal organisation' of the historical writing on this subject, he notes that 'analysis is restricted to the problem of "origins" or causes . . . Narrative begins with the "events", in 1787 or 1789 and runs through to the end of the "story" . . . as if, once the causes are set out, the play went on by itself, propelled by the initial upheaval.' A phenomenon like the French Revolution, Furet goes on to say (and the point applies with equal force to Partition), 'cannot be reduced to a simple cause-and-effect schema . . . Let us assume for a moment that these causes are better

---

[7] For one discussion of this, see Lynn Hunt, *Politics, Culture, and Class in the French Revolution* (Berkeley and Los Angeles, 1984), Introduction.

[8] Cf. the major writings on refugees which initially came mainly from officials: Tarlok Singh, *Land Resettlement Manual (for Displaced Persons in Punjab and PEPSU)* (Shimla, 1952); M. S. Randhawa, *Out of the Ashes: the Rehabilitation of Refugees from West Pakistan in Rural Areas of East Punjab* (Bombay, 1954); U. Bhaskar Rao, *The Story of Rehabilitation* (Delhi, 1967); and for non-official examples, Stephen L. Keller, *Uprooting and Social Change* (Delhi, 1975); V. N. Datta, 'Panjabi Refugees and the Urban Development of Greater Delhi', in R. E. Frykenberg, ed., *Delhi Through the Ages. Selected Essays in Urban History, Culture and Society* (Delhi, 1993); and Karuna Chananana, 'Partition and Family Strategies: Gender-Education Linkages among Punjabi Women in Delhi', *Economic and Political Weekly*, 'Review of Women's Studies' (24 April 1993); among others.

understood than they actually are, or that some day it will be possible to list them in a more functional order; the fact remains that the revolutionary event, from *the very outset*, totally transformed the existing situation and created a new mode of historical action that was not intrinsically a part of that situation.'[9]

Koselleck makes the same sort of argument at a more abstract level. 'One introduces for the understanding of a particular occurrence *causae* which are not contained by this occurrence.' There are two kinds of objections to this procedure, he suggests. First,

such a form of proof can be infinitely extended. There is no rational and unambiguously demonstrable boundary of possible origination beyond which causes are no longer valid . . . Whoever becomes involved with causality naturally enough cannot explain everything by means of everything, but it is possible to advance as many causes for each event as one wishes.

In addition, Koselleck posits a structural feature of history, which points to another difficulty that is not 'causally soluble': that every historical constellation contains 'both more and less' than is embedded in any particular historical occurrence. It is here that he locates history's 'surprising singularity, transformability, and its changeability', without which, one would have to say, history – as change – would not be possible. Hence his conclusion: 'If one wishes to comprehend the singularity of a historical event, one can only use causal inferences in a subsidiary role.'[10]

It is not my contention that socio-economic explanations, or wider ranging investigations of origins, have nothing to say about Partition. However, that is hardly an end to the history of the event. As W. C. Smith puts it, in another context, 'If you wish to understand oaks, you should study more than acorns!'[11] The historian's enterprise needs to go beyond providing a statement of the genesis of Hindu–Muslim antagonisms, and hence (?) of the Pakistan movement, and hence (?) of the violence that occurred as it neared its end. It surely needs to explore the meaning of Partition in terms of the new social arrangements, new consciousnesses and new subjectivities to which it gave rise.

In spite of the acknowledgement of colossal violence in northern India in 1947, however, and the repeated statement that no one had – or could

[9] Francois Furet, *Interpreting the French Revolution* (1978; Cambridge, 1981), pp. 18, 22 (emphasis in original).
[10] Reinhart Koselleck, *Futures Past. On the Semantics of Historical Time* (Cambridge, Mass., 1985), pp. 227, 228.
[11] Wilfrid Cantwell Smith, 'The True Meaning of Scripture: an Empirical Historian's Nonreductionist Interpretation of the Qur'an', *International Journal of Middle East Studies*, 11, 4 (1980), p. 499.

have – anticipated what happened at the time, Partition historians remain overwhelmingly concerned with causes. It is neither the genocidal murder and suffering, nor the issue of the consequences for Indian and Pakistani nationalism and nation building, that provides the charge in this body of writings, but the question of India's unity. What caused the breakup of the country? What are the implications of different historical interpretations (indeed of different historical questions) for the furthering of Indian unity and disunity?

One major history after another harks on the reasons for Hindu–Muslim antagonism, for the decision of the leading Muslim party to go a separate way and, to a lesser extent, on the causes of the unprecedented violence of the mid-1940s. Mushirul Hasan has it as follows in a recent articulation: 'For many of us in the subcontinent, still confronted with and troubled by the bitter legacy of Pakistan, the critical and unresolved issue is how Jinnah and the League were able to secure the support of so many Muslims in so short a time.'[12] Seeking to explain 'the transformation of patriots into power-hungry politicians', Sumit Sarkar writes: 'The bait of complete transfer of power by a definite and fairly early date proved too tempting to be refused – particularly as the only real alternative for the Congress was to plunge into another mass confrontation, difficult in the context of communal riots and very dangerous socially in view of what appeared to be a growing Left menace.' And in another summary statement in the same essay: 'Indian business groups ... [also] fell short of the "national bourgeois" ideal-type ... in their frequent preference of sectional over country-wide class interests. This became very important indeed during the last years of British rule, for, as the events of 1945–47 tragically proved, the price of a negotiated transfer of power was an encouragement of divisive forces culminating in Partition.'[13] 'How did a Pakistan come about which fitted the interests of most Muslims so poorly?' asks Jalal, adding that this is the central problem to which her book addresses itself.[14]

Sarkar finds a good part of the answer in dereliction of duty on the part of the British Indian government in the face of the 'unprecedented ... riots' of 1946–7 – 'the British, who as late as June 1946 had been making plans to bring five army divisions to India in the context of a possible Congress movement, made no such move while presiding over this awesome human tragedy' – and in the growth of 'lumpen elements' (as a result of years of famine-related malnutrition) who provided 'ample combustible material for communal riots on a totally unprecedented

---

[12] Mushirul Hasan, ed., *India's Partition*, p. 42.
[13] Sumit Sarkar, *A Critique of Colonial India* (Calcutta, 1985), pp. 144, 139 and 120.
[14] Jalal, *The Sole Spokesman*, p. 4.

scale from August 1946 onwards'.[15] Suranjan Das's study of the 1946 Calcutta riots follows Sarkar's account closely. He borrows the very same phrase that Sarkar had taken from Penderel Moon for a more general characterisation of the times – the 'edge of a volcano' – to describe the condition of Calcutta in mid-1946: 'Destitutes collected from the city streets almost doubled between March and June 1946, and the months preceding the August outbreak witnessed a steady rise in Calcutta's mortality rate . . . These developments reduced the value of human lives.'[16]

Violence and civilisation

Furet has suggested that historians of the French Revolution would do better describing the ways in which the Revolution was represented than troubling about causes or consequences. In his reckoning, the event was made not so much by social upheaval as by rhetorical claims about the Revolution's meaning.[17] In fact, of course, historians cannot but attend to 'facts' and rhetoric simultaneously: for the extent of a social upheaval is determined by rhetorical claims and vice versa.[18] It becomes necessary, therefore, to construct a more layered account of the struggle against particular kinds of domination – and the institution of new kinds of domination, new contradictions, new subjects and new subject positions – that is the history of Partition. And in seeking to recover the meaning of these, the moment of violence will require greater attention than Indian historians have as a rule been willing to give it.

Overwhelmingly, 'violence' and 'Partition' ('riots' and 'politics', the 'primitive' and the 'modern'?) have been seen as being two quite separate things in this historical enterprise. Scholars have spoken commonly of the bloodbath, the violence or simply (and frequently) the 'riots' that *accompanied* Partition in 1947. Thereby they have made a judicious, if not always conscious, separation between a 'partition' that was *history* ('historical', consequential, explicable) and an exhibition of violence that was not – that was, indeed, more or less an aberration.

---

[15] Sarkar, *Critique of Colonial India*, pp. 119 and 133–4.
[16] Suranjan Das, *Communal Riots in Bengal*, p. 162. Das stresses too the prominence of goondas – 'an umbrella-term used to denote a broad spectrum of social groups, ranging from various marginalized elements to habitual criminals' – in the actual carrying out of violence; and the abdication of responsibility by the State – 'Important British civilians reportedly "enjoyed" themselves in the Calcutta Club whilst the city was ablaze'; pp. 184–5 and 187–8. See also I. Talbot, *Freedom's Cry. The Popular Dimension in the Pakistan Movement and Partition Experience in North-West India* (Karachi, 1996), p. 50, for another statement along similar lines.
[17] Furet, *Interpreting the French Revolution*, pp. 14–17 and *passim*.
[18] I elaborate this point in ch. 5.

In cutting their historical canvas in this way, subcontinental historians are by no means exceptional, but Indian historiography has its own particular reasons for making the emphatic distinctions that it makes. One particular political circumstance goes a long way towards setting the limits in this aspect of Indian historical endeavour. Communalism – 'the opposition to each other of religious communities', as Dumont provocatively if inaccurately described it[19] – has found a place in Indian political discourse as possibly the most important obstacle to be overcome in the evolution of a just, progressive and modern society in the subcontinent. The battle against communalism has thus been at the centre of the struggle for nationalism and democracy in India, no less notably in the last decade and a half as fifty years ago. This has deeply and understandably coloured all of the most serious historical work on nationalism and the nation-state coming out of the country (and, I would add, out of Pakistan and Bangladesh too).

Serious historians are right to maintain, Dumont notwithstanding, that communalism is not in the main about religion. Indeed Dumont acknowledges as much when, immediately after proffering the definition cited above, he goes on to speak of communalism (in W. C. Smith's words) as 'that ideology which emphasises as the social, political, and economic unit the group of adherents of each religion, and emphasises the distinction, even the antagonism, between such groups'.[20] Once this move has been made, the insistent search for the causes of historical events leads the historian of communal violence away from any interest in the ideological power of religion to detailed investigation of the importance of politics and of social and economic circumstance.[21]

'Religion' is put in its place, as it were, in the effort to combat communalism and build a modern, progressive nation. As Athar Ali, a major authority on Mughal history, put it time and again in his undergraduate lectures: 'Religion was a matter of convenience for Aurangzeb [the last of the 'Great Mughals', and by common consent a deeply pious and orthodox Muslim], not a matter of conviction.'[22] Or as another leading historian has it, in a survey of writings on medieval Indian history in which he notes the shift of historical investigation 'towards society's lower end, indeed towards its lowest end' and the increasing attention to labour processes and socio-economic conditions more broadly, 'the very

---

[19] L. Dumont, *Religion/Politics and History in India* (Paris, 1970), p. 89.
[20] *Ibid.*
[21] For a fuller discussion of this point, see my *Memory, History and the Question of Violence. Reflections on the Reconstruction of Partition* (Calcutta, 1999).
[22] Personal communication from Muzaffar Alam.

complexity of this [kind of] study allows religion merely the share that is its due in social life [*sic*]'.[23]

The result, I suggest, is to consign 'religion' to oblivion in the best general histories of pre-modern, as of modern India. Much the same thing happens to the question of 'violence' – and here the criteria seen to be making for self-respect, rationality and progress are very much more widely shared, in India and abroad. In its most common representation (or self-representation) modern civilisation has been equated with a state of non-violence, where mature, adult human beings negotiate with one another and determine their rights and duties through rational argument. Elias's account of the 'civilising process' fits well with this view. Through the civilising process, Elias has suggested, the 'necessary control of impulses' is increasingly transferred from an exterior prohibition, imposed often by force, to an almost unconscious self-restraint. However, 'the peculiar stability of the apparatus of psychological self-restraint which emerges as a decisive trait built into the habitus of every civilized human being, stands in the closest relationship to the monopolization of physical force and the growing stability of the central organs of society'.[24]

'Civilisation' is the absence, then, or at least the strict restriction, of violence. Of the two controlling elements, the state and self-control, however, the first may be said to have the upper hand. This is what underlies Europe's 'civilising mission' in the rest of the world. But it would seem to apply at an earlier stage in Europe too – before Europe became 'Europe'. It is the state and its laws that ultimately ensure self-restraint. In a more extreme version of the thesis, the state assures civilisation. At the same time, of course, the state equals 'history'. Let me quote Hegel once more, for he puts the argument squarely.

History is the progress of freedom. Freedom is possible only in the state. The life of peoples, as individuals and even communities before the state belongs to *pre*-history. As a translator of the philosopher has it, for Hegel 'the story of individuals alone, and even of individuals in the still emotional, irrational community of the family, is not yet history'.[25] And Hegel himself:

India not only has old books of religion and brilliant works of poetry but also old codes of law – which above were mentioned as a condition of the formation of history – and yet it has no history. In that country the impulse of organization, which begins to differentiate society, was immediately petrified into the natural

---

[23] Harbans Mukhia, 'Communalism and the Writing of Medieval Indian History: a Reappraisal', *Social Scientist*, 123 (August 1983).

[24] Norbert Elias, *The Civilizing Process. Sociogenetic and Psychogenetic Investigations*, revised edn (Oxford, 2000), pp. 369, 373 and *passim*.

[25] Hegel, *Reason in History*, pp. 74–5 and *passim*; and Hartman's introduction, p. xxxi.

distinctions of caste . . . Because of that bondage of the caste system, in all historical relation there is wild arbitrariness, ephemeral bustling, indeed, raging without
a final purpose of progress or development.[26]

The proposition was, of course, in line with the predominant colonial
view of Indian society before the coming of the British: with or without
the restraining influence of caste, this was a society of un-civilisation, pre-
history and primitive passions. Untamed violence – and its exact opposite,
complete passivity (immobility, unchangingness) – was a mark of the
Indian past: that is, until India came up against the civilising influence
of the modern state in the form of British rule and western education.
Unfortunately, this predominant colonial knowledge went on to assert,
that 'past' – marked by an intemperate and pretty much indiscriminate
violence – lived on in the colonial Indian 'present', in spite of the best
efforts of British administrators and western educators.

James Mill's comments on the 1809 'riot' in Banaras are a classic in
this genre: 'The disturbance was characteristically illustrative . . . of the
discordant elements of Indian society, which are alone restrained [*sic*]
from frequent and destructive conflict by the vigilance, vigour and im-
partiality of the ruling power.' And again:

The resort of persons of all descriptions from every part of India, and the dissolute
and riotous conduct of a large proportion of its inhabitants or visitors, rendered
the maintenance of order and tranquillity in the sacred city of Benares, for some
time at least, a troublesome and imperfectly accomplished task; but the unrelaxing
firmness of British rule, a better knowledge of the British character, and the
improving intelligence of the people, gradually lightened the labour, and, ten
years after the transactions described, Benares was regulated with as much facility
as any other city in the territories of the Company.[27]

Hunter's account of *The Indian Musalmaans* written fifty years later is
informed by the same understanding of the seeds of 'civilisation'. It was
only through rigorous statecraft, careful education and 'the sober and ge-
nial knowledge of the West' that the anarchic violence of the East could
be curbed. 'By this path, the rising generation of Mohammedans would
tread the steps which have conducted the Hindus, not long ago the most

[26] *Ibid.*, pp. 75–7. Imagine, as Dubois does, what this country would have been without the
institutional restraint and codes of caste, Abbe J. A. Dubois, *Hindu Manners, Customs
and Ceremonies*, tr. by H. K. Beauchamp (1897; reprinted Oxford, 1928), pp. 29–30.
[27] James Mill (and H. H. Wilson), *The History of British India. From 1805 to 1835. In Three
Volumes*, vol. I (London, 1838), pp. 336 and 338–9. To this Wilson adds the following
footnote for good measure: 'In 1820 the writer was in the habit of traversing every part
of Benares without fear of molestation or insult. The materials for the beautiful map
of Benares, executed not long afterwards by . . . Mr James Prinsep, were collected by
him in the city, in fearless reliance upon the goodwill of the people, which he invariably
experienced', p. 339n.

bigoted nation on earth, into their present state of easy tolerance.'[28] Historiography, I wish to suggest, has long been in line with this view of the centrality of the state in 'history'.

The 'ahistoricity' of violence

'History' follows from the organisation of the state and its archive and has been designed in its disciplinary form to produce a coherent narrative of civilisation. The civilising state may use 'force' – in war, in counter-insurgency operations or simply expanding the frontiers of production and profit – but it never, apparently, uses 'violence'.[29] It is as though 'real' violence, of which the 'riot' might be described as the quintessential form, lies outside the domain of the state, outside progress and history. It is this disorganised, chaotic, 'irrational' violence – and, lest we forget, its opposite, apathy and resignation – that the historian of medieval and early modern Europe comes up against periodically. It was this that the colonial state supposedly encountered even more emphatically in its Indian colony, as elsewhere in Asia, Africa and the New World. And it is this untamed violence that has threatened to surface once more, whenever the state power has been weakened or has broken down.

An early account of Partition violence in Delhi will serve to make explicit the connection between the state, rational order, masculinity and civilisation upon which so much of our inherited modern political understanding is based. In the second volume of his autobiography, Nirad Chaudhuri quotes a detailed private account of events that he wrote in September–October 1947 after living through some three weeks of horrifying violence in Delhi. 'Periodically', he wrote then, '. . . a situation develops in India which neither Prime Minister nor Grand Vizir is able to control.' When looting continued in spite of the personal, even physical intervention of Prime Minister Nehru, and under the very noses of the military pickets on duty, it was, according to Chaudhuri, not the first time such things had happened.

In India, when empires decline, such things inevitably happen [*sic*]. In 1729, when the Mogul Empire was breaking up and Muhammad Shah was Emperor, there was a notorious Hindu-Muslim riot in Delhi, which has passed into history. Its centre was the great Jami Mosque built by Shah Jahan, which was nearer to the seat of the Emperor – the *Qala'-i-Mubarak*, 'Fortunate Citadel', present Red

---

[28] W. W. Hunter, *The Indian Musalmaans* (1871; reprint, Calcutta, 1945), p. 205.

[29] State violence is often written into the narrative as the unfortunate but necessary cost of progress. Marx's writings on India fall into this category, although they may be exceptional in their acknowledgement of the violent character of British rule in the subcontinent.

Fort – than Connaught Place [where looting occurred in September 1947] is to the seat of the Governor-General. At the request of the Emperor the Grand Vizir himself, Qamar-ud-din Khan Itimad-ud-daulah, went down to the Jami Mosque to quell the riots, but all he could do was to stand helplessly near the north gate, while even the men of the Imperial artillery joined in the fray.[30]

The writer signals his own modernity (and 'masculinity') when he expresses his personal preference for organised war over what he might have called 'infantile disorder'. 'Today', he wrote in his reflections on those three weeks of violence and the reactions to them, 'war is outlawed by solemn treaty and public opinion, [but] there is neither Kellogg Pact, nor Covenant of the League of Nations, nor UN Charter to outlaw riots. So, while *honourable war is in disgrace*, dishonourable rioting can be extolled as an instrument of policy . . . There is interminable and sickening bluster in the true Nazi manner from men who do not possess a hundredth part of the only virtue the Nazis had – guts [*sic*].'[31]

Nine months or so earlier, in a piece written for *The New English Review*, Nirad Chaudhuri had already compared conditions in early eighteenth century India, when the Mughal Empire was in decline, with those existing in late 1946. Three of the seven points he set down as showing the similarity of the two ages (nos. 1, 6 and 7 as published in his autobiography) concerned the collapse of state power and its consequences; another three (nos. 2, 3 and 4) were only a little less directly related to the decline of state power and probity. Here are brief extracts from the former three:

1. Complete ineffectiveness of the state. It could not resist foreign invasion, put down internal rebellions, suppress Hindu-Muslim riots (there were Hindu-Muslim riots even in those days [*sic*]), could not ensure efficient administration and was not successful in any project it initiated . . .
6. The effect of the decline of the power of the state on the masses was twofold. It made one part predatory and the other panicky . . .
7. Lastly, there grew up a habit of tolerance of anarchy and corruption, or at all events resignation to them . . . [32]

Historians far and wide have shared this association of statist order, masculinity and civilisation. Historical scholarship in India has been no

---

[30] Nirad C. Chaudhuri, *Thy Hand, Great Anarch! India 1921–1952* (London, 1987), p. 843.

[31] *Ibid.*, pp. 857–8, emphasis added. Compare with this the Hindu Mahasabha's call for 'violence on the most up-to-date western scientific lines [*sic*]' in its campaign for the 1945–6 elections: 'It would be wise if Congress were to take up . . . to meet the [Muslim League] threat of a Civil War, the Mahasabha slogan of "Train the Youths in Horse Riding and Rifle Shooting"'; cited in Joya Chatterji, *Bengal Divided*, p. 238.

[32] Chaudhuri, *Thy Hand, Great Anarch*, pp. 859–60.

exception. One needs only to re-read Jadunath Sarkar's account of the fall of the Mughal empire to have the point forcefully demonstrated. 'The Mughal Empire and with it the Maratha overlordship of Hindustan, fell because of the rottenness at the core of Indian society. This rottenness showed itself in the form of military and political helplessness. The country could not defend itself. . .' War, he writes further, is 'the supreme test of a nation's efficiency': it is a view that has been echoed over and over again in India since 1947. Happily for India, Sarkar went on to say, the 'middle ages' here (in the form of the Mughal empire) gave way directly to the 'modern'. 'In Europe the fall of the Roman empire was followed by a thousand years of disorder and darkness, out of which Europe struggled back into light only in the fifteenth century.' In India, on the other hand, 'the death of her old order was immediately followed by the birth on her soil of modern civilization and thought . . . First of all, *an honest and efficient administration was imposed on the country* and directed by a British agency to ensure peace and economic growth . . .'[33]

The requirements of a history of Partition

If Indian historians have long since moved away from this rather convoluted celebration of the benefits of British rule, they seem nevertheless to have remained tethered to certain fundamental tenets of the colonialist narrative on history, violence and civilisation. An Indian Marxist, political scientist and political activist, Javeed Alam, has reiterated the case very sharply indeed in the context of the recent resurgence of interest in Partition, arguing for the importance of *not* studying Partition violence, but focussing rather on the centrality of the state and other 'large organisations', of long-term historical processes, and of 'history' in this sense. An examination of his argument may be an appropriate way to close this discussion of the professional historian's reconstruction of Partition. 'Looking at Partition', Alam says,

there is something which strikes us as a particularity. There are innumerable cases of large-scale massacres mutually indulged in by people at a moment of loss of judgement, of a sense of proportion, at a moment of frenzy. There is no involvement of large organisations or the state as the instrument of mass killings. You can't therefore talk of these events as a general phenomena [*sic*].[34]

---

[33] Jadunath Sarkar, *Fall of the Mughal Empire. Volume Four. 1789–1803* (1950; Delhi, 1992), pp. 289–90, and 292–3, emphasis added.
[34] The quotations that follow are all taken from 'Remembering Partition', a dialogue between Javeed Alam and Suresh Sharma, *Seminar*, 461.

The works of Joya Chatterji, Suranjan Das, David Gilmartin, Mushirul Hasan, Ayesha Jalal, Ian Talbot and others[35] suggest different findings on the involvement of 'large organisations', but that is not the point I wish to make here. Let us attend, instead, to Alam's notion of the 'general' and the 'particular', which is readily translated into the 'historical' and the 'unhistorical'.

'There are large historical forces behind the little events that happen', Alam states at one point. 'The breach between Hindus and Muslims in the 19th century, it becoming politicised, leading through a very tortuous course to Partition. I think, for example of the role of the British state and its policy of systematic divide-and-rule, of playing one community against the other . . . ' The 'little events' – violence and rape, mass murder and the expulsion of whole communities – thus appear irrelevant. They are the product of other forces and other processes, which is what requires study. The 'little events' themselves are, in this view, best forgotten.

It is not that every instance of large-scale violence should be so treated. Indeed, there are certain types of violent events that we are enjoined to remember. The critic distinguishes three different kinds of violence. At a time when the complicity of the state in acts of brutal and apparently meaningless violence is all too well established, the first kind he identifies refers to those occasions when a state or state-like body directly carries out genocide or massacres: as in Germany, Serbia and Russia, he tells us. India in 1984 provides a variant, when 'the state became a part of the violence against the Sikhs'.

A second brand of collective violence that requires notice is of the kind witnessed in India in 1992–3, when the Vishwa Hindu Parishad, 'a very large organisation', incited mass killings over the Babri Masjid issue: 'The state wasn't there as perpetrator but it could have controlled [the violence] and it did not.' There is a third category, however, 'where people become victims of violence where at a moment of a loss of sanity they start killing each other. It is this third type of violence which we saw at Partition. This should be left behind, should be forgotten, so that people may live in peace, socially normal everyday life, politically as well as individually . . . '

'What remains crucial', Alam concludes, 'is the presence of a state which is the perpetrator [as in Nazi Germany] . . . It is right, even morally necessary, to institutionalise the memory of the Holocaust.' One point that is perhaps not adequately appreciated in this context is that the Holocaust now appears a distant event – something that occurred 'there', not 'here', and therefore something that may now be faced. Habermas

[35] See references cited in ch. 1, nn. 4 and 7.

says as much in his celebration of 'the political morality of a [German] community that – after being liberated by Allied troops... – has been *established in the spirit of the occidental conception of freedom, responsibility and self-determination*'.[36] If modern Indian historians or political scientists could similarly distance themselves from 1947 – if the 'violence of Partition' was not an ongoing presence and an ever-present threat in present-day India, or if the historians and political scientists were located far away (say, in the United States) – we might have seen moves towards the institutionalisation of the memory of Partition, in the way of Holocaust museums, Vietnam memorials and reconstructions of Hiroshima. As it happens, given the history of the subcontinent since 1947, this has not been possible. The historian or political activist therefore clings to a number of hackneyed nationalist propositions about what is singular about India, and appropriate to Indian history.

If it is the question of guilt and the necessity of the remembrance of suffering that has animated the German debate on the historiography of the Holocaust, it is – as I have stressed – the question of India's unity, and the need to *forget* in the interests of that unity, that Indians are asked to take (and to a large extent have taken) as guide in their historical scholarship on the Partition of 1947. 'When we go to people and ask them to remember all that has happened, to recount it for the record...', Javeed Alam declares, 'it seems to me morally indefensible.' He frankly expresses the reasons for this feeling of outrage: 'A new generation has emerged for whom the Partition is a distant historical event. It has gone back into their memory [*sic*], which is important for our politics, for our social lives, for normal interaction between communities. The everydayness of life becomes normal when you forget this experience [*sic*].'

Alam's concern, then, is with the history of the state and 'large organisations', and the need to preserve 'socially normal everyday life' from contamination. Other scholars have expressed this fear of contamination, and argued for the need to preserve the singular aspects of India's heritage, in slightly different ways. Thus, in his dialogue with Javeed Alam on the matter of 'remembering Partition', Suresh Sharma returns again and again to one such aspect of the Indian legacy – an ethos of pluralism which he calls 'the distinctive nature of our civilizational ground'.[37] In doing so he reverts, I submit, to the well-worked nationalist theme of the exceptionalism of India – an exceptionalism which was once called 'spiritualism'.

To make his case, Sharma draws some comparisons between the Indian subcontinent and the Mediterranean region. When the Christians

---

[36] Habermas, *Forever in the Shadow of Hitler?*, p. 170, emphasis added; see also p. 43, and for others' comments along similar lines, *ibid.*, pp. 67, 129, 140 and *passim*.

[37] Quotations from Sharma also from 'Remembering Partition', *Seminar*, 461.

reconquered Spain, he notes, they wiped it clean of Muslims. In North Africa, exactly the reverse happened. In Spain, indeed, after the first mass expulsion, a large number of Moors who had converted to Christianity still remained: but this was not something that was palatable. The ex-Moors were given a special name – Moriscos – and 'sixty years after the expulsion of the Moors', there was another mass expulsion of Moriscos.

Not so, we are told, in India. Even after all the violence of 1947, the historian notes, after the large-scale expulsions and ethnic cleansing, 'the lines still stay blurred' in the subcontinent. This may be seen not only in India and Bangladesh, but also in what is now Pakistan, even if the number of non-Muslims left there is relatively small. 'It is a suffused and intense kind of blurring which constitutes the historical ground called India.'

One wonders what Suresh Sharma has to say about the presence of Coptic Christians in Egypt, or for that matter the continued resi-dence of Palestinian Muslims in Israel, or even the survival of a small number of Jews in Germany; and again, what he feels about the Hindu right wing's slogan trumpeted repeatedly in the 1980s and '90s – 'fifty' years after that first expulsion of Indian Muslims – that there are only two resting places for the Muslims: Pakistan or the grave (*'Musalman ke do hi sthan – Pakistan ya kabristan'*). But in a sense that is irrelevant to the famil-iar nationalist rhetoric that he, consciously or unconsciously, reproduces here – rhetoric that underlines the fundamental unity, the distinctiveness, and the greatness, of this old nation (or civilisation) called India.

Along with other analysts of Indian history, society and politics, Alam and Sharma also emphasise the 'gestures of kindness' and protectiveness that are recorded along with accounts of killing and rape in 1947. 'For every instance of killing that we hear of', as Alam puts it, 'we also hear of somebody's attempt to help, to rescue, somebody giving a shoulder to lean on.' Such individual gestures and acts of sensitivity require societal sustenance to be effective, notes Sharma: 'Even a minimalist gesture ac-quires effectiveness only when this blurring happens on a scale wider than the person who is giving expression to it. This is the distinctive historical civilizational ground from which the blurred demography, the blurring of the Partition line itself... has happened.'

It is this inheritance that must be carefully protected and preserved; and it is this that is endangered by the currently fashionable projects of recovering memories and writing histories of Partition violence and suffering. 'We have to be sensitive', says Sharma, 'to what a project of recovering memory may do to [this inheritance].' Here, as in Alam's commentary, colonialism's passive victim returns: the innocent masses who (astonishingly, for a radical perspective) have no will of their own, from whom anything may be prized out and in whose heads, apparently, anything may be planted; who have in addition only 'frenzy', 'insanity' and the provocation of short-sighted recorders of memory as possible motives for their own violent actions; who have to be given 'history' – by the state, by other 'large organisations' and by us; and who must be allowed to forget so that they can return to their normal, everyday lives.

Over the last several years, as research on the Partition violence has increased, there has been growing criticism that this recent work pays too much attention to one aspect of the history of the times – and that, not the most significant. If Alam and Sharma make the argument in one way, Alok Bhalla makes it in another. Referring to my observation that what constituted Partition was the rape, abduction and killing, Bhalla comments:

> To say that there was enormous violence during the partition is tautological. There is violence in every civil strife. Any encyclopedist of terror can compile an endlessly cumulative dossier of barbarity in times of social and political turmoil. One turns to a historian or a novelist, not to learn how to add sorrow on sorrow, but to hear in 'unqualified horror or despair' the more difficult cadence of 'tragedy'. The best of the fiction writers about the partition are not concerned with merely telling stories of violence, but with making a profoundly troubled inquiry about the survival of our moral being in the midst of horror.[38]

Bhalla does not wish to underplay the violence of 1947, as this same paper of his shows very well. I am left wondering, nevertheless, whether his emphasis on 'the survival of our moral being' is markedly different from Sharma's emphasis on the 'distinctive nature of our civilizational ground' and Alam's foregrounding of gestures of kindness. Does not Bhalla's argument too merge into the same nationalist proposition about the secondariness of violence, its essential *irrelevance* compared to the tortured search for our moral being – even in the midst of terror? This violence, then, becomes no more than a 'local' detail – of the moment, or of the place – as against the universal struggle to uphold 'humanity'.

I do not wish to suggest that pornographies of violence present no danger in this context. There are enough chauvinist accounts, fictional as well as non-fictional, that have worked to do nothing other than spread the poison. Yet the question remains whether we are to surrender the entire field of the history of Partition – remembered as violence by so many survivors, and by others who have read or heard the tales of survivors and of right-wing historians – simply to those right-wing historians? Does

---

[38] Alok Bhalla, 'Memory, History and Fictional Representations of the Partition' (forthcoming).

the proposition that violence made the Partition of British India what it was – a critical (traumatic, and repeatedly re-cited) moment in the establishment of two nation-states and the life of their newly constituted peoples – automatically amount to 'telling stories of violence' and accumulating a 'dossier of barbarity'?

Rather, such a proposition may be used to ask precisely the kinds of questions that Bhalla wishes to focus. Is there not a need to explore the construction, and unfolding, of this particular tragedy? How is the tragedy of Partition played out, understood, told – and, therefore, made – in 1947 and afterwards? Has the eternal (natural?) character of our moral being been too easily assumed? Does this moral character simply survive through such periods, overcoming in the process those evil forces that threaten to pull it under, or is it in fact significantly reconstituted in these moments of unprecedented fury? Is this a matter of mere 'local' detail, or is it perhaps rather more central to an investigation of our times, and of our past and future politics?

The view that harmony and mutual understanding are the norm (until challenged from the outside, especially by powerful states and large organisations) rests on an unduly sanguine and ahistorical construction of human nature and human society. If the 'masses' are allowed to live undisturbed, this view seems to suggest, all's right with the world. The thought fits well with a common sense, liberal discourse in which 'disturbances' are precisely a sign of the breakdown of state control and 'normalcy'. Such an interpretation inevitably detracts from any close investigation of the history of specific conflicts and specific resolutions in so-called 'enlightened' ('civilised') societies.

If the portrayal of 1947 India and Pakistan as a battle between 'pure evil' and 'pure virtue' is obviously naïve, it is not a great advance on this to say that the two co-exist at the same time and often in the same person. One needs to carry the argument somewhat further and recognise the indeterminacy, the ambiguity and the historical reconstruction of notions of both 'good' and 'evil' – much like the constitution, and reconstitution, of the individual subject him- or herself. At moments like 1947 (or 1984) in the subcontinent – or in Hitler's Germany, Pol Pot's Kampuchea and the 1990s Rwanda and Bosnia, not to mention the white man's colonisation of the Americas and Australasia – 'good' and 'evil' do not simply co-exist. Rather, doubt arises as to what is which: over the meaning of the good society and of moral order. If the Enlightenment and the struggle for democracy produced one kind of (new) human spirit, imperialism and colonialism produced other notions of civility and appropriate behaviour – on both sides of the colonial divide.[39] It will scarcely do to leave the diverse consequences of this centuries-long encounter unexamined.

Returning to the subcontinent, it is not my argument that the coexistence of many different communities and of several major world religions in India, or reports of mutual support and kindness even at times of great bloodshed, are simply untrue or unimportant. However, these facts must not be allowed to obscure the *history* of changing Hindu–Sikh–Muslim relations, of emerging right-wing formations and attitudes, of a state that has become increasingly partisan and, indeed, of a growing societal tolerance of violence and brutality. They must not become an excuse for a retreat into the tired nationalist proposition that 1947 (or 1984, or 1992) was an aberration, the handiwork of 'outsiders' and 'criminals'.

One might even propose that it is India's fortune, and singularity, that the country was (and is) riven by numerous crosscurrents and contradictions – anti-colonial feelings, regional and linguistic aspirations, conflicts between upper castes and lower castes and Dalits ('Untouchables'), the desire to keep women in their place, to name a few.[40] This has often meant that when one particular obsession, or conflict, threatens to take over its politics and its history, other concerns and other contradictions act as a hindrance. Yet, if that is true, it has not made the society any less violent or any more tolerant in recent times. On the contrary, all the evidence of open, brazen and brutal atrocities points the other way: witness, the well-documented violence of the state against peasant and other rebels who have readily been labelled 'naxalites' or 'terrorists'; of nativist parties against migrants from other regions of India who are seen as challenging the 'sons of the soil'; of communalist parties against religious minorities; of men (and women) against women; of upper castes (and lower castes) against 'Untouchables'. Neither the old nationalist affirmation of a distinctive culture of coexistence, nor sentimental claims of the survival of a universalist humanity, are

---

[39] There is, of course, a vast literature on this subject now. For just a few important statements, see Cesaire, *Discourse on Colonialism*; Frantz Fanon, *The Wretched of the Earth. Offenses against the Person* (London, 1963) and his *Black Skin White Masks* (New York, 1967); Talal Asad, ed., *Anthropology and the Colonial Encounter* (London, 1973); Edward Said, *Orientalism* (New York, 1979); Gayatri Chakravarti Spivak, *In Other Worlds: Essays in Cultural Politics* (New York, 1988); Walter Mignolo, *The Darker Side of the Renaissance: Literacy, Territoriality, and Colonization* (Ann Arbor, 1995); and the several volumes of *Subaltern Studies. Writings on South Asian Society and History*, vols. I–X (Delhi, 1982–1999).

[40] One must qualify this: multiple divisions and contradictions obviously exist in most countries. Such plurality has not prevented the emergence of particular divisions or identities as the overriding ones at particular times and places – in India as elsewhere.

particularly helpful in historical or political investigations of the present conjuncture.

A final word

One last comment regarding Alam's critique of recent research on Partition. In criticising the method of 'doing history . . . via memory', as he calls it, Alam posits an important distinction between 'memory' and 'oral history'. The latter is, in his reckoning, perfectly honourable, for it 'has been a part of the larger historical project. It helped fill up the paucity of data or [went] to enrich it, but it never positioned itself as an alternative to conventional history.'[41] There, I suggest, lies the rub. The 'historical project' has long ago been laid down for us and is apparently unquestionable. The jurisdiction of history is already known, however great the evidence that the way in which we have circumscribed its concerns is excessively narrow and, now, perhaps deadening.

The fact remains that neither 'original causes', nor 'states' and 'large organisations', exhaust the domain of 'history'. The unity and progress of the nation or the state is not all that counts in our pasts, even in those countries that came to be called the 'Third World', and that continue in various ways to live under the sway of imperialism. Mentalities – long-lasting attitudes of mind, social practices, memories, rituals – are made by more than the ruling classes and their initiatives: they are made through many 'little histories', long neglected by the historical academy. The need to pay closer attention to these should be self-evident by now.

This is where some of the recent work on Partition violence and the history of women (and children) has marked such a refreshing, and significant, break.[42] What this work has done is to recognise and document the scale of this violence. It has turned aside from an exclusive concentration on high politics, and the question of ultimate responsibility, to reopen other issues crucial to an understanding of our recent history and politics: the suffering of bewildered and angry men, women and children in 1947 (and since); the construction of women and children as community and national property; the isolation of religion as the sole mark of a citizen's identity; the unashamed patriarchalism of the state. It has re-established 'everyday normality' as a product of history – a history in which state and society are both implicated.

---

[41] Surprisingly, given how much her account of Partition has helped to challenge received histories of the event, Butalia wants to make the same sort of argument, see *The Other Side of Silence*, p. 10.

[42] I refer especially to the writings of Veena Das, Ritu Menon and Kamla Bhasin, Urvashi Butalia and others cited in n. 7 of ch. 1.

What it has not done quite so forcefully, perhaps, is to look at Partition not simply as a happening, but as a category of understanding a happening. We need to ask how the different ways in which 1947 is remembered and written about are implicated in the making of the event and the heritage called Partition. How have the communities and nations of the subcontinent employed the limiting case of Partition to construct and reconstruct themselves? Is it in the character of limit cases that their history is ever being told and retold, that they are constantly being reinvented – until a new limit case is found (for a new community)?[43] No less important: what are the sources upon which 'histories' of the limit case are based? The next chapter considers this question.

[43] Bangladesh provides an obvious instance. The invasion and massacres perpetrated by the Pakistani army in 1971 created a new history of cataclysmic birth, displacing 1947 to a large extent. The crisis of 1857, and then the losses in the 'Great War' of 1914–18, provide something of a parallel in the case of imperial Britain; Gallipoli, and now the issue of responsibility for the wiping out of indigenous inhabitants and cultures – which has recently become a major political question – have played a similar role in Australia and New Zealand. (I should add that in certain circumstances, the limiting case might not even be explicitly discussed; its presence is often assimilated into everyday vocabulary, bureaucratic and social procedures, and taboos. The recent politics of India and Pakistan provide good examples, but there are parallel examples in many other parts of the world.)

4   The evidence of the historian

Genocidal violence leaves but a broken historical trace. The surviving records of Partition are marked by their fragmentariness.[1] They move, in fits and starts, through jerks and breaks and silences – incoherent, stuttering, even incomprehensible – between the poles of testimony and rumour. Testimony, Langer notes, is 'a form of remembering'. Rumour, by contrast, is a form of doing – of making happen – by telling.[2] The record of Partition clearly bears the mark of both. The importance of first-person testimony (for the judge, as for the historian) requires no underlining. 'I was there . . .'; 'I saw . . .'; 'I can name . . .'; 'I recognise . . .'; and (more than occasionally for the historian and the journalist, though perhaps less commonly for the judge) 'I learnt from the most reliable witnesses . . .' Testimony's method is that of particularising and individualising, specifying sites and bodies that carry the marks of particular events, making real in everyday, physical, nameable terms. Its difficulty in the limit case is that it needs to articulate an unparalleled, unthinkable history struggling to find a voice. How does the witness share 'the particularity, the unshareability, and the incommunicability of pain in torture'?[3] How can we speak for the dead, who are no longer present? How can we testify on behalf of the dead, if we are not dead? How can anyone who is not a *Muselmann* know what it is to be a *Muselmann*, as historians of the Holocaust have repeatedly said?[4]

---

[1] As I shall suggest, this is only partially because the violence destroyed much of its own evidence, and because the successor regimes have refused to release the documents that still exist.

[2] See Lawrence Langer, *Holocaust Testimonies. The Ruins of Memory* (New Haven, 1991), p. 2; and Veena Das, 'Official Narratives, Rumour, and the Social Production of Hate', *Social Identities*, 4, 1 (1998), p. 117.

[3] Daniel, *Charred Lullabies*, p. 142. Daniel goes on to talk of the 'drone of silence' that persists in many interviews, 'a silence that does not settle for the anthropologist whether it is a silence of a not-being-able-to-speak or of an ought-not-to-speak' (p. 150); and again, in the words of Steven Shaviro in the same work, of a violent convulsion, a catastrophe that 'overwhelms all sound and all speaking' (p. 210).

[4] Cf. Giorgio Agamben, *Remnants of Auschwitz. The Witness and the Archive* (New York, 1999), pp. 41–86. 'Muselmann' is a term used in Holocaust writings for the 'living dead'.

The importance of rumour in the record of violence is also established, though perhaps more in the matter of its making than in that of its evaluation or reconstruction. Rumour moves in a direction almost contrary to that of testimony: generalising, exalting to extraordinary (even miraculous) status and employing the sweeping terms of deluge and just deserts (actual or impending). In rumour, language is transformed from a mode of (possible) communication to a particular kind of imperative condition – communicable, infectious, possible (and almost necessary) to pass on. The impact of this anonymous, mercurial, fleeting figure is well attested in accounts of the history of violent uprisings – from Lefebvre's and Rude's writings on the French Revolution, to Guha's analysis of peasant insurrections in colonial India, to Veena Das's account of the 1984 massacre of the Sikhs.[5] That rumour is no stranger to the written records or oral accounts of 1947, too, is hardly surprising. How seriously has all this affected our assessment of that moment?

It is the purpose of this chapter to examine the extent to which historical discourse on Partition, from 1947 to today, takes the form of testimony or rumour – or hovers between the two. I focus for this purpose on the twin questions of violence against women and casualties, both of which loom large in the annals of the event. 'The figure of the abducted woman became symbolic of crossing borders, of violating social, cultural and political boundaries', Menon and Bhasin write. By the time the rape and loot and migrations were finished, 'about eight to ten million people had crossed over from Punjab and Bengal . . . and about 500,000–1,000,000 had perished'.[6] 'Estimates of the dead vary from 200,000 (the contemporary British figure) to two million (a later Indian estimate) but that somewhere around a million people died is now widely accepted', writes Butalia. She goes on to note the statistical evidence of 'widespread sexual savagery': 'about 75,000 women are thought to have been abducted and raped by men of religions different from their own (and indeed sometimes by men of their own religion)'.[7]

Several observers described the violence that erupted so fiercely between Hindus–Sikhs and Muslims in 1946 and 1947 as 'a war on each other's women' or, alternatively, a war waged 'especially' on women and children. 'Unless Hindus and Muslims stop this war on each other's

---

[5] Cf. Georges Lefebvre, *The Great Fear* (London, 1973); George Rude, *The Crowd in the French Revolution* (Oxford, 1972); Ranajit Guha, *Elementary Aspects of Peasant Insurgency in Colonial India* (Delhi, 1983); Homi K. Bhabha, *The Location of Culture* (London, 1994); and Veena Das, 'Official Narratives, Rumour, and the Social Production of Hate', *Social Identities* 4, 1 (1998), It will be clear that I have derived many of my comments on rumour from the work of the last three.

[6] Menon and Bhasin, *Borders and Boundaries*, pp. 20 and 35.

[7] Butalia, *Other Side of Silence*, p. 3.

women folk', F. V. Wylie, the governor of Uttar Pradesh, wrote immediately after the Garhmukhteshwar massacre of November 1946, '... the
whole country may go mad.'[8] As a result of a number of important recent
writings, including the two quoted above, the extent and brutality of this
war is now fairly well known.[9]

That this concentrated and extended violence against women was glo-
rified all round is also established. The celebrations emphasised the pride
and valour of the community. They included recitations of the 'unparalleled sacrifices' of 'our' women, as well as boastful tales of the capture,
disfiguring, rape and humiliation of the 'other's' women – even, one sus-
pects, in cases where the women concerned were later made into 'our'
own, adopted, married and settled into the 'victorious' local community.

The discourses surrounding this war on women – on the issue of both
rape and sacrifice – require some reflection, for they had much to do with
the progress of the war itself and crucially conditioned the fate of its
women victims. New tales of bravery and new accounts of tradition were
now retailed. These were developed in large part to restore pride and
self-respect in the midst of humiliating circumstances. If this entailed the
gathering of testimony, the remembering of sacrifices to preserve and
strengthen the community, it also entailed a fight against rumour – the
hushed insinuations and the extravagant claims that became the primary
mode in which the 'shaming' questions of women's honour and community losses were discussed in 1946–8. Yet the disciplining of rumour, and
the (re-)imposition of self-respect and order, was accomplished, paradoxically, by the reproduction of the conditions in which rumour flourished
and by the incorporation of rumour into the 'historical' accounts of the
period.

Primary discourse: the signature of rumour

In his writings on peasant insurgency, Ranajit Guha distinguishes between three levels of 'historical' discourse: a 'primary' level, referring to
reports from the front, as it were; a 'secondary' that refers to commentaries and memoirs that aspire to the status of history; and a 'tertiary',
which might be described as history proper, with the full paraphernalia
of referencing and footnotes, objective distance and 'scientific' language.
Of primary discourse, Guha notes that it is marked both by its immediacy

---

[8] (IOR) L/P&J/8/650, Wylie to Viceroy (21 November 1946); see also (IOR) Mss. Eur.
F200/168, Wylie to Mountbatten (18 May 1947). The Garhmukhteshwar violence is
discussed in ch. 5.
[9] See works cited in n. 7 of ch. 1; also Andrew J. Major, '"The Chief Sufferers": Abduction
of Women during the Partition of Punjab', *South Asia*, 18 (1995), pp. 57–72.

and its official character.[10] This is certainly the case with the first reports we have regarding many individual instances of looting and killing. The 'First Information Reports' found in the police records, for example, belong to a form of reporting crime in the police posts of the Raj, whose very condition of existence was a bureaucratic–judicial context, language and imperative. Yet statements of this kind are not always the first that we come across regarding the occurrence of 'riots' or 'disturbances', especially in the twentieth century.

The first reports we have of major incidents of violence, faithfully (or not so faithfully) reproduced in newspaper reports and official documents, are often rumours. '*Something* has happened there.' 'Don't go further, it is not safe just now.' 'A disturbance has broken out.' 'People are fleeing.' 'The shutters are down.' 'Curfew has been imposed.' 'Two (or ten, or a hundred, or hundreds of) people have been killed.'[11]

The state usually makes its appearance only in the wake of these rumours and other fleeting reports. And many of its inaugural reports – the first that historians often have to hand – are marked by the signature of rumour, jostling now with a vocabulary of 'civilisation' and 'counter-insurgency'. Rumour is marked characteristically not only by indeterminacy, anonymity and contagion, but also by a tendency to excess and 'certainty'[12] – a 'certainty' confirmed when the report moves from a verbal to a graphic or filmic mode. As Lefebvre has it on revolutionary France,

It goes without saying that (this mode of transmission) favoured the spread of false reports, the distortion and exaggeration of fact, the growth of legends . . . In the empty silence of the provinces, every word had the most extraordinary resonance and was taken as gospel. In due course, the rumour would reach the ear of a journalist who would imbue it with new strength by putting it into print . . . [13]

Consider one of the first reports in a Delhi newspaper on the massacre of November 1946 in and around the Garhmukhteshwar fair, not fifty miles from the capital: 'PILGRIM TRAIN ATTACKED NEAR MEERUT. 50 BUTCHERED, OVER 100 INJURED. Another Forty-Five Perish in Neighbouring Village', apart from 'about 200' killed at Garhmukhteshwar on

---

[10] In the double sense that it originated often with officials and other attendants of colonialism, and was meant primarily for administrative use, Guha, ed., 'The Prose of Counter-insurgency', in *Subaltern Studies*, vol. II, p. 3.

[11] For just two examples, see the report of the People's Union of Democratic Rights on Bhagalpur, *Bhagalpur Riots* (Delhi, 1990); and the Sahmat collection of reports on Ayodhya, *Resources against Communalism and Religious Fundamentalism in India* (comp. by Harsh Kapoor; New Delhi, n.d.).

[12] As Bhabha puts it, 'rumour produces an infectious ambivalence, an "abyssal overlapping", of too much meaning and a certain meaninglessness', *Location of Culture*, p. 202.

[13] Lefebvre, *The Great Fear*, pp. 73–4, cited in Guha, *Elementary Aspects*, p. 253.

7 November.[14] The rounded-off figures are one indication of the persistence of rumour, *precise* and yet *extravagant* – suggestive of so much more than the numbers themselves. And of course such numbers are easily multiplied for reasons of journalistic or political advantage, as observers have noted in the case of more recent 'riots' in India.[15]

Or the following report from the commissioner of Meerut, the senior-most ICS official in the area, writing after a personal inspection of the site of the massacre. Baynes described some of the worst horrors: '3 women and 9 babies all dead in one well, a child of three or four with its face kicked in and then charred with fire, a woman beaten to death while in the act of producing a baby, girls of twelve or thirteen raped, and then killed by thrusting spears up them and ripping them apart . . .'[16] The description perhaps outdoes the *Hindustan Times* in its precision and its extravagance. It appears as an eyewitness account. What is notable, however, is that every part of this sentence, except for the clause relating to the number of bodies found in one well, depends on hearsay. Hearsay transformed into truth – the 'truth' of the riot, and the 'truth' about India in the last days of the Raj.

Here rumour serves to reinforce an argument about the need for British rule. If this reads like testimony, it is not *testimony on behalf of* the victims, but *testimony to* the 'goodness' of colonialism. Much the same kind of report emanated from colonial officials even when they were writing to intimate relatives far removed from the scenes of the violence. Here is one providing details to his wife in England of what he described as the 'carnage indescribable' in south Bihar in October–November 1946: '. . . little Mahomedan girls of four or five with their throats cut from ear to ear. One wretched Muslim woman . . . ripped up, the knife being stuck in her vagina to start with . . .'[17] How shall we read this? As an eyewitness account? The considered narrative of an investigating magistrate? Or another rumour parading the 'truth' of the departing regime, contrasting this bestiality with its own implicit humanitarianism – through a particular kind of reporting of facts?

It was not only British colonial officials, however, who reproduced the structure of rumour in interpreting and describing the violence of these years. Indian and Pakistani officials worked in a very similar way. The following report from a liaison officer of the government of India,

[14] *The Hindustan Times* (10 November 1946).
[15] Cf. Charu Gupta and Mukul Sharma, 'Communal Constructions: Media Reality vs. Real Reality', *Race and Class*, 38, 1 (July–September 1996).
[16] (IOR) L/P&J/8/650, FWW Baynes, Commissioner, Meerut to Wylie (18 November 1946).
[17] (IOR) A. W. Flack coll., Mss. Eur. D1060/19, Flack's letters to his wife Joan (4 and 11 November 1946).

describing a column of Muslim refugees marching out of Kapurthala state, provides one illustration. The refugees walked in rows of ten or twelve, the officer wrote. The women and children walked in the centre, flanked on either side by men. 'Groups of armed Sikhs stood about in the fields on either side of the road. Every now and again one of the groups would make a sally at the column, drag out two or three women and run away with them.' The men and women who sought to resist were killed or wounded. The military guard accompanying the refugees did little to interfere. 'By the time the column arrived at Jullunder [Jalandhar]', we are told, 'almost all the women and young girls had been kidnapped in this manner.'[18]

There is no suggestion in this report that the liaison officer accompanied the refugees the whole way from Kapurthala state to Jalandhar. He saw them leaving. Yet the account he provides is striking precisely because of the details of happenings at every stage of the journey, and the condition of the refugees when they arrived in Jalandhar. Almost certainly, this is based on what he had heard – hearsay, now compounded by an emerging narrative on the *pattern* of attacks and the deployment and methods of the attackers in this part of the country.

Non-officials and leading political figures were no less guided by the structure of these emerging narratives, which rapidly became part of the circumstances and discourses – the escalating panic and the escalating brutality – that made Partition. Indeed, the clearest statement I have found on the 'Sikh method' of attack on Muslim villages in East Punjab comes from the Bengal Muslim League leader, Husain Suhrawardy. He described the procedure in a letter to Gandhi written at the peak of the killings in Punjab and north-western India in August–September 1947. The method consisted, he wrote, in surrounding a village on three sides, leaving one side 'open', and then creating an uproar, opening up with gunfire and setting fire to the houses. When 'Muslims [*sic*] and their families and children' tried to escape towards the open side, they found themselves confronted by 'gunners . . . and by a special group of young men who separate the women. These women and girls are abducted . . . and the men shot dead.'[19]

The detail is graphic and, in the circumstances, inevitably dependent on stories widely disseminated at this time. Suhrawardy was not an eyewitness to any of the happenings in Punjab. However, people far and wide across the subcontinent (not to mention Britain) now spoke on behalf of the South Asian nation/s or the most dispersed 'emotional communities'

[18] Cited in G. D. Khosla, *Stern Reckoning. A Survey of the Events Leading up to and Following the Partition of India* (1949; reprinted Delhi, 1989), p. 289.

[19] (IOR) Mss. Eur. F200/129, Suhrawardy to Gandhi, bulletin no. 4 (Lahore, 21 September 1947).

of the region. The mood of people belonging to different religious denominations, whether they were rural or urban, privileged or unprivileged, and their understanding of the tradition and character of other religious communities, was built up – or renewed – to a considerable extent on the basis of incendiary and rhetorical, but certain, knowledge about the untold violence let loose on 'our' unsuspecting brothers and sisters in faraway places.

Women social workers who devoted themselves in the last months of 1947, and the years that followed, to the work of tracing, recovering and taking care of women and children who had been abducted, raped and traumatised, were also subject to the influence of such stories. The genre of rumour feeds on itself at moments like this, escalating in the repetition, becoming part of the violence and serving to produce new kinds of 'truth'. A reference to the report of one leading social worker on an issue that has now come to be seen as emblematic of the degradation and brutality, as well as the crass nationalism of Partition, will help to illustrate the proposition.

'The volunteers told me', Begum Anees Qidwai wrote in her memoirs based on a diary she maintained at the time, '*of many, many women* who had "Pakistan Zindabad" tattooed on their foreheads and the names of numerous [rapists] cut into their arms and breasts ... *Hundreds of Muslim girls* were [also] brought to me, on whose arms hoodlums had tattooed their names and even the date of their crimes'.[20] How are we to read the details provided in the italicised portions of this quotation? We know that tattooing is the work of specialists, a job that usually requires the services of more than one individual and, with that, some minimal facilities and time. The branding and tattooing are clearly further indicators of the collective character of this assault and the collective character of its celebration. What are we to make of the numbers mentioned here, however? Do we read Qidwai's remarks on this mode of scarring and humiliation as a statement of empirical truth? It is more likely that 'hundreds of girls' is a figure of speech. As such, it is even more overpowering than a verifiable statistic; for it shares the power contained in rumour, which worked to produce the new beliefs and emotions of the day, with all their deadly consequences.[21]

---

[20] Begum Anees Qidwai, *Azadi ki chhaon mein*, Hindi tr by Nur Nabi Abbasi (New Delhi, 1990), pp. 156–7, emphases mine.

[21] A related point may be noted here. The castration of men, which is commonly insinuated in oral accounts, is not taken up for discussion or even recorded anywhere in written documents of the time. Perhaps the symbolic status accorded to the branding of women, and the simultaneous silence on the castration of men, tells us something about patriarchal fantasies and the patriarchal preservation of male honour. (I am grateful to Veena Das for this suggestion.)

As the last two examples will already have indicated, the contagion of rumour carries over very easily into the secondary discourse produced by political commentators and memorialists at this time. The signature of the fleeting, panic report, *precise* and yet *extravagant*, appears to have been especially marked in accounts of attacks against women – for reasons of 'culture' that produced considerable shame and censorship, but also considerable hyperbole. What emerged in this context was a particular kind of heroic narrative and political reportage that contributed to emptying the struggles and experiences of women of much of their content. To trace the crystallisation of these different forms, it may help to look at the first written reports we have of some contemporary instances of violence, and then to follow them through to their later (written and oral) versions.

First Information Reports

I shall begin by examining three 'First Information Reports' (or FIRs) filed with the police by the victims of attacks in the rural areas of Rawalpindi district in West Punjab in March 1947. Given the destruction, and suppression, of Partition records and the very difficulty of filing reports with an administration that was collapsing and, in places, hostile, very few FIRs have survived from the time. The three I analyse here are found not in the police records but in the manuscript collection of a major political party.[22]

These FIRs were filed within a week or so of the March 1947 incidents by a woman from village Mughal, a man from Bewal and an unspecified number of villagers from Bassali, who had found refuge in different refugee camps of Rawalpindi district. All three refer to large Muslim mobs that surrounded their respective villages from all sides: the numbers quoted are over 1,000 in the case of Mughal, 3,000 in the case of Bassali and 5,000 to 6,000 attackers in the case of Bewal, armed with guns, rifles, axes, swords, spears, sticks and, in two cases, some hand grenades as well. The attacks, we are told, were accompanied by shouts

---

[22] (NMML) Hindu Mahasabha papers, File C-165, 'Report about Village Mogul (Sikh Dhok), Police Station Rawat, Tahsil Rawalpindi (as stated by Satnam Kaur, wife of Puran Singh)' (n.d.); 'First Information Report regarding the arson, looting and murders committed in village Bassali, P. S. Rawat, district Rawalpindi' (filed from refugees' camp, Rawalpindi, 18 March 1947); and 'FIR of Moti Ram Singh, s/o Bk. Nihal Chand, caste Gupta, resident of village Bewal, Police Stn, Gujarkhan, District Rawalpindi (at present refugee at Gujarkhan Khalsa School)' (n.d.). (I use the acronym FIR for all three reports made by sufferers from these three villages within days of the attacks, even though the report from village Mogul (or Mughal) was not lodged with the police and is, therefore, not technically an FIR.)

of 'Pakistan Zindabad' and 'Allah-ho-Akbar'. The initial object seems to have been the loot and destruction of Sikh and Hindu houses and shops. However, those who came out to try and appease the attackers or to return brickbats and gunfire were killed, and a number of women were abducted even at this initial stage.

Having worsted those who were brave or able enough to defend and demoralised the rest by looting and arson, individual killings and abductions that went on for hours – 'throughout the night' according to two of the reports – the attackers then turned on those who had taken collective shelter in the local gurdwara or the stronger, more substantial houses of village notables. This meant the majority of the Sikhs and Hindus, especially women and children. As the attack on their places of shelter began, prominent attackers (or 'mediators', as they claimed to be) called on the villagers to come out of their hiding places and reach some settlement – a demand, in every instance, for the surrender of arms and, in a couple, for payment of a specified sum of money. This did not, however, satisfy all the attackers. Along with the surrender of arms, or immediately after, several people demanded that all the Hindus and Sikhs embrace Islam or give up their lives.

In Mughal, 180 men, women and children, who had taken refuge in the gurdwara, surrendered when they were targeted with gunfire, stones and then the setting on fire of the gurdwara.'The mob was asked to forgive the inmates their lives [sic]', states Satnam Kaur in her deposition to the police.[23] The attackers replied that their lives would be spared if they handed over their arms: two guns, swords and sticks. 'This was readily agreed to and the guns and swords etc., was handed over to the muslim mob.' The 'inmates' were then taken to the house of a Sikh notable. Here, a Muslim from a neighbouring village shouted that 'either we are forcibly converted into Islam or mercilessly butchered'. 'All the Sikhs yielded', she adds in a pithy statement.

Even after this, Satnam Kaur went on to say, part of the crowd was not satisfied. They suggested that the Sikh–Hindu women should be separated from the men and taken to another place: 'Our men refused to do this.' The Sikhs and Hindus were allowed to seek shelter with Muslim families that would take them in. As some of them moved to find shelter, however, 'more people from the surrounding villages poured in who persisted that every sikh women and child must be killed and the body giving shelter will be similarly dealt with'. Satnam Kaur's family, consisting of eleven members, hid in a grainfield until dark, when a Muslim neighbour

---

[23] I have retained the grammar and spellings of the original reports in all quotations in the following paragraphs, and shall therefore refrain from any further use of *sic*.

was able to hide them in his house – only to ask them to leave again early the next morning, as he feared for his own life. Spotted in the grainfield where they hid again, they were forced back into the village and taken to the place where 'the dead bodies of the inmates of the Gurdwara were burning'. She and a sister of her husband's (both 'young girls', as she tells the police) were pushed aside, and the rest of the family was stoned and burned to death. 'My husband's brother's wife, Sujan Kaur was thrown into the burning fire by Channu, son of Mohd Shaffi, after he had taken off her clothes.' Satnam and her sister-in-law were forcibly taken away by two Muslims of the village, but then protected by some kindly relatives of theirs until a military rescue party arrived two days later.

In Bewal a large number of men, women and children had taken shelter in the house of Sardar Gokul Singh. They were besieged for a day and a night before some of the more prominent Muslims offered a settlement whereby their lives would be spared if they surrendered their arms and embraced Islam. After this statement, the report is in two parts. One deals with the sixty or seventy men, women and children who came out at the attackers' bidding, among them Moti Ram Singh, the complainant in this case. The other refers to those who did not surrender at this stage. The former group was surrounded by '150/200 rioters' as soon as they came down, and taken to the main mosque in Bewal. 'From Juma Mosque we were taken to the house of Fazal Karim Barber. Under threat of immediate death our Keshas [hair, which Sikh men must wear uncut] and beard[s] were cut by Fazal Karim barber.' They were then taken to another house, from where a few of them escaped to hide for one night in the house of a Muslim in a nearby village and then for eight or nine days with a Muslim well-wisher in a place somewhat further away. It was from here that they were rescued by the military.

Those left behind in Gokul Singh's house, who had not agreed to conversion, were attacked periodically through the rest of that day and night, with guns, grenades and that other deadly weapon – arson. When the house was set on fire, those hiding there escaped along the rooftops to the village gurdwara. The attack shifted here, and was reinforced with a Sten gun. Around 4 a.m. the next day, the attackers succeeded in blowing a hole in the side of the building, whereupon some fifty assailants entered the gurdwara and a general massacre ensued. 'Some 200 to 300 persons were killed in that Gurdwara', Moti Ram Singh declared. The village had a population of 500 Hindus and Sikhs, according to him. Of these only 'seventy-six' had been 'accounted for': eight men or boys who had escaped; twenty-nine who had been 'converted' and were now in a refugee camp; thirty-one 'converts' who were still with the Muslims (eight of them identified as daughters, seven as sons; another six or possibly seven were female – judging from the names); and four women who had been abducted and were believed to be alive in the custody of Muslims (making a total of seventy-two). Perhaps 361 had been killed, and the remainder were 'missing and are believed to have been murdered'. 'There were about 150 houses and 60 shops belonging to Hindus and Sikhs', Moti Ram added. 'All excepting one home belonging to Sukha Singh (who has been forcibly converted to Islam [and was still in the village, according to this account]) have been looted and burnt.'

Several aspects of these FIRs need to be noted. First, these statements to the police are primarily to identify the attackers (the perpetrators of a crime), name other witnesses who can corroborate their testimony and appeal for justice and compensation. In spite of the fact that they were produced in desperate circumstances in makeshift refugee camps, lawyers or magistrates (or people conversant with the law and magistracy) will have had a hand in drawing up, writing down and/or translating these accounts, asking particular kinds of questions and eliciting particular kinds of answers as they did so.

The commonality in the pattern of the reports, and in their language, is in part a by-product of this. The attackers are 'Muslim ruffians', including (in the attack on Mughal) the 'babares [barbarous] tailors of Dhok Daraian'. Those who sought shelter in a gurdwara or other solid house are 'inmates'; and it is 'some ladies' who hide in the house of Dr Attar Singh in village Bassali. The repeated identification of individuals killed, individual attackers and individual witnesses is a product of judicial requirements. Moti Ram Singh names twenty-six 'leaders' of the 'five to six thousand Muslim rioters' who attacked village Bewal, identifying them by their occupations and home villages. 'Besides these leaders', he says, 'I know the persons shown on annexure to this report who were amongst the rioters and I can recognise many others whose names I do not remember.'

The first person who was murdered was Dalip Singh S/O Sunder Singh who was done to death by a sword blow by [blank] S/O Subedar Mutwali of village Dhera Kalian. Bakshi Balmukand['s] Grandson Kuldip and Brahm[?] Dass were murdered by Talib Sheru S/O Mangu Hav[aldar] with the aid of others. Lochan Singh who was at the roof of his brother's house, was killed by Banka with a sword blow. Banka belongs to village Bewal.

Again: 'While we were in Juma Mosque I saw Mohinder Kaur daughter of Girdit Singh, Amrit Kaur daughter of Ishar Singh, Basant Kaur Daughter of Raja Ram and Har Kaur, d/o Bishan Singh, all grown up girls being taken away by Abdul Wahid s/o Sh[eikh] Mohd, Shafi and Ditta Khan s/o Fazal Ghumar village Dhore Kanian...'

Reporting another detail of the attack, Moti Ram Singh names four individuals ('s/o . . . ') who 'witnessed and have narrated the incident to me'. Another occurrence was 'witnessed by Trilochan Singh, s/o Hoshiar Singh also'; and 'the following facts have been narrated by those persons who are alive and were left behind in the house of S[ardar] Gokul Singh'. Finally, of the attack as a whole: 'A list of some of those persons who are still alive is given below and these persons will support the facts stated [above].' This is followed by a list of names of eight people who had 'escaped'; twenty-nine who had 'converted and reached refugee camp by now'; thirty-one who were 'converted [and] still with Mohammedans'; and four abducted women, 'taken away and still believed to be alive with Mohammedans'.

In their turn, the villagers who filed the FIR 'regarding the arson, loot-ing and murders committed in village Bassali' name some fifty villages and hamlets from where the alleged attackers came, adding that the Muslims of Bassali joined them. They named individuals who carried particular arms. 'Hadishah, Bhaiya alias Mir, Dost Mohd. And Ajaib Khan of Chak Jogian, were armed with revolvers and Subedar Fazardin, Shera Muzaffar Ali of Jabbar Darvesh and some others had guns with them.'

The first casualties in Bassali, by this account, were two Sikh youths, Nanak (s/o Hira Singh) and Mangat (s/o Narain Singh). They were wa-tering cattle at the village pond when they were attacked 'with spears and hatchets': Nanak by Hadi Shah and Shera, Mangat by Jehandad and Dost Mohd. 'This assault was witnessed by Gurdit Singh, Parmanand and Bhai Dhian Singh.' The same kinds of details are provided for later incidents. 'Gurcharan Singh's haveli was looted and set on fire by Amirkhan alias Bhai, Mohd. Zaman tailor of Bassali, Mohd. Sharif of Bassali. This was witnessed by Sujan Singh, Kishan Singh and Mehr Singh. Mehr Singh has since died.' 'Gurdwara Singh Sabha was attached [attacked] and set on fire by Allahadad of Dudhian, Master Mohd. Din, Master Abdul Majid, Hassan Khan of Kalri. This was witnessed by Sujan Singh, Pt. [Pandit] Tara Chand and Sadhu Singh.' And so on.

At the end, the report lists all those whose houses were looted and burnt, along with the names of the perpetrators in each instance; the four 'ladies' who were burnt to death; the fifty-two others who were 'murdered by the mob'; and 'about 40' who were still missing. It concludes with the plea that 'our report be recorded and investigation started. If the houses of these persons are searched, majority of looted property can be recovered.'

We have seen that Satnam Kaur of village Mughal similarly specified the sites and times of different incidents and named those who could corroborate her evidence. Two final examples: 'Petrol and Kerosin oil was freely used by the mob. Our house was set on fire by babares [barbarous] tailors of Dhok Daraian. Prehlad, Mehtab, Gurbachan and others saw this.' Further: 'All of us were taken into the Haveli [of] Makhan Singh where Kazim of Daducha village shouted to the mob that they should see either we are forcibly converted into Islam or mercilessly butchered. Man Kaur, Ishar Prehlad, Gurbachan, Joginderkaur and some others are still alive and can tell about this occurance.'

The entreaty to government in every one of these cases, the continued expectation (however muted) that the state would still perform its duties of protection and punishment, even in these extraordinary circumstances, is noteworthy. For a short while in August–September 1947, such a move would seem impossible: but for large numbers of people, the collapse of local institutions and communities meant that the state was left as the last resort of appeal.[24] Yet, alongside that appeal to the state is an urgent concern to mark a loss. The FIRs cited above follow the path of insistently individualising the experience, naming all of the dead (the living dead and those physically obliterated), and revisiting each site of violence. The testimony also contains an essential lacuna at its core. Satnam Kaur strives to speak from an inside that is no longer available, seeking to recover community when community has disappeared. This is a struggle that remains a mark of survivors' testimony then and later. It is largely absent, however, from the subsequent political reportage which is more readily given over to grand statistic and hyperbole.

The criminal charge in the reports cited above is already over-determined by a political charge. We see this in the references to slogans of 'Pakistan Zindabad' and 'Allah-ho-Akbar'. We see it much more clearly, however, in the first reports of other affected, or interested, contemporary observers, whose commentaries belong somewhere between Guha's categories of primary and secondary discourse.

Secondary discourse: rumour politicised

A press statement issued by Hansraj Sethi and three others after a 'rescue expedition' to villages Kallar, Thamali and Dubheran of Rawalpindi district on 21 March 1947 provides indications of the first steps away from an act of remembrance (political in its own way) to a different kind of political commentary. Accompanied by a military man from Dubheran, two residents of Thamali and an escort of a head constable and four other constables provided by the superintendent of police of Rawalpindi

---

[24] Cf. in this context the direct appeals and letters written to Gandhi, Nehru and other top leaders of the new nations, by individuals of different classes and communities, calling for some action (any action) on the part of the state to restore loved ones and provide compensation, refuge or minimal opportunities for a new beginning.

district, the 'rescuers' reached Kallar to find the main bazaar and other shops, houses, a timber depot and an oil-pressing establishment burnt and gutted. 'Only a few isolated houses [were] standing complete.' The first thing they saw on reaching Thamali was the 'ghostly' sight of eight half-burnt corpses lying by a house on the roadside. All of Thamali had been 'cordoned [off] by thorny fences': so as to prevent the flight of Sikhs and Hindus, the investigators believed, but it could equally well have been part of the latter's defence. 'Fields on all sides of the village were littered with dead bodies of Sikhs. We saw some Keshas cut off lying near the dead bodies as if persons have been murdered after their heads had been shaved ... There were also female clothes lying about at many places – such as shalwars and dupattas.' However, 'the most ghostly sight' still awaited them, in the gurdwara. 'It was burnt from outside from all directions', Harbanslal and his associates stated. 'We removed some of the debris and found ... it covering a large tragic sheet of dead bodies.' The total number of corpses they felt was not less than 250, although it was difficult to make any estimate. All the Muslim houses and shops were intact, but the inhabitants had fled.

At Dubheran, the last place they went to, the same grizzly sights greeted them. 'The smell of dead bodies was virtually intolerable.' 'Not a single building, shop, house or Gurdwara was standing. The Muslim houses lying at a distance were standing intact all of them.' In a room of one gurdwara, which had been used to store musical instruments, they saw 'heaps of keshas cut off', and in a courtyard opposite this 'heaps of burnt corpses'. The narrow street to one side was filled with corpses, and a big house on this street had at least fifty half-burnt corpses. 'In another room in this house the corpses of a whole family including a child of about three were lying dead, their corpses full of vermin giving out [a] horrible stench.' The bigger gurdwara of the village was also full of corpses, and the total number of corpses in the village could not have been less than 425, the visitors stated. 'The whole village was so full of stench that we had no patience to visit the third Gurdwara.'[25]

The attention to specific sites, bodies, hair and clothes remains urgent and disconcerting. Yet the figure of speech is already changed in some respects: 'ghostly sight', 'tragic sheet of bodies', 'corpses full of vermin' letting out an unbearable stench. The dead are now an indistinguishable mass: not less than 250 in one place, over 425 in another. And the new communities that were being erected are brought into focus: 'The Khalsa School reduced to ashes presented a strange contrast to the District Board

---

[25] Hindu Mahasabha papers, File C-136, 'Statement of M/S Hansraj Sethi, Harbanslal Kandhari, Dharampal and [blank] regarding their rescue expedition to villages Kallar, Thamali & Dubheran, on 21st March, 1947'.

School which has not been touched at all.' 'The Muslim houses lying at a distance were standing intact all of them.'

'Shorn of contemporaneity', Guha writes, '[secondary] discourse is . . . recovered as an element of the past and classified as history. This change, aspectual as well as categorial, sites it at the very intersection of colonialism [one might say, 'politics'] and historiography.'[26] Other commentators, observing the effects of the violence from one remove, illustrate the point, which has to do with the intersection not only of colonialism (or politics) and historiography, but the intersection of both of these with rumour.

Frank Messervy, the general officer of the Northern Command of the British Indian Army, described the violence of March 1947 as a 'concerted attack, and very widespread throughout the rural areas, which suggested that it had been planned, and made it very difficult to deal with . . . ' The general flew in a small plane low over the villages of Rawalpindi district, while the attacks were still continuing or very soon after that. 'It was a horrible sight', he wrote. 'You could see corpses laid in the fields just outside a village, like rabbits after a shoot.'[27] The hunting analogy is common enough in colonialist writings on native conditions. 'A horrible sight' from the heights of an aeroplane, with corpses laid out 'like rabbits after a shoot'. These were 'natives' after all.[28]

However, the president and general secretary of the All India Hindu Mahasabha who, along with a number of Punjab leaders, visited the refugee camp at Wah, thirty miles outside Rawalpindi city, on 25 March 1947, a couple of weeks after the worst of the violence, presented their findings in equally gross terms. They spoke to the 12,000 refugees accommodated in the camp, they said, and got from them a mortifying account of the terror and devastation visited upon them. 'Several thousands of Sikhs were found whose hair have [been] completely cut off and beards shaved.'[29] 'Several thousands' of 12,000 leaves out very few, if one excludes women and children, but again statistical truth is not the main point at issue. What is at stake is a grim political message, bolstered by an axiomatic 'history'.

Consider another petition, addressed to the governor of Punjab by a deputation of over one hundred Sikhs and Hindus of Rawalpindi, which describes the destruction visited on the rural areas of the district in the

---

[26] Guha, 'The Prose of Counter-insurgency', p. 7.

[27] Cited in Stephens, *Pakistan*, p. 145.

[28] Consider one official's suggestion, soon after the March violence in Multan, of possibly 'laying on a riot' for the entertainment of potential visitors from home, (IOR) Mss. Eur. D943, A. J. V. Arthur's letter to his parents (7 April 1947).

[29] Hindu Mahasabha papers, File C-154, 'Punjab Tour' of L. B. Bhopatkar and Ashutosh Lahiry.

following terms. 'Huge mobs numbering several thousands have been pillaging villages and massacring people on [a] large scale', the petitioners wrote. A large crowd of some 5,000 people, consisting of discharged army men 'armed cap-a-pie with rifles, tommy guns and steel helmets', had attacked the villages of Thoa Khalsa, Bewal and Dubheran. It met with some resistance, especially in Thoa Khalsa, where the Hindu and Sikh inhabitants fought the raiders for three long days but could not hold out longer.

During all this time, however, the civil authorities did nothing to ask the military for help, chiefly because the district magistrate relied on the advice of the Muslim additional district magistrate whose sympathies lay openly with the Muslim League campaign for the establishment of Pakistan. 'The result was that all the inhabitants (Hindus and Sikhs) [of Thoa Khalsa] succumbed and refusing to accept such peaceful Islam gave up their lives . . . a few managed to escape to tell the people here of a specimen of Pakistan and the protection which Jinnah has all along been promising to the minorities.'[30]

'Huge mobs', 'armed cap-a-pie'; *none* of the Hindu and Sikh inhabitants gave up their faith; *here* was a specimen of Jinnah's promised Pakistan. Reports such as these, like the desperate accounts and disfigured bodies of fleeing refugees, served to multiply the most common kind of reporting at this time – rumours of panic and slaughter, relayed in 'excess' and 'certainty' – and served, of course, also to multiply the attacks and counter-attacks.

The following summary of the Rawalpindi events written in May 1947 by a Hindu social worker of Lahore, who himself came from Rawalpindi division and had spent the previous weeks visiting the violence-torn areas and refugee camps in Rawalpindi, Wah, Campbellpur and elsewhere, reinforces the 'history' and politics of the above. Chhabil Das makes the point that it is an abuse of language to call these events 'riots':

They are in reality broad day-light organized acts of gangsterism, working under the instructions of the Muslim League Feudal Lords and [f]renzied Muslim priests – who in normal times are pillars of the British imperialism . . . The whole

---

[30] From Thoa Khalsa, the statement goes on, the Muslim crowd advanced to Dubheran 'to give this helpless village the boon of Islamic culture'. In Dubheran, too, the defenders suffered a similar fate, except that 'here the devout and pious votaries of Islam caught hold of some 70 girls as victims for their lustful attentions and murdered the rest of the population irrespective of their age and sex – thus adding another feather to the cap of Islam', (NMML) Diwan Chaman Lal papers, file no. 142, petition to H. E. Sir Evan Jenkins, Governor of Punjab and Dependencies, signed by Bhagat Laxmi Narayan, President, Hindu Sabha, Dev Raj Anand, President, Central Relief Committee, R. P. Dewan, General Secretary, Central Relief Committee, Sardar Uttam Singh Duggal, President, Singh Sabha, and 100 other Hindu and Sikh residents of Rawalpindi.

region being an arid and barren plateau, lives on the military services and military pensions. The demobilized soldiers, pensioners (civil and military), Lumberdars or Patels, Zaildars and Jagirdars and Inamkhors, all fell prey to the vicious communal virus indiscriminately spread by the Muslim League Feudal Lords, and armed with spears, axes, tommy guns, hand grenades and incendiary bombs [they] pounced upon the peaceful populations.

The object seemed to be to terrorise and thus drive away non-Muslims from the lands and homes they had occupied 'since time immemorial'. For the time being, Das observed, the attackers had succeeded in their 'nefarious designs': he estimated that something like 80 per cent of the non-Muslim population of these districts had migrated to UP, central India and the hill states of the Punjab. The ostensible cause of the Muslim League's civil disobedience movement earlier in the year was for the restoration of civil liberties and the bringing down of the Khizr ministry in Punjab and that of Dr Khan Sahib in NWFP: in fact it was used for 'terrorizing, intimidating and exterminating the Hindu and Sikh minorities, whose interests they were so loudly proclaiming to protect. Could Duplicity and Devilry go further?'[31]

A few years later, G. D. Khosla, a Justice of the Punjab high court engaged by the government of India to produce 'a true and authoritative account of the happenings in West Punjab, the North West Frontier Province and Sind . . . for the future student of History', gave to this picture of attacks by fanatical Muslims and the martyrdom of brave non-Muslims the stamp of 'authentic history':

A mob of Muslims armed with all kinds of weapons shouting slogans and beating drums, approached a selected village and surrounded it from all sides. A few non-Muslim residents were immediately killed to strike terror throughout the village. The rest were asked to embrace Islam. If they showed reluctance a ruthless assault was launched upon non-Muslim life and property. Some members of the mob started looting and burning their houses and shops. Others searched out young and good-looking girls and carried them away. Not infrequently young women were molested and raped in the open, while all around them frenzied hooligans rushed about shouting, looting and setting fire to houses. Most of the non-Muslims would leave their houses and run to the local Gurdwara or a house affording some measure of protection or defence and there men, women and children, huddled together, would hear the noise of carnage, see the smoke rising from their burning homes and wait for the end . . . Some women would commit suicide or suffer death at the hands of their relations with stoic indifference, others would jump into a well or be burnt alive uttering hysterical cries. The men would come out and meet death in a desperate sally against the marauders.[32]

[31] (NMML) B. S. Moonje papers, file no. 58, 'The Punjab Riots and the Lessons', from Chhabil Das, ex-life member, Servants of the People Society (Lahore, 5 May 1947).
[32] See Khosla, *Stern Reckoning*, pp. vii and 107.

The canonisation of particular acts of violence is a notable feature of this 'secondary' discourse. One major example mentioned above is that of the collective suicide of some ninety women and children of Thoa Khalsa, in Rawalpindi district. Perhaps this instance became especially well known because of the scale of the martyrdom; perhaps because it was one of the earliest instances of the suicide and murder of one's own relatives in the course of Partition. The petition presented to the governor by over one hundred Sikhs and Hindus of Rawalpindi in March 1947 singled out the incident. Hindu and Sikh villagers had, to the last man, refused to give up their religion, it said. 'Some of the women preferring death to dishonour jumped into a well, some others were butchered for their refusal to accept the culture of Islam.' It is fascinating to observe how quickly news of this 'sacred' occurrence spread after that.

The genealogy of Thoa Khalsa

The story of Thoa Khalsa has recently been recovered for Partition historiography by Urvashi Butalia and Sudesh Vaid. A prominent survivor gave them a vivid account of the mass suicide at the site:

In Gulab Singh's haveli twenty-six girls had been put aside. First of all my father, Sant Raja Singh, when he brought his daughter, he brought her into the courtyard to kill her, first of all he prayed (... did *ardaas*) saying '*sacche badshah*', we have not allowed your Sikhi to get stained, and in order to save it we are going to sacrifice our daughters, make them martyrs, please forgive us ...

About the sacrifice at the well later the same day, Bir Bahadur Singh had this to say:

There was a well ... at the well Sardarni Gulab Kaur ... in my presence said '*sacche badshah*', let us be able to save our girls ... This incident of 25 girls of our household [being killed] had already taken place ... she knew that Sant Raja Singh had killed his daughters and other women of his household ... those that are left, we should not risk their lives and allow them to be taken away ... After having talked among themselves and decided, they said, we are thirsty, we need water, so the Musalmaan took them to the well. I was sitting with my mother ... Mata Lajwanti, who was also called Sardarni Gulab Singh, sitting at the well, she said two words, she did *ardaas* in two words, saying '*sacche badshah*' it is to save our Sikhi that we are offering up our lives ... forgive us and accept our martyrdom ... and saying those words, she jumped into the well, and some eighty women followed her ... they also jumped in. The well filled up completely ... one woman whose name is Basant Kaur, six children born of her womb died in that well, but she survived. She jumped in four times but the well had filled up ... She would look at her children, at herself ... Till today I think she is alive.[33]

---

[33] See Butalia, 'Community, State and Gender', p. ws-14.

The structure of this narrative was, however, already in place in the 1950s. A statement recorded at the time from the leader of the Thoa Khalsa Sikhs, Sant Gulab Singh himself, detailed this deed of unparalleled piety. 'Sardarni Lajwanti asked for permission for the women to go and sit at the well', he says, describing his own wife in the formal third person. 'Water was drawn up and all the assembled washed themselves, and the recitation of the scriptures began. There were 90 women in all, all of one lineage [Gulab Singh's own] . . . they included young unmarried girls, my granddaughters and grandsons, little children and their mothers.'

When the Muslim assailants surrounded the women and children at the well, Gulab Singh went on to say, and declared their intention of taking away the young women, the *sardarni* (Sikh woman) warned them that no earthly power could destroy the honour of the women of this community. Then, 'taking a five-year old granddaughter by one hand and a grandson by the other, and calling out *"Sat Siri Akal"*, she leapt into the well, so that I should not have to witness the dishonouring of any (Sikh) daughter. Upon this, the young daughters and old women of the clan all followed suit, and the entire well filled up within a minute or two.'

A man came running to tell Gulab Singh of what had transpired. 'On hearing his tale, all the Sikh young men and women [sons and daughters] cried out in one voice, *'Dhanya Guru Kalgidhar'* ['Blessed is the Guru Kalgidhar' – a reference to Guru Gobind Singh].' Seeing what had happened, 'the Muslims fled in terror': Pathans and 'other tyrannical groups', every Muslim present 'shivered with fear' – fear of a community that could sacrifice an entire clan in this way for the faith. Gulab Singh says he thanked the Almighty and asked for guidance for his own actions. 'At that time, I saw Baba Nanak in person, and it seemed as if he said to me: "there are other tests yet to come – you must face these, and you must look after [the community] . . . " '[34] Thus Gulab Singh, like Bir Bahadur, translates the bravery and suffering of the women of his village into a hallowed martyrdom and, the tasks remaining after this, into a religious duty for himself and the remainder of his community.

Other reports had contributed to the sanctification. 'The story of 90 women of the little village of Thoa Khalsa, Rawalpindi district, who drowned themselves by jumping into a well during the recent disturbances, has stirred the imagination of the people of the Punjab', *The Statesman*, Calcutta, reported in April 1947.[35] In July of the same year,

[34] Account of Thoa Khalsa, based on Sant Gulab Singh's statement, in Kirpal Singh, comp., *Shaheedian* (Amritsar, 1964?), pp. 69–71. (I am grateful to Mr Brij Mohan Shangari for providing me with a Hindi translation from the Gurmukhi text, and to Dr Mohinder Singh for making this possible.)
[35] *The Statesman* (Calcutta, 15 April 1947).

leaflets distributed among the Sikhs of Delhi celebrated the martyrdom and sacrifices of the women of Thoa Khalsa and other brave Sikh women and men. 'THE MEMORY OF THE HEROES OF JAITO AND NANKANA [who died in the non-violent Sikh struggle to regain control of their gurdwaras between 1920 and 1925] HAS BEEN ENLIVENED ONCE AGAIN BY THE "SISTERS OF THE SPINNING WHEEL" – THE DEATH-DEFYING SISTERS OF RAWALPINDI – THE PRIDE OF POTHOHAR – THOSE BRAVE DAUGHTERS OF GURU ARJAN – WHO PREFERRED VOLUNTARY DEATH – SELF-INFLICTED OR AT THE HANDS OF THEIR DEAR ONES TO AN IGNOBLE LIFE. THEY ARE PHYSICALLY GONE. THEIR SPIRIT IS AN UNDYING FORCE.'[36]

A Shiromani Gurudwara Prabandhak Committee (SGPC) report on the 'Muslim League' attack on Sikhs and Hindus in 1947, published in 1950, was equally ardent in its acclaim of the 'epic resistance' offered by Sikh men and women in village after village throughout Punjab. Of the village of Thoa Khalsa, it said: 'The Sikh ladies in their extremity either committed suicide or entreated their husbands and fathers to kill them. This was done. Thus the ladies saved their honour.'[37]

Sikh histories written three and a half decades later continue this glorification. In March 1947, writes one historian,

The sledge hammer of Muslim violence fell most disastrously on the Sikhs in Rawalpindi division. In the rural areas, where they were severely outnumbered, they faced total annihilation. Frenzied Muslim mobs would assemble from all over, beating drums and shouting their religious war cries. They would trap the scanty Sikh populations in their villages and start making short work of them. Sikhs were hunted down in their homes, in *gurdwaras* and in the shelters offered by friendly local Muslims . . . Neither woman nor child was spared. The holocausts Sikhs had suffered in the eighteenth century were thrown into the shade by this organized butchery.

Against this 'ruthless onslaught', he adds,

The Sikhs did not fail to reproduce their inheritance of courage and heroic action . . . Many won laurels of martyrdom while trying to protect their *gurdwaras* from desecration. The women jumped into wells to save themselves [from] . . . dishonour . . . In the village of Thoha [*sic*] Khalsa alone, ninety-three Sikh women immolated themselves in this manner. To their *ardas* [prayer], which recounts deeds of Sikh heroism and martyrdom, the Sikhs now added new stirring lines as . . . they had done at all difficult periods of their history.[38]

[36] (NMML) CID Papers, 3rd instalment, F1, copy of cyclostyled handbill being distributed among the public (accompanying note is dated 7 July 1947).
[37] By contrast, it declared, 'Most of the Hindus under pressure accepted Islam', Gurbachan Singh Talib, comp., *Muslim League Attack on Sikhs and Hindus in the Punjab, 1947* (Amritsar, 1950; reprinted, Delhi, 1991), p. 352 and *passim*.
[38] Harbans Singh, *The Heritage of the Sikhs*, revised edn (Delhi, 1994), pp. 288–9.

The actions of the Thoa Khalsa women would be written of in history 'in letters of gold', a leading woman social worker associated with the Indian National Congress, Rameshwari Nehru, wrote in December 1947.[39] 'A country that has such courageous women among its inhabitants can never die', she declared, as she appropriated the sacrifice at the well to the greater glory of an ancient – new – nation.

Nehru visited Thoa Khalsa along with several associates on 30 March, two and a half weeks after the incident of collective suicide. In her newspaper account, published in December 1947, she described the evidence of destruction and the putrid air that still hung over the village when she visited it. The habitation of 2,000 to 2,500 Sikhs contained nothing but the skeletons of houses, she noted, and in them human skulls and bones and huge heaps of ('once beautifully kept', and now 'shorn') hair. She and her companions had gone to the well where the mass suicide had taken place, and she refers to the overpowering stench that made it impossible to stand at the site for any length of time. But all of this was of little significance in an article that set out to honour the glory of India's pure and brave womanhood.

The scene is set by an alluring description of the wonderfully clean, prosperous and well-ordered character of a village, set on a cliff, with beautiful orchards beneath it, green fields of rice and wheat and, behind them, hills laden with small trees and bushes. When Nehru and her colleagues reached there, 'a cool and gentle breeze was blowing': 'I had never before seen such a clean, beautiful and well-organised village in my life.' It was this idyllic village that was attacked by 10,000 to 12,000 armed Muslims on 12 March.

This appears to have been the date on which the final attack on Thoa Khalsa occurred, but Nehru's account collapsed the attacks and struggles of the preceding days onto this one date. Houses and shops were looted and burnt, she writes, and a number of Sikhs were forcibly converted, with their hair and beards being shaved off. Those who could do so fled, under cover of darkness or when they saw a chance. The rest, unable either to persuade the Muslims to cease their attacks, or to continue the fight for more than a few days, adopted harsher – and braver – methods. Several prominent youths of Thoa Khalsa 'killed one another and their own women with their own swords'. And further: 'Finding no other way out, 105 women saved their chastity and religion by committing suicide.' 'What these illiterate village women showed to the world by their actions was in no way less momentous than

---

[39] 'Punjab ka bhayankar hatyakand' by Rameshwari Nehru, Deshdut (28 December 1947), in (NMML) Rameshwari Nehru papers, 'Speeches and Writings', s.n. 5. The name of the village is mistakenly given as Choa Khalsa in this article.

[the legendary Queen] Padmini's *jauhar* or the self-sacrifice of Rajput [noble-] women.'

Indeed, the urban nationalist became positively lyrical in her description of what she and her companions found at the well where the mass suicide of women and children had occurred:

> It was eighteen days after the incident that we arrived at this sacred spot. The bodies of those beautiful women had become swollen and floated up to the surface of the water. Their colourful clothes and long, black hair could be seen clearly. Two or three women still had [the bodies of] infants clinging to their breasts. There was not a man or woman in our party who did not have tears in his/her eyes . . . All of us bowed down to these *sati* [pure, sacred] women . . . We thought of it as our great good fortune that we had been able to visit this site and worship these *satis* . . .

The *testimony* here is, again, not a witnessing for the dead, but a testimony to the grandeur of something 'larger' – 'Indian' tradition, and 'Indian' womanhood, from which these particular victims (women and children, and men) are now excluded.

The question of casualties: a note on tertiary discourse

The FIRs that I have cited as one example of primary discourse are appeals to the state, reporting criminal attacks, identifying specific crimes, perpetrators and victims, and calling for justice, redress and compensation. At the same time, they constitute a form of remembrance, struggling as they do to preserve a memory of the dead, of the houses and sites they inhabited, and of communities that are crumbling. This latter impulse remains a part of survivors' testimony even years later, when the memory of these events, people and places has been sanitised and flattened in various ways. Testimony both participates in rumour and seeks to overturn it: the former because, in times of collective violence, it must acknowledge the practices that rumour initiates; the latter since it seeks to reinsert subjectivity, one that has been denied by rumour. This struggle to recover individuality and specificity is not a prominent feature of secondary discourse, however, or of the tertiary – whose subject is almost invariably far more abstract and general.

The political commentary/reportage that constitutes a good part of the secondary discourse on Partition available to us is primarily concerned to assign responsibility for 'disorders' to particular political movements. It develops a rhetoric of blame towards what was now coming to be seen as an 'enemy' nation (already in March–April 1947, and much more clearly later). Another instance of such secondary discourse, contemporary 'histories' written to record events for future enquirers, shares with political reportage the object of assigning guilt. Almost uniformly, they glorify or vilify local violence/sacrifice and local traditions. In all these genres of writing, prejudice and hearsay is barely sifted from demonstrable fact. Rumour appears to cast a spell over the proceedings.

There is much in the tertiary discourse relating to 1947 that perpetuates the message – and method – of rumours. Consider the most basic data that our histories of Partition present on the question of casualties. I cited two important recent studies at the start of this chapter. Recall what Butalia tells us. Estimates of the dead 'vary from 200,000 . . . to two million . . . ': a considerable margin of error, to say the least. However, 'that somewhere around a million people died is now widely accepted'. What is the basis for this acceptance? That it appears like something of a median? Menon and Bhasin choose '500,000–1,000,000'. Mohammad Waseem accepts a figure of 'about half a million'. Wolpert settles for 'approximately one million'.[40]

In his popular biography of Mountbatten, Ziegler provides the following summary statement. ' "A million dead" was the propagandist's slogan, but none of those who have made any attempt to base their calculations on serious analysis of the sources . . . puts the figure so high.' He notes that G. D. Khosla, the judge appointed by the Indian government to prepare a comprehensive report out of the records of its fact-finding committee, estimated a death toll of 400,000–500,000; and Chandulal Trivedi, the first Indian governor of East Punjab, 225,000; adding that 'probably the most systematic attempt to work out a correct figure was that of Penderel Moon, who suggested the most likely total was 200,000'.[41] It is worth considering how the latter, a noted Indian Civil Service (ICS) official from Punjab, worked out this estimate.

Based as he was then in Bahawalpur, he had 'a pretty-accurate knowledge', Moon wrote, 'of the casualties both in Bahawalpur State itself and in the immediately adjacent West Punjab districts'. A historian ploughing through the records of the government of the time, of military and other intelligence, as well as the findings of journalists and other non-official observers, might be somewhat less sanguine than the colonial administrator. But Moon was at least trying to establish the bases of a calculation. Regarding a number of other districts, he claimed to have

---

[40] See nn. 6 and 7 on p. 68; Mohammad Waseem, 'Partition, Migration and Assimilation: a Comparative Study of Pakistani Punjab', in Ian Talbot and Gurharpal Singh, eds., *Region and Partition. Bengal, Punjab and the Partition of the Subcontinent* (Karachi, 1999), p. 207; Stanley Wolpert, *A New History of India* (New York, 2000), p. 348.

[41] Philip Ziegler, *Mountbatten* (New York, 1985), p. 437. It will be clear from the following paragraphs that Moon was citing this figure only for Punjab and neighbouring princely states.

'good information from old subordinates', especially among magistrates and police. On the basis of this information, he arrived at 'fairly precise figures' for about half the districts of West Punjab. On the basis of these, he went on to make 'fairly intelligent guesses' regarding casualties in the remaining districts. His calculations led him to a figure of 60,000 as the number of those killed between August and December 1947 in West Punjab and Bahawalpur. The author adds that he was gratified to learn that the governor of West Punjab, Sir Francis Mudie, had quite independently arrived at 'exactly the same result' – though one would have to note that the latter was, by his very position, cushioned from happenings in the countryside.[42]

As to East Punjab and the many princely states in that region, from where many of the Sikh attacks against Muslims appear to have been launched, Moon had 'no detailed information'. He 'knew', however, that casualties there had been 'considerably heavier than in West Punjab'. He 'assumed . . . that they might have been twice as heavy, i.e. 120,000 . . . Subsequent inquiries have led me to think that the casualties in East Punjab, though undoubtedly higher than in West Punjab, were not, as I had assumed, twice as high and consequently my final figure of 200,000 [for those killed in the two Punjabs and neighbouring states] was somewhat inflated.'[43]

Among other early estimates, Ian Stephens, the editor of the Calcutta *Statesman*, who had seen the Calcutta killings at close quarters in August 1946, provided the figure of 'about 500,000' killed between August 1946 and December 1947.[44] On the basis of published and unpublished materials and oral evidence provided to him by officials and non-officials in Pakistan, Symonds declared that, 'at the lowest estimate', half a million people perished and twelve million became homeless.[45] Like others, I have in an earlier essay accepted something like the latter figures as the most 'likely'.[46] Nothing in the surviving records, in the calculations made at the time, or in the contentious debates that have gone on since then, gives us anything like a persuasive basis for such an inference. Is it, rather,

---

[42] Cf. Mudie's own comment in October 1947: 'How many have already died no one knows. No one will ever know', letter to *The Times* (17 October 1947). More than one observer also noted the narrowness that flowed from Mudie's bureaucratic approach. 'The snake in the grass in the West Punjab is Mudie. He is inveterate against Congress. He tries to govern himself. Thus he thwarts his Cabinet, above all in their attempts to bridge the gulf between West and East Punjab . . .' (IOR) Mss. Eur. F200/129, 'Note' by W. Short (17 October 1947). See also Khalid bin Sayeed, *Pakistan: the Formative Phase*, p. 264.

[43] Moon, *Divide and Quit*, p. 293.

[44] Stephens, *Pakistan*, p. 107.

[45] Richard Symonds, *The Making of Pakistan* (London, 1950), p. 74.

[46] Gyanendra Pandey, 'Can a Muslim be an Indian?', *Comparative Studies in Society and History*, 41, 4 (1999).

a question of what one can live with? Yet it is not entirely clear why it is easier to live with 500,000 dead than with a larger or smaller figure. Is this the 'median' that allows one to emphasise the enormity of Partition and point to our surviving humanity at the same time? Or is it a figure that has gained credibility in academic circles simply by repetition?

I want to stress that the question here is not one of 'truth' or 'falsehood'; for who can deny that there was incredible loss of life, dislocation and devastation? It is rather to consider the structure and the power of the discourse that surrounds and makes up the history of this violence. In the tertiary discourse, as in the primary and secondary, at the level of the nation, as at that of smaller, local groups of victims, 'facts and figures' of this kind continue to be reproduced. The historical discourse continues to bear the stamp of rumour, aggregating the power not so much of verifiable truth, as of a rumoured statistic – extravagant, expandable, unverifiable, but credible. The accounts live on in this form, rooted as they are in deeply held suspicions and beliefs, which are of course further reinforced by such 'rumoured histories': 'truths' produced by prejudice that further accentuate prejudice.[47]

The most 'likely', 'consensual' 'estimates' are thus accepted as true and recycled – because they have been heard, or heard repeatedly, in various forms and contexts. These are 'oral' reports that approximate to gospel, and that are then confirmed in the writing. Is it far-fetched to suggest that the general discourse on Partition still functions as something like a gigantic rumour, albeit a rumour commonly presented as 'testimony' (or 'history')? The process of its transmutation from one to the other requires closer investigation, however. The next chapter examines the move in relation to a widely reported event that took place in November 1946, nine months before the official Partition and Independence of India and Pakistan.

---

[47] Cf. Veena Das's comment that rumour 'naturalises the stereotypical distinctions between social groups and hides the social origins and production of hate', 'Official Narratives', p. 117.

5   Folding the local into the national: Garhmukhteshwar, November 1946

Historians of Partition have written of the 'overtly "communal" violence' that 'erupted in terrifying proportions' from August 1946. As Sumit Sarkar puts it, 'the whole Indian scene was rapidly transformed by communal riots on an unprecedented scale: starting with Calcutta on 16–19 August, touching Bombay from 1 September, spreading to Noakhali in East Bengal (10 October), Bihar (25 October), Garmukteswar in UP (November), and engulfing the Punjab from March 1947 onwards'.[1]

I want, in this chapter, to deal with one minor place that finds mention in this reconstructed arc: Garhmukhteshwar, alternatively described as a 'small town' or 'village' in the Meerut district of western UP, the site of a massacre of Muslims on the occasion of an annual fair (the *Kartik Purnima mela*) held in November 1946. Like Calcutta, Noakhali, Bihar and Punjab, Garhmukhteshwar has become a metaphor for the atrocities of Partition; and Partition itself a metaphor for the kind of extraordinary, genocidal violence that was not witnessed again in India, perhaps until 1984: so that in a curious and little explored way, 'Garhmukhteshwar' (or 'Noakhali', or 'Bihar', or 'Punjab'), 'Partition' and 'violence' come to stand in for one another.

Among the numerous ways of stripping events of their historical significance, I have suggested, one is that of localising them, another that of banishing them to the domain of an alien nation or community's history. The process of 'localising' – or 'nationalising' – however, requires further discussion. The 'local' and the 'global' are often mistakenly understood to be questions of scale; sometimes they are better seen as perspective.[2] Let us begin by making a clear distinction between locality as a spatial

[1] Sumit Sarkar, *Modern India, 1885–1947* (Delhi, 1983), p. 432. See also Judith Brown, *Modern India. The Origins of an Asian Democracy* (Oxford, 1994), pp. 337–8; S. M. Burke and Salim al-Din Quraishi, *The British Raj in India. An Historical Review* (Karachi, 1995), pp. 464–7; Suranjan Das, *Communal Riots in Bengal, 1905–1947*; Mushirul Hasan, ed., *India's Partition*, p. 38.

[2] Cf. Arjun Appadurai's consideration of locality 'as primarily relational and contextual rather than as scalar or spatial' in his *Modernity at Large. Cultural Dimensions of Globalization* (Minneapolis, 1996), pp. 178ff.

entity and the local as specifying a social condition. In a sense, of course, the vast majority of historical events have been *local* events – at least before the current epoch of 'virtual reality' and 'virtual communities'. They have occurred in particular, designated, definable geographical spaces – Montaillou, Meerut, the Midlands, the American south, western India – with particular, identifiable, culturally defined actors, under particular, varied but specific conditions.

There are events (and places), however, that are not classified as local because they supposedly represent the national, universal, global, metropolitan. The bankers of the City of London are, in this sense, never local.[3] On the other hand, other events (and places) are readily consigned to the local, as they are judged to be of little significance – meaning, of course, of little significance in the advance of the narrative of the national (or the global). Even where a locality is thoroughly globalised, efforts are sometimes made to dismiss major events as essentially 'local': such is the case of the Union Carbide industrial disaster in Bhopal.[4] Alongside that, and sometimes in the same moment, when 'recalcitrant events'[5] cannot be brushed aside in this manner, they are presented as belonging to an altogether different tradition and history – of little relevance or (if that is hard to maintain) of only negative significance in the development of our particular history. How does all this affect Partition?

The historians tell us that the communal riots of 1946–7 were no longer 'local' disturbances – in that they had come to be distinctly tied up with wider political movements and demands.[6] Indeed, the relationship between the 'local' and the 'national' is a matter of some importance in discussions of this violence. How did national forces affect the local? And local forces appropriate the national? How was the national perceived, and constructed, in particular instances – by local participants as well as by outside commentators? The meaning of the 'national' and of the 'local' is, however, itself not in question. This remains the case, I suggest, even in studies that produce sophisticated arguments about the interpenetration of the 'local' and the 'national' (or indeed 'global'), and the presence of the one in the other.

---

[3] Cf. Brackette F. Williams, 'A Class Act: Anthropology and the Race to Nation across Ethnic Terrain', *Annual Review of Anthropology*, 18 (1989).

[4] For one important analysis of this, see Das, *Critical Events*, ch. 6.

[5] I take the phrase, 'recalcitrant events', from Shahid Amin – to refer to events that are not easily accommodated within the terms of a particular narrative.

[6] Suranjan Das describes the process as the forging of a growing link between 'organised' (modern) and 'unorganised' politics, but adds that, as this happened, there was a shift from a 'strong class orientation' (in earlier, 'local' communal riots) to a more overt communalism (which made them part of wider, communal/national struggles), *Communal Riots in Bengal*, pp. 6, 11, 207 and *passim*.

One point that needs to be noted about events like the 'riots' of 1946–7 is that the historical records do not generally allow us to answer the kinds of 'local?'/'national?' questions that scholars ask of them. For by the time such an event gains a place in 'history' (and in the state's archive), the 'local' and the 'national' are so inextricably intertwined in it as to make their disentangling a practical impossibility. What we might more fruitfully ask, on the basis of this kind of historical record, is *not*: what was the 'local' and what the 'national' in this event, *but*: how does historiography itself proceed to *localise* or *nationalise* the event: or both? This is what I seek to do in the following pages through a detailed consideration of contemporary and later writings on the violence that occurred in the village, or small town, of Garhmukhteshwar in November 1946.

The 'bare facts' of a 'riot'

In his book on Chauri Chaura, Shahid Amin writes of the peasant–police clash there in February 1922 as both an event and a metaphor. 'Chauri Chaura, a place name, has . . . become a figure of speech, a trope for all manner of untrammelled peasant violence . . . I write about the riot as an event fixed in time . . . and also as a metaphor gathering significances outside this time-frame.'[7] Unlike Amin, I am not sure that I can separate event and metaphor in the case of Garhmukhteshwar, even though (like Chauri Chaura) this event is localised to one place and one major instance of violence.[8] For Garhmukhteshwar, the *event* is made by its apprehension – in both senses of the term. The historical incident named 'Garhmukhteshwar' is a metaphor from the very beginning, perhaps because of the heavily politicised nature of all reporting and all interpretation in the year leading up to official Partition and Independence, perhaps because any event that attains the status of 'event' (that is to say, of 'history') functions as metaphor from the start.

Here is an outline of the Garhmukhteshwar event, as it appears in what might be considered an authoritative official account, the provincial government's report of political events in UP in the first half of November 1946. The report notes the 'desire for revenge' that took hold of both Hindus and Muslims in the province in the wake of the mass

---

[7] Shahid Amin, *Event, Metaphor, Memory. Chauri Chaura 1922–1992* (Berkeley and Los Angeles, 1995), p. 3.

[8] To be fair to Amin, he states categorically that 'interpretations of the evidence, archival as well as oral, are a necessary part of the history of [the] event', *ibid.*, pp. 3–4. My point would be that it is not only 'interpretations of the evidence' (archival and oral), but interpretations of the event at the time of its occurrence as well that go to make up the event.

killings in Calcutta, Noakhali and Bihar, made worse in the eastern districts of UP by the arrival of refugees from neighbouring Bihar. The tension exploded, however, at the western end of the province, at the Garhmukhteshwar *mela*, or fair, which was attended on this occasion by 700,000 to 800,000 people from western UP and eastern Punjab.[9] The disorders started on 6 November 1946, with an attack by Hindus upon Muslim shopkeepers in the *mela*. Forty-six people were killed and thirty-nine injured in the attacks that evening. On 8 November, when the Muslims attending the fair were waiting for organised transport to take them away, there were still reports of sporadic assaults and arson, and the police were compelled to open fire.

Meanwhile, 'a well organised Hindu crowd from the *mela*' had attacked Garhmukhteshwar town, three miles away, on the afternoon and evening of the 7th. They destroyed the Muslim section of the town and inflicted heavy casualties. 'There was mass slaughter of Muslim men, women and children accompanied by arson and other gruesome atrocities', the official account states. There were further attacks on the town, and on the 9th morning the cloth shops of Hindu shop-owners were also attacked, in spite of police firing. By that time, according to the provincial government, the dead bodies of 214 Muslims had been recovered.

Reports and rumours of what had happened in Garhmukhteshwar quickly spread and precipitated incidents of violence in other towns and villages in the vicinity. According to the same fortnightly report, five Muslim bus passengers were killed on the road to Hapur; twenty-three Hindus and two Muslims in a large village called Shahjahanpur, between Garhmukhteshwar and Meerut; nine others (probably mainly Hindus) killed and eight injured at Dasna railway station; thirty-seven Muslims killed in Harson and nine more (with twenty injured) in village Gadri;[10] plus fifteen Hindus and Muslims killed and sixteen injured in Meerut city by 9 November, and another fourteen killed and nineteen injured on 11 November. The government account concluded that thirty-seven Hindus, 230 Muslims and 127 people whose religious affiliation was not known, that is, a total of 394 people, had been killed in the course of these incidents in Meerut district alone: there were casualties in some neighbouring districts too, on a smaller scale.

The precision of these figures should not mislead us. That 127 among the dead are listed as being of unknown religious affiliation speaks both

---

[9] (Imperial War Museum, London) papers of Lt Gen. Sir Francis Tuker, 71/21/4/4, 'Fortnightly Report for the first half of November, 1946', government of UP, confidential dept (Lucknow, 25 November 1946). The reports differ on whether this attendance was larger or smaller than usual.

[10] Other reports suggest the name Garhi, or, more likely, Indragarhi.

of the fact that this 'riot' was hardly a local affair – that large numbers of strangers were caught up in it – and that the authorities did not go to a great deal of trouble to identify the victims. The total number of Muslims killed computed by the UP government does not tally even with the breakup it provides in the paragraph immediately preceding its totals: 214 killed in Garhmukhteshwar, five on the road to Hapur, thirty-seven in Harson, nine in Gadri (Indragarhi?); and this excludes the casualties counted in Meerut city, not to mention those reported in other accounts. Rumour and precise statistics went together.

Muslim League sources put the figure of those killed in the fair and the town at 'upward of 2,000'.[11] Lieutenant General Sir Francis Tuker, writing a couple of years later – while 'memory' still served, as he stressed – declared it 'certain that one thousand Muslims died, perhaps two thousand'.[12] Not to be outdone, Hindu right-wingers came up with their own preposterous statistics. 'Six' Muslims were killed in the riots at the Garhmukhteshwar fair and town, one of their papers declared; by contrast, numerous Hindu women were killed, and 'hundreds' were thrown into the river at Dasna and Shahjahanpur – the sites of the two major Muslim counter-attacks in the district.[13] It is necessary to compare these diverse constructions of Garhmukhteshwar at somewhat greater length.

Explanations and omissions

What stands out in the Indian National Congress and related nationalists' accounts is a proposition about the unfortunate, but nonetheless *limited*, character of the 'riot' at Garhmukhteshwar. To a large extent, the narrative goes, the violence here was sparked off by reports of riots and of losses suffered at the hands of the 'other' community in other places. Extreme right-wing organisations were behind the trouble; as always at such junctures, criminal elements took a leading part; and the simple, innocent peasant folk were misled. In addition, the Congress would note, the administration failed to do its duty.

The Congress largely reproduced the provincial government's assessment of casualties and destruction, as well as its minimalist account of what transpired at Garhmukhteshwar between 6 and 9 November 1946. The provincial administration, then serving under a Congress ministry, went to some lengths to underplay the scale of the violence and casualties,

---

[11] *Dawn* (23 November 1946), editorial.
[12] Francis Tuker, *While Memory Serves* (London, 1950), p. 200.
[13] (NMML) All India Congress Committee (AICC) papers, G-10/1947, DO no. 68/S-47, collector, Meerut to home secretary, government of UP (13 February 1947), citing a Meerut bulletin called *Sunday Times*.

whether from fear of provoking further revenge attacks, or sullying the name of the Congress ministry, or simply in order to maintain peace at the annual session of the Indian National Congress which was to meet later in November in the same Meerut district. Congress spokespersons and the pro-Congress press highlighted the incidents that followed *after* Garhmukhteshwar: events at the *mela* and town thus became merely the starting point for this round of violence; and 'Hindus' and 'Muslims' were represented as being equally to blame – if that.[14]

Thus, *The Hindustan Times*, a Congress newspaper published from Delhi, reproduced the UP government's casualty figures as well as its general account of the violence in Garhmukhteshwar, except that it made no direct reference to the communal identity of the victims (perhaps as a matter of general newspaper policy, as encouraged by the Indian government at this time).[15] In the previous chapter, I cited its headlines of 10 November 1946: 'PILGRIM TRAIN ATTACKED NEAR MEERUT. 50 BUTCHERED, OVER 100 INJURED . . .' The body of the report noted that following a 'riot' in Garhmukhteshwar on the 7th in which 'about 200' people lost their lives, 'hooligans' had attacked a passenger train 'mostly full of pilgrims returning from Garhmukhteshwar', and so on. The front-page headline on 11 November said: 'MEERUT SITUATION NOW UNDER CONTROL. Pant and Kidwai Supervise Relief Work.' In other words, the Congress government had acted immediately and effectively, and the violence, which was already spiralling, had quickly been stopped.[16]

Important nationalist commentators argued that there was some conspiracy or organisation behind these incidents. Major General Shah Nawaz Khan, the acclaimed hero of Subhas Bose's Indian National Army, and Mridula Sarabhai, a general secretary of the Indian National Congress, along with other local leaders and workers, toured through Meerut district in the days immediately following the Garhmukhteshwar massacre. Their finding was that the 'disturbances' were created mainly

---

[14] Tuker put it as follows: 'The provincial government, willingly helped by its Indian administrators, soft-pedalled these outrages committed by Hindus, and the Hindu papers purposely emphasised the far smaller acts of retaliation by Muslims in the area of the disturbances, in order to cover up the misdeeds of their co-religionists', *While Memory Serves*, p. 196.

[15] See *The Hindustan Times* (12 November 1946); and also its reports on 10 and 11 November.

[16] The *Aj* (Banaras), probably the most important nationalist Hindi daily of UP, published a similar account to that of *The Hindustan Times* (only briefer) and similarly small casualty figures, in its only report of the Garhmukhteshwar events, on 9 November 1946. All other reports from Meerut, published that month in *Aj*, have to do with preparations for the AICC session – for example, *ibid.* (12 and 19 November 1946) – except for a report that the UP government had sanctioned Rs. 15,000 for the relief and rehabilitation of the Meerut refugees, *ibid.* (20 November 1946).

by pilgrims from the Rohtak and Hissar districts of Punjab (what the military intelligence would specify as 'Rohtak and Gurgaon Jats'). These returning pilgrims 'systematically' destroyed villages that lay in their path, observed Shah Nawaz, 'far exceed[ing] any of the atrocities and cruelties committed by the Japanese in the three years of their occupation of East Asia [*sic*]'. They were 'incited' by extreme right-wing communalists, 'in all probability members of the RSS [Rashtriya Svayamsevak Sangh]'.[17]

In addition, it seemed to these nationalist leaders that the police had been seriously negligent in their duty. They had done precious little to discipline, let alone disarm, the returning pilgrims, many of whom carried lethal weapons. Both Shah Nawaz Khan and Mridula Sarabhai observed mounted horsemen patrolling the area and directing the attacking crowds. However, the police made no move to arrest the ringleaders when these activities were pointed out to them.[18] 'Had the police acted more vigorously and promptly, much of the destruction to life and property could have been prevented.'[19]

On both these points – about the organisation that lay behind the violence and administrative ineptitude or negligence – Muslim Leaguers and Communists, and colonialist observers too, were in agreement with Congress critics; indeed, they expressed themselves far more strongly than Shah Nawaz and Sarabhai. As the monthly security intelligence report of the army headquarters for the UP area for November 1946 put it in a summary assessment of the violence at Garhmukhteshwar, 'What originated as a petty incident developed into a massacre of the Muslim population... Calcutta was revenged in Noakhali, Noakhali in Bihar, Bihar in Garmuktesar, Garmuktesar in ???'[20]

The brutality of the Garhmukhteshwar violence is underlined in the chronological account that follows in an appendix to this report. On 6 November, Hindus – 'mainly Rohtak and Gurgaon Jats' – who were watching a death-defying ('wall-of-death') motor-cycling show – raised a

---

[17] AICC papers, G-10/1947, Shah Nawaz Khan's statement to the press (13 November 1946). The proposition that the disturbances were 'well planned' had been made by the local district magistrate, among others; see (NAI) Home Poll (I) file 5/5/47, 'Summary of Dist. Magistrate's Report on Disturbances in Meerut District'. For a later expression of doubt by the government, see the report of a debate in the provincial legislative assembly, *Dawn* (19 April 1947).

[18] 'They were afraid rather than apathetic', Tuker was to suggest, *Memory*, p. 198.

[19] AICC papers, G-10/1947, Shah Nawaz Khan's statement (13 November 1946). A somewhat different construction of the event comes through in the earliest official accounts, which seek to underscore administrative integrity and full official effort to maintain law and order, (NAI) Home Poll (I), file 5/5/47, 'Summary of Dist. Magistrate's Report on Disturbances in Meerut District', covering the period 6–17 November 1946.

[20] Francis Tuker papers, 71/21/4/4, 'Extract from Monthly Security Intelligence Report for November 46 of HQ UP Area'.

cry about an alleged insult to a Hindu woman, looted and burnt the show, killing its proprietors, and proceeding to loot other shops and 'massacre all the Muslims they could find in the Mela'. Forty-seven Muslims were reported killed, and thirty-nine injured, but (according to the military intelligence) many more corpses were recovered later. About fifty Muslim girls were thought to have been abducted.

On the afternoon of 7 November, a large body of 'Rohtak Jats' led by local Hindus went to Garhmukhteshwar town, where they 'mingle[d] unnoticed' with returning pilgrims and 'wiped out [the] Mohamedan Quarter of the town, killing all Muslim men, women and children with disgusting bestiality'. Between 9 and 12 November, 'returning Jats' assaulted Muslims at several spots, inflicting severe losses, and groups of Muslims too attacked returning pilgrims in a few places.[21]

A Communist Party correspondent, O. P. Sangal, wrote after conducting personal investigations and interviews in Garhmukhteshwar and other places in Meerut district that the attacks on the town and fair 'were both well-organised affairs'. There was no doubt that the RSS was responsible; they had organised rallies and meetings (in Rohtak, in Delhi, in Meerut, and at the fair itself) to incite people. Finally, not only the police, but also the military – and the regime as a whole – was negligent. 'The military was sent very late to Garhmukhteshwar . . . after a lot of haggling between civil and military authorities'; and again, 'The riot stopped for some time on the first day but owing to indifference and negligence on the part of the military that was posted on the road between the fair and the town, a mob succeeded in raiding the town on the second day.'[22]

Muslim League spokespersons were even sharper in their response. A report in the Muslim League newspaper, *Dawn*, on 22 November noted the statement of a UP government spokesman that 'mass murder, arson, and conversion of girls, was done by Jats of Rohtak district and volunteers of the Rashtriya Sewak Sangh [*sic*], who are held responsible for the riot'.[23] Its own independent evidence of pre-planning was, however, far more damning. In its very first report on what it described as another 'Killing' (a term that had gained currency from the 'Great Calcutta Killing'), the newspaper quoted an eyewitness (a Muslim itinerant trader who had managed to escape from Garhmukhteshwar by disguising himself as a Hindu) as saying that when the attack began at one of the entertainment enclosures on the 6th, 'simultaneously trouble started all over the fair, an area of 12 square miles. Shops owned by Muslims were

[21] *Ibid.*
[22] *People's Age* (22 December 1946).
[23] *Dawn* (22 November 1946).

attacked and burned. Many of the shopkeepers including their women were thrown live into the flames. Stray Muslims were chased and killed.'[24] Muhammad Aslam, the joint secretary of the Meerut City Muslim League, is quoted at the end of the same report: 'From the fact that the assailants and hooligans were all armed and trouble started all over the fair at the same time and the large mob which attacked the village had all the requisites for arson, it is clear that the whole thing has been planned beforehand.' The police, he noted, 'did not intervene at all'.

Ghazanfar Ali Khan, Muslim League member for health in the interim government established at the centre in 1946, drove the point home after a mission of inquiry that he led to Garhmukhteshwar on 17 November.[25] 'Without any kind of interference or check' by either the police or the military, he observed, the massacre, looting and burning went on throughout the night of the 6th and into the afternoon of 7 November. 'The killing and arson ended only when there remained no Muslim to be killed and no Muslim shop to be burnt... The mob did its work most systematically and with surprising precision', his report noted. The assailants carried petrol, other chemicals and 'equipment' for the sprinkling of houses – evidence surely of the involvement of ex-servicemen, perhaps belonging to the Indian National Army. On the 9th, the 'mob' proceeded to launch a second attack on the village, looting and demolishing several Muslim houses and shops opposite the village police outpost that they had bypassed on the first occasion, even though the police strength had meanwhile been increased from six to twenty. He found, moreover, that they had even demolished a Muslim *idgah* (site for Id prayers) near the main police station, a couple of furlongs from the village. In both places, the police 'silently watched'.[26]

Ghazanfar Ali quoted Rafi Ahmed Qidwai, the UP Congress minister, as having told him that the whole affair was clearly 'pre-meditated' and 'carefully planned'. Ghazanfar's own view was that three parties cooperated in the 'long-drawn-out butchery and destruction'. One, in which a number of sadhus or religious mendicants were prominent, was instrumental in planning and instigating the violence, shouting slogans like '*Noakhali ka badla lenge* [We shall avenge Noakhali]' and '*Gandhi ki jai* [Victory to Gandhi]'. A second group did the actual killing, looting and

---

[24] *Dawn* (10 November 1946).

[25] The delegation included Nawab Mohammad Ismail Khan, president of the UP Muslim League, and other leaders. On the basis of this investigation, Ghazanfar Ali wrote a 'Report on the Massacres at Garhmukhteshwar, UP, November 1946', which was widely publicised and published as an 'Appendix' in (IOR) L/P&J/8/575, *Reports on the Disturbances in Bihar and the United Provinces, October–November 1946* (Muslim India Information Centre, London, n.d.), hereafter Ghazanfar report.

[26] *Ibid.*, pp. 16, 17, 18.

burning: the 'Jats of Rohtak' were prominent in this. Finally, there were the local Hindus, who marked houses and shops, and provided 'active guidance' to the attackers.[27]

The Congress's position

The Congress response to Garhmukhteshwar involved a shifting of attention away from the violence that had occurred at the site. This was done, consciously or unconsciously, by the attempt to blame an extremist organisation like the RSS, identify ringleaders, and proclaim the innocence of the bulk of the population. The same result – of defusing the seriousness of Garhmukhteshwar – was achieved by representing the massacre at the fair and town as one point in a chain of events set off by 'outside' forces, and by suggesting that the object was to derail the Congress struggle for Indian independence.

Part of the rioters' aim, Shah Nawaz and Sarabhai declared, was to discredit the Congress. Some of the attackers wore Congress caps and carried Congress flags. 'Nowhere did we hear the Hindu religious slogans; but there were the Congress slogans like "Mahatma Gandhi ki Jai", "Jawaharlal Nehru ki Jai", "Bharatmata ki Jai", "Jai Hind".'[28] The object was apparently to make local inhabitants believe that the Congress had organised, or at least sanctioned, the violence. 'In some places, I regret to say', said Shah Nawaz Khan, 'local Congressmen assisted them.' Both leaders spoke of the urgent need to counter such malicious and damaging propaganda being spread in the name of the Muslim League and the Congress: 'If we are to have real peace and unity, then appeals to Jehad by irresponsible elements in the name of the Muslim League, and the senseless destruction of life and property in the name of the Congress and Mahatma Gandhi, must be stopped immediately.'[29]

It is noteworthy that, in spite of the reports that came out of the investigations undertaken by Mridula Sarabhai, Shah Nawaz Khan and others, the All India Congress Committee (AICC) files dealing with Meerut in late 1946 and early 1947 contain far more correspondence on the disturbances of November and December 1946 in Meerut city and at Hapur, an important trading mart in the district, than they do on the Garhmukhteshwar massacre.[30] Over all of this looms the shadow of the forthcoming Meerut session of the Congress. The other major issue seems

---

[27] *Ibid.*, pp. 18–19.
[28] AICC papers, G-10/1947, Mridula Sarabhai's statement issued to the press (Delhi, 13 November 1946).
[29] *Ibid.*, Shah Nawaz Khan's statement (13 November 1946).
[30] See AICC papers, CL-10/1946-47 and G-10/1947.

to have been the question of the extent of punitive fines and compensation to be demanded from the Hindus and Muslims respectively in different localities. Behind this lay the question of who was ultimately responsible for the ongoing strife. In the end, it is the thesis of revenge upon revenge, and the equal complicity of Hindus and Muslims – if not, implicitly, the greater responsibility of the 'Muslims' for their willingness to stir up hatred and violence in their campaign for Pakistan – that is retailed repeatedly.

'[The] Garhmukhteshwar riot took place on 6th and 7th November 1946 in which many muslims [*sic*] were killed and their property looted,' wrote Thakur Phool Singh, Secretary of the UP Provincial Congress Committee, in his report on the 'Hapur riot'. 'On the 9th November, 1946, the muslims of Shahjahanpur and Dasna attacked the Garhmukhteshwar pilgrims on their way home. The Hindus in their turn retaliated by killing muslims of Harson and Indergarhi on the 10th of the same month.'[31] The respected Congressman, Algu Rai Shastri, had made the same kind of statement more movingly in an earlier report on the Hapur riot, upon which the provincial Congress secretary's account was probably based:

A chain of events was set off by the Garhmukhteshwar riot which took place on the occasion of the *Kartik ka mela* on 7 November, before the Meerut session of the Congress, and as a result of which the Muslims of Garhmukhteshwar suffered severe losses of property and wealth: that chain of events has lasted a long time . . . The Muslims of Shahjahanpur and Dasna sought to take revenge for Garhmukhteshwar, and did so to a great extent. Revenge for this revenge was taken by the Hindus in Harson, Indragarhi and one or two other places. And thus human beings became animals and went around killing one another.[32]

The general secretaries of the Indian National Congress (including Mridula Sarabhai) noted, in their report to the fifty-fourth annual session held at Meerut on 23 and 24 November 1946, that 'unspeakable acts of brutality' had been committed in Calcutta, in East Bengal, in Bihar and 'some parts of Meerut District'. The Congress itself passed a resolution saying that 'the responsibility for this widespread brutality must rest with the preaching of hatred and violence for political purposes and the degradation and exploitation of religion for political ends.'[33] J. B. Kripalani, a right-wing Congressman, who was president of the party

---

[31] AICC papers, CL-10/1946-47, Thakur Phool Singh's report on 'Hapur Riot' (23 January 1947).

[32] *Ibid.*, *'Hapur, Zila Merath (UP) ke Sampradayik Dange ki jaanch ka vivaran'*, Algu Rai Shastri (18 January 1947).

[33] A. M. Zaidi, ed., *The Story of the Congress Pilgrimage. Volume 4: 1940–55* (Delhi, 1990), p. 111.

at its Meerut session, made the case even more directly and dangerously: 'Whoever... preaches, sanctions, encourages, or uses violence [a reference to the Muslim League], specially of the sort that was practised in East Bengal [an example of violence by Muslims against Hindus], be he an individual or be it a group, party or community, does the greatest disservice to the nation.'[34]

The central government failed to nip the trouble in the bud in Calcutta, he went on to say. The result was that 'the provinces became virtually independent [sic]. The neighbouring province of Bihar under the circumstances was entitled to protest against what happened to the Biharis in Calcutta. The Bihar Government should have made it plain to Bengal that the Hindus in Bihar were profoundly agitated over the fate of their co-religionists in Bengal and that with the best will in the world the Government might not be able to control the situation if the feelings of the people were strained beyond a certain pitch.'[35] As – unfortunately – they were!

Congress sympathisers went out of their way, however, to emphasise that not everyone fell prey to this communal madness, that there were important counter-examples of Hindu–Muslim humanity and solidarity. Stories of the 'atrocities' committed by Hindus on the minority community in Garhmukhteshwar and other villages 'sometimes alternate with inspiring tales of how Hindus protected Muslims during these pogroms', wrote the special correspondent of *The Hindustan Times*, in a despatch captioned 'Hundreds of Muslims Saved by Hindus.' A sub-inspector of police in village Modinagar had reported that the local Jat peasants 'disguised their Muslim fellow villagers as "Jat women" by making them wear their women's large, loose garments so that unsuspecting murderers passed them by'. The only Muslim killed in Modinagar, the newspaper noted, was the village surgeon who was wearing a fez cap when he went to treat a Jat villager: when the mob attacked him, 'his Hindu patient stretched himself fully on the surgeon's body, and received many a blow intended for the surgeon. The latter was finally torn away from him and killed. His Hindu defender is lying in Modinagar with several deep wounds in his back.'[36]

Shah Nawaz Khan and Mridula Sarabhai also pointed out examples of cross-communal unity and the triumph of a nationalist idealism. In spite of some regrettable lapses, Shah Nawaz stated, 'there were... cases where Congressmen did their duty and in some places both the Hindus

---

[34] A. M. Zaidi, ed., *Congress Presidential Addresses. Volume 5: 1940–85* (Delhi, 1989), p. 57.
[35] *Ibid.*
[36] *The Hindustan Times* (21 November 1946).

and Muslims put up a joint defence and protected the lives, property and honour jointly'.[37]

The Muslim League's response

Accounts emanating from the Muslim League have a different perspective on Garhmukhteshwar. Like 'Bihar', 'Garhmukhteshwar' was central to these accounts – as a sign of Hindu perfidy and the implacable hatred and division that marked the existence of the 'two nations' that the proponents of the Muslim League believed existed in the subcontinent. As of course, 'Calcutta' or 'Noakhali' were, with the site of perfidy relocated, in right-wing Hindu accounts (with which, as we have seen, Hindu Congressmen and women also frequently agreed). Indeed, as contemporary and later records show, even Garhmukhteshwar could be recast in the Hindu account as an event providing evidence of inborn Muslim villainy. In all of this, right-wing commentators (Hindu and Muslim) shared a great deal with the colonial perception of Indian society and politics.

For all of these parties, as for the Congress, 'Garhmukhteshwar' remains an empty signifier – the incidental ground upon which a battle of claimed national worthiness/unworthiness is to be fought. 'Garhmukhteshwar' is no different from 'Bihar' and later 'East Punjab', as 'Noakhali' (and later 'West Punjab') is a repetition of 'Calcutta'. It was his 'unenviable task', wrote a correspondent who had accompanied the Muslim League inquiry team to Garhmukhteshwar on 17 November, to describe the 'tragic drama' enacted by 'pilgrims' who 'after taking dips into the holy water of the Ganges, cast their vengeful eyes on the village of Garhmukhteshwar . . . to avenge the alleged Noakhali atrocities'. The number of people at the *mela* 'who saw and acted in this ghastly drama' was estimated 'between 8 and 10 lakhs', he wrote. 'According to reliable sources the number of dead of the minority community who kept stalls at the Mela runs into four figures, while in the village the number of dead is several hundreds . . . The police it is alleged stood and watched the grim drama like bemused spectators and made little or no endeavour to stop . . . [the] miscreants.' Another report had it, on the testimony of eyewitnesses, that 'women were made stark naked and paraded in the streets and indiscriminately raped. Some of them were forcibly converted. While others

---

[37] AICC papers, G-10/1947, Shah Nawaz Khan's statement (13 November 1946). The correspondent of the Communist party paper made the same kind of point more emphatically in a detailed report on 'What Happened at Garhmukteshwar', *People's Age* (22 December 1946).

who resisted . . . were subjected to various forms of sadism and done to death.'[38]

The differences between the Congress and the Muslim League position on Garhmukhteshwar are all too evident. They begin with the question of casualties and the numbers of those involved in the attack at Garhmukhteshwar, compared with what had gone before. Congress spokespersons generally stood by the government version that perhaps 250 to 275 Muslims had been killed in the fair and the village, with a relatively smaller number of Muslim and Hindu casualties occurring in the violence that followed at other places in the vicinity. For League commentators – as for Tuker when he wrote his *Memory* a couple of years later – it was the massacre at Garhmukhteshwar that deserved undivided attention, and a conservative estimate would put the number killed there at 1,000. The killing, both Tuker and the League observed, stopped only because there was no one left to kill.[39] Probably over 1,000 were killed at the fair itself, Ghazanfar Ali wrote. Very few of these were women: the victims in this first stage were 'mostly shopkeepers, lorry drivers, bullock-car drivers, who had brought Hindu families to the *mela*, and performers at various amusement shows'.[40]

The spokespersons of the Muslim League emphasised the fact of the complicity, and worse, of the local Hindu inhabitants. It was not only the police who watched: 'between 8 and 10 lakhs [800,000 and 1,000,000]' villagers and pilgrims 'saw and acted' in the 'ghastly drama'.[41] 'The houses of [the] minority community were singled out, marked with chalk and shown to the marauders by the villagers of the majority community.' Indeed, the preparations and the guidance were so good that shops belonging to Hindu landlords, but tenanted by Muslim shopkeepers, were not burnt – though their contents were looted; and a Muslim landlord who had let out shops to Hindu as well as Muslim shopkeepers found that only the latter were burnt.[42]

League sources focussed too on atrocities against Muslim women, and noted the latter's resistance – neither of which government and Congress sources had emphasised. The Congress press noted that the question of abducted women was a 'rankling' source of bitterness and potential strife in the Meerut countryside, both for 'Muslims who lost their women

---

[38] *Dawn* (19 November 1946).
[39] See Tuker, *Memory*, p. 198.
[40] Ghazanfar report, p. 16.
[41] *Dawn* (19 November 1946). Note that Congress and government sources put the total number of those attending the fair on this occasion at 700,000–800,000.
[42] *Ibid.*; and Ghazanfar report, p. 19. The UP government later denied that any markings had been made on Muslim houses and shops, *Dawn* (19 April 1947).

during the Garhmukhteshwar disturbances' and 'Hindus who lost their women in [the] retaliatory outrage at Dasna'.[43] Ghazanfar Ali Khan, on the other hand, cited detailed reports of women being stripped, raped and murdered. Muslim rescuers had recovered the dead bodies of women without a strip of clothing on them from several wells. Other women and children had simply disappeared: no one knew their fate. He also learnt of a 'weird ceremony' of *shuddhi* ('purification' or, as some would have it, 'conversion' to Hinduism) that was performed on captured Muslim women.

One woman at a time would be stripped naked and marched as a captive in the midst of a crowd of 200 men or so to the Ganges, the crowd shouting slogans of triumph to the accompaniment of musical instruments. The procession would reach the bank of the river, the woman would be dipped into it and after this 'purification' handed over to a Hindu as his chattel. After one woman had been disposed of, the ceremony of 'appropriating' another would begin.[44]

Other statements underlined these charges. 'The plight of women was terrible', read the account of the Muslim trader who escaped, published in bold type on the front page of *Dawn*:

I saw a girl of about 15 or 16 being taken by a huge mob towards the Ganges. She was ducked in the river and asked to take 'Ram nam' [the name of the Hindu deity, Ram]. She cried out, 'Ya Khuda' [invoking Allah], and refused to say anything else. She was beaten to death.

I saw other women whose clothes had been removed. They were taken round the fair in that helpless condition, the brutes making fun of them and treating them in indescribable fashion... Not a single one of them agreed [to get converted] ... and they were murdered.[45]

Another account, published in the issue of 12 November, again on the front page, told the story of a respectable Muslim woman, the wife of a health officer who was on duty at the Garhmukhteshwar *mela*. Their camp was surrounded at about 2 p.m. on 7 November, while the woman's husband was out – and perhaps already killed. The subordinate Hindu officials and workers at the camp did nothing to help her, while the crowd burnt the hospital and the camp and then asked her to choose one of them as a husband. 'On her refusal, she was dragged from one camp to another and subjected to humiliation and indignities', the paper reported.

[43] *The Hindustan Times* (21 November 1946). Government reports spoke simply of the Rohtak and Gurgaon 'pilgrims' getting away with 'a certain number of abducted Muslim girls'; see, for example, Tuker papers, 71/21/4/4, commissioner, Meerut division to chief secretary, government of UP (16 November 1946).
[44] Ghazanfar report, pp. 16, 17 and 19. The report also observed that the police watched these proceedings from afar and did nothing to intervene until late on 8 November, p. 18.
[45] *Dawn* (10 November 1946).

After some time, 'when they found her defiant they tore off her clothes and made her naked'. She was throttled, had sand shoved in her mouth, was belaboured with lathis and then thrown into the Ganges in the belief that she was dead. 'With one of her arms broken', the doctor's wife swam across the river, where a conscience-stricken constable gave her his coat to 'cover her shame'.[46]

All of this added up to a powerful indictment of the Congress for its commissions and omissions, and of the Hindus whom, in the League view, the Congress represented. As Iskandar Mirza wrote to Jinnah in early 1947: 'The Bihar and Garhmukhteshwar massacres...show beyond a doubt what we have to expect unless we find ways and means of meeting a numerically stronger enemy on more or less equal terms.'[47] The fundamentals of this argument lay in the proposition that Hindus and Congress could not be trusted, that they were well organised and had the government on their side and that as long as the Muslims lived with them as a minority, under the same regime, they were liable to suffer severely.

Dawn, the mouthpiece of the Pakistan movement, had laid out these charges in its first reports on the Garhmukhteshwar violence. What had happened at the fair and the 'village' on 6 and 7 November showed, it said, that 'here again took place murder, arson, looting, rape and other brutalities on one community by another on a major scale, and that the news agencies and the UP Government have blacked out the truth'.[48]

What made matters worse, in the League's argument, was that Garhmukhteshwar was a stronghold of 'nationalist Muslims'. Most of the Muslims who had come to the fair had voted for the Congress in the last elections: they felt they were safe, wrote the *Dawn* correspondents, which was why they came in spite of reports of the 'Great Bihar Killing'.[49] The view was entirely mistaken. Among those killed was the Muslim president of the local Congress committee, as the UP ministry later acknowledged.[50] 'The tragedy of Garhmukhteshwar has been no less serious than that of Bihar', declared the Lucknow correspondent of the newspaper. Only, it happened in 'more concentrated form...This was admitted by a UP Government spokesman who has toured the riot-stricken area though he preferred to call Garhmukhteshwar as Noakhali in the reverse in almost every detail.'[51] In their turn, the editors of *Dawn*

[46] 'Muslim Heroine Defies Hindu Mob', *Dawn* (12 November 1946).
[47] Z. H. Zaidi, ed., *Quaid-i-Azam Mohammad Ali Jinnah Papers. Prelude to Pakistan. 20 February–2 June 1947*, 1st series, vol. I, part 1 (Islamabad, 1993), p. 143.
[48] *Dawn* (10 November 1946).
[49] *Ibid.* (10 and 22 November 1946).
[50] See *ibid.* (19 April 1947).
[51] *Ibid.* (22 November 1946).

dubbed it the 'Great Garhmukhteshwar Killing': 'the greatest Killing in UP's recorded history', with a death toll of 'upwards of 2000... many times more serious than incidents in East Bengal'.[52]

The colonial account

Nothing fits the colonial view of India better than the more extreme of these right-wing Muslim (and Hindu) statements. 'Primitive' and 'bestial' are the adjectives that surface again and again in colonial reports on Garhmukhteshwar. In the words of the military intelligence, 'Gruesome atrocities appear to have been perpetrated but the news has been amazingly hushed up and although accounts appeared in the local press, it was not made out to be half the immensity that it actually was.'[53]

The colonial account does not understate the cycle of revenge, or the 'definite organization and planning' that went into the attacks. It notes the presence of criminal – goonda – elements, and emphasises the fact that the administration had in some senses collapsed (as collapse it must on the departure of the British). However – another reason why the British withdrawal from India was premature – such violence was also, in this view, the inevitable product of age-old animosities and of deep-seated savagery: it was a boiling over, the periodic expression of peoples unable to help their own barbarity. This was what accounted for the gruesome quality of so much of what happened – at Garhmukhteshwar and elsewhere. Let me briefly elaborate these points.

According to British Indian military sources, 'the Gurhmekhtesar [sic] incident was carefully planned and organised'. Large numbers of people knew about the plans, the military authorities averred: among those in the know was a Hindu lieutenant-colonel from Meerut who later said that 'so many people knew about it that it never occurred to him that he should report it'.[54] 'The indications are that it was organised and preconceived', wrote the commissioner of Meerut division.[55]

The Punjab Jats, more especially those of Rohtak and one or two other districts, emerge as the undoubted villains of the piece. The massacre was 'almost entirely the work of Jats from the Punjab', declared one official.

[52] *Ibid.* (23 November 1946). The Bihar killings, and with them Garhmukhteshwar, were described as 'the worst bloodshed ever in India's history... not "communal rioting", but massacre of the minority by large masses of the majority, organized and armed', (IOR) L/P&J/8/575, 'Reports on the Disturbances in Bihar and UP', p. 3.
[53] Tuker papers, 71/21/4/4, 'Extract from Monthly Security Intelligence Report for November 1946 of HQ UP Area'.
[54] *Ibid.*, 'C' to Tuker (26 July 1947).
[55] (IOR) L/P&J/8/650, F. W. W. Baynes, commissioner, Meerut division to F. V. Wylie, governor of UP (18 November 1946).

The Rohtak Jats first massacred all the Muslims they could find in the Fair. Next day they massacred all the Muslims they could find in Garhmukhteshwar Town. When they left the Fair, they massacred Muslims on the various roads leading from the Fair towards Bulandshahr, Delhi etc., and even in villages near the roads. They started trouble in Delhi when they got there, and finally indulged in communal rioting in their own home district of Rohtak.[56]

However, while the Jats loom large in this story, the local (Indian) administrators are part of the network responsible for the crime. 'The massacres were committed by Jats, without provocation. Jaitly, the Superintendent of Police . . . had a Jat Sub-Inspector in charge of the Mela Kotwali, and another Jat Sub-Inspector in charge of Garhmukhteshwar Town Thana. When the trouble broke out, the Military sent down two Companies of Jats . . . [sic!]'[57] Unfortunately, wrote Tuker, 'there was not a single British officer in control of the area of the trouble. The Senior Superintendent of Police, the District Magistrate and the Super-intendent of Police were all Hindus.'[58] In making the charge, Tuker conveniently overlooked the senior-most police official of the region, the deputy inspector general of police, Robinson, whom other senior officials (including his own British superiors) were to find equally culpable.

Similarly, the British commissioner commented that Shankar Prasad, the Indian district magistrate, was 'completely' inefficient and deceit-ful, never in fact doing what he said he would do. Jaitly, the super-intendent of police, was (in the same superordinate's view) more effi-cient, but not very trustworthy either. 'The main object of these two and Robinson is to curry favour with the Ministry.'[59] It seems indeed to have been Robinson's suggestion that the ex-members of the Indian National Army (INA) should be made special constables for the Meerut session of the Congress, and issued with arms. Pant and Qidwai, pre-mier and home minister of the province, agreed only after some resis-tance; and the order was reversed after the violence at Garhmukhtesh-war and other places in which, it was suspected, the INA people had a hand.[60]

Thus a number of different (Indian) elements were thought to have contributed to the violence at Garhmukhteshwar. Among these, the en-mity between Congress and Muslim League, and therefore for colonial

[56] The quotations are from *ibid.*; and Tuker papers, 71/21/4/4, commissioner, Meerut division to chief secretary, government of UP (16 November 1946).
[57] *Ibid.*
[58] Tuker, *Memory*, p. 198.
[59] (IOR) L/P&J/8/650, Baynes to Wylie (18 November 1946).
[60] See *ibid.*, Secret UP- 66, governor to viceroy (21 November 1946); and Ghazanfar report.

officials between Hindus and Muslims, was not the least important. Jinnah had stayed at Baghpat in Meerut district between 18 and 21 October 1946 to condole the death of the local landlord's brother. According to British officials, this had given rise to 'wild rumours' about 'Muslim plans' to disrupt the Congress session.[61]

After Garhmukhteshwar, the officials observed, there was a definite move to blame local Muslims for provocation. When Baynes (the commissioner) and Robinson went to Garhmukhteshwar on the 8th, a day after the massacres, along with numerous 'Hindus and Congress leaders', Baynes noted, no such charge had been made. Since then, however, Congress circles had started spreading the story of how the riots broke out when a Hindu shopkeeper was looted and murdered. Jaitly, the superintendent of police, stated that 'Muslim Defence' volunteers started the trouble by attacking Hindus with spears; and Robinson quoted a rumour of local Muslims killing a cow, which he had not mentioned earlier.[62]

Beneath it all lay the congenital hatred of Hindus for Muslims, and Muslims for Hindus, colonial observers would argue. Moreover, a propensity to irrational violence (on the part of both Hindus and Muslims – in turn!), a deep-rooted mendacity, the presence of evil in the soul one might say. For these were the marks of this society and this politics. The argument comes together in Lieutenant General Sir Francis Tuker's much vaunted volume, *While Memory Serves*.

'By the 15th November the pilgrims [from Garhmukhteshwar] had passed on their locust-stricken way leaving devastation behind them and the peace of the desert reigned on smoking village and bereaved children', he wrote. 'I was never able to find out the casualties. The Indian administration minimised them and the whole affair. It is certain that one thousand Muslims died, perhaps two thousand [*sic*].'[63]

It was not just the killing, however, but the manner of it that was telling. On 6 November, when a Muslim performer 'threw a jest' at a Hindu woman, now in this narrative specifically identified as a Jat (or 'Jatni'), a 'sudden shout' went up: at this a number of small bands of Jats 'rushed out and, in concerted fashion, set to work to massacre the Muslim stallholders at the *mela*, spattered all about the Fair grounds quietly plying their trade'. On the next day, a large number of these same fiends – now specified as 'Rohtak Jats' – entered Garhmukhteshwar town: 'All of a sudden they fell upon the Muslim quarter of the town, slaughtering with disgusting brutality all Muslim men, women and

---

[61] Tuker papers, 71/21/4/4, Baynes to Wylie (16 November 1946).
[62] This paragraph is based on (IOR) L/P&J/8/650, Baynes to Wylie (18 November 1946).
[63] Tuker, *Memory*, p. 200. Page references for quotations are given in the text in the following paragraphs.

children. Women were raped and murdered and the houses burnt...'
(198–9).

'Practically every Muslim man, woman and child [in Garhmukhtesh-war] was murdered with appalling cruelty...', the general further observed. 'Even pregnant women were ripped up, their unborn babies torn out and the infants' brains bashed out on walls and on the ground. There was rape, and women and children were seized by the legs by burly fiends and torn apart...' (198). Here is rumour transformed into British 'memory'. At the end of the day, Tuker concluded, all that remained of the Muslims in Garhmukhteshwar were a handful of miserable survivors, awaiting a similar end at the hands of their devilish enemies. 'There was nowhere for them to go. All around were these same blood-thirsty enemies. They returned to await in the Devil's good time their inevitable end, death at the hands of their enemies or the eternal slavery of a scheduled caste' (200).

'Garhmukhteshwar', I have suggested, becomes but a matter of merely 'local' significance in the nationalist account. No attempt is made to understand the particularity and consequences of such a 'riot'; and (as we shall see) there is no real place for it in the chronicles of the nation. In the colonial construction, too, it is a 'local' affair – but here in the sense that all of India, and the East, is 'local': that is to say, not yet modern or rational. To illustrate this fully, we need to dwell a little longer on Tuker's classic text.

Recall that the general's account appears in the form of a story, more or less personally witnessed by the author. As the title of his book indicates, Tuker claims to add to the documentary record of the last months of British rule while his 'memory' is fresh. 'Today it seems to me that it would be a pity to lose forever the emotions and happenings of those last anxious months, months which will go down to history in the school books of ages to come...' (3). 'To conserve my forces I was compelled to write almost daily a commentary on the situation in my Command as a whole [the Eastern Command of the Indian Army, which covered the provinces of Assam, Bengal, Orissa, Bihar, UP and, in 1947, Delhi and eastern Punjab as well], affected as it was by events and plans in the India outside.' It is these daily memorandums, he informs us, that provided the basis of his book. Further, 'I could not be witness to all the events of which I write, but I have been lucky in being given personal accounts by my officers written especially for myself' (3–4).[64] The archivist himself as witness, or relying on the direct testimony of witnesses.

---

[64] For the personal accounts and other documents upon which Tuker bases his book, see Tuker papers.

Much of what Tuker records comes, often word for word, from the reports that he received from military informants he trusted. But Tuker's own interpretation of 'India' – perhaps shared, but not so fully articulated by his informants – runs through the pages of his *Memory*. One of his informants had noted: 'An interesting feature of the killings was that a large number were by means of strangulation.'[65] There is no doubt that this piece of information tells us much: about the unarmed nature of some of the attackers, and hence about the (at least partly) 'spontaneous' nature of the violence and the participation of ordinary pilgrims; about the fighting that must have taken place at close quarters; and about the time that it would have taken to perform many of these 'murders'.

However, Tuker puts a rather different gloss on it: 'Most were killed with spears but some of the killings were by strangulation which, it will be recalled, was the ritual method of the Thugs'(198). One needs to pause a little over this statement about Thugs, made *en passant*, in the account. The reference to 'ritual method' alludes to the outlandish character of this land called India. This is not to say that ritual has nothing to do with this event of killing. As scholars have demonstrated, all kinds of massacres do bear the signature of ritual.[66] Bodies too are constructed through ritual as, say, 'Hindu' or 'Muslim' bodies; and they are redefined in moments such as these precisely as 'Hindu' or 'Muslim', and nothing else.[67] The question is what this British reduction to particular ritual modes accomplishes.

The answer is that it is supposed to establish several things at once: the essential 'otherness', the unchanging character, the cruelty and irrationality of the Oriental – here represented by the Thug and the society that tolerates his existence. The methods of this mysterious group, made famous (and mysterious) by Sleeman above all others in the nineteenth century, naturally survive into the middle of the twentieth. 'The Thugs' thus account for an interesting part of what happened in Garhmukhteshwar.

Thug: 'member of religious organisation of robbers and assassins in India suppressed about 1825' (*The Concise Oxford Dictionary*);

---

[65] Tuker papers, 71/21/4/4, 'Extract from Tour Notes of Major W. Moorshead 14–20 Nov. 1946'.

[66] Among major historical writings on this theme, see Peter Burke, *Popular Culture in Early Modern Europe* (London, 1978); Emmanuel le Roy Ladurie, *Carnival in Romans* (New York, 1979); Guha, *Elementary Aspects of Peasant Insurgency*. On the sacrificial origins of different kinds of violence, see also Rene Girard, *Violence and the Sacred* (Baltimore, 1972), p. 40 and *passim*.

[67] For one study of this kind of ritual constitution of the body, see Deepak Mehta, 'Circumcision, Body, Masculinity. The Ritual Wound and Collective Violence', in Veena Das and Arthur Kleinman, eds., *Violence and Subjectivity* (Berkeley and Los Angeles, 2000). See also ch. 6 below.

'It is by the command, and under the special protection of the most powerful goddesses that the Thugs join themselves to the unsuspecting traveller, make friends with him, slip the noose round his neck, plunge their knives in his eyes, hide him in the earth, and divide his money and baggage' (Macaulay, 1843);[68]
'There are Thugs at Jubulpore from all quarters of India; from Lodheeana to the Carnatick, and from the Indus to the Ganges. Some of them have been in the habit of holding, what I may fairly call unreserved communication with European gentlemen for more than twelve years; and yet there is not among them one who doubts *the divine origin of the system of Thuggee* – not one who doubts, that he and all who have followed the trade of murder with the prescribed rites and observances, were acting under the immediate orders and auspices of the Goddess Devee, Durga, Kalee, or Bhawanee, as she is indifferently called [*sic*], and consequently there is not one who feels the slightest remorse for the murders which he may, in the course of his vocation, have perpetrated or assisted in perpetrating . . . A Thug considers the persons murdered precisely in the light of victims offered up to the Goddess' (Sleeman, 1836).[69]

What the Thugs illustrate – murder as religion, uncontrolled force of habit, a violence sometimes submerged but ever present – applies in more diffuse but nevertheless definite form to much of the rest of the population too. Tuker lays out the depths of their 'bestiality', 'fiendishness', 'devilry' – the words are all his – at length. 'Women and their babies were cut up, butchered, with an obscene devilry that a civilised people cannot even conjure forth in their imagination', he wrote in his reminiscences of the large scale violence that had occurred in Bihar in October–November 1946 (182). All of this recalled for Tuker the Great Mutiny of 1857, another nineteenth-century moment that the British could never forget. 'If this was what was done to our own people in the Mutiny then there was no punishment that we could have inflicted on such cruel ruffians that would have fitted the deed . . . All we can do', he added magnanimously, 'is to forget' (*ibid.*).

Adjectives of inveterate evil and devilish behaviour provide the terms that move the colonialist account along. In his Garhmukhteshwar chapter, Tuker found more specific application for them, as he had done in that on Bihar. The applications came from his knowledge and experience of the British Indian army. 'They were [not surprisingly] Biharis' who moved with 'such obvious, fiendish intent from victim to victim' in the Bihar massacres. 'They were Biharis,' he notes in the next sentence,

[68] Cited in Henry Yule & A. C. Burnell, eds., *Hobson-Jobson. A Glossary of Colloquial Anglo-Indian Words and Phrases, and of Kindred Terms, Etymological, Historical, Geographical and Discursive* (new edn, William Crooke, ed. London, 1903), pp. 916–17.
[69] W. H. Sleeman, *Ramaseeana, or a Vocabulary of the Peculiar Language used by the Thugs, with an Introduction and Appendeix, Descriptive of the System Pursued by that Fraternity and of the Measures Which have been Adopted by the Supreme Government of India for its Suppression* (Calcutta, 1836), p. 7, emphasis Sleeman's.

'whom we expelled from our Army after the Mutiny of 1857–8 and never again enlisted' (182): testimony to the perspicacity and prescience of the British.

However, even the most sterling qualities of the British could not overcome all that lay in the heart of the beast – as Garhmukhteshwar demonstrated. Here it was by so many accounts the Jats (of 'Punjab', of 'Rohtak and Hissar', or 'Rohtak and Gurgaon', variously) who were the main culprits. Yet these same Jats had provided recruits for the British Indian army for generations. Tuker managed to work the riddle out to his own satisfaction: 'It seems that beneath the discipline which has been the cause of their good behaviour in the Army there yet remains a horrid vein of inhuman, merciless ferocity [*sic*]' (195). Another colonial official had made the point in another way in a report immediately after the Garhmukhteshwar violence: 'In view of [the Jats'] bestial behaviour, it is surprising that Muslims have indulged in so little retaliation.'[70] In this country of irrational violence, moderation in any quarter was a thing to be marvelled at.

'Garhmukhteshwar' was in the end, then, little different from 'Bihar' for the British. 'The tale of horror now takes us northwards [to Garhmukhteshwar].' This is the opening sentence of Tuker's chapter on Garhmukhteshwar. 'This terrible deed is marked by the savagery of the Jat men who did the brutal work . . .' (195). 'The murderers' women stood about, laughing with glee at the burning booths, egging on their menfolk', he added (198). It is not clear how he found this out. Perhaps it was simply that this is how Tuker expected that they would behave in this land of 'the Mutiny'.

Nationalist historiography at work

There is an interesting convergence between the colonialist method of constructing this massacre and, by extension, all Partition violence, and that of a number of Pakistani and Indian commentators: and this is not only because Tuker's high colonialist account was as strong an argument in favour of Pakistan as any that a Muslim Leaguer could have made. This convergence of attitudes in Indian, Pakistani and British writings on Garhmukhteshwar points to a common effort at distancing the writer's own 'history' from such 'extraordinary' and brutal violence.

The official history of the freedom movement in Pakistan, and more recent Pakistani histories too, have relied wholly on Tuker's authority in

---

[70] Tuker papers, 71/21/4/4, commissioner, Meerut division to chief secretary, government of UP (16 November 1946).

their writing up of Garhmukhteshwar. Both Sharif al-Mujahid's chapter on 'Communal Riots' in the official history, published in 1970, and Burke and Quraishi's 1995 history of the British Raj quote Tuker's statement of how 'practically every Muslim man, woman and child' was murdered, 'even pregnant women were ripped up ... and ... infants' brains bashed out on walls' and 'the murderers' women stood about, laughing with glee ... ' The former goes on to cite Tuker on how not a Hindu raised a hand or voice to protect the Muslims, the latter on how every single police officer was Hindu.[71] This is the sum total of the information they provide on Garhmukhteshwar: but it is, of course, from one point of view, enough.

As I have noted, Garhmukhteshwar had become, for many, a sign of deep-rooted hatred – of an undying enmity and antagonism between two different kinds of people who were in fact, and always had been, two 'nations'. What League spokespersons in 1946–7, as well as more recent Pakistani writers, would not have acknowledged was that barbarity was inborn in *all* the peoples of the East. For the advocates of Pakistan, as for Pakistani historians, the killings at Garhmukhteshwar and Bihar were more a matter of Hindu design, of Hindu discrimination against Muslims, of the Congress (Hindu) ministries' refusal to fulfil their duty of protecting all citizens – in a word, of *politics*, even if this politics rested on the fact of deep-seated animosities between Hindus and Muslims.[72]

Both Pakistani and Indian historians have sought to emphasise the alienness of this kind of violence to their respective traditions and national struggles. This may be seen in the way in which Congress and other Indian nationalist historians report Garhmukhteshwar, and the way in which Muslim League and Pakistani historians report other such events in which Muslims were the aggressors. The proposition is the same in both camps. Violence was the product of a thirst for revenge, of conspiracies and instigation by extremist groups; and an innocent people was overcome with (legitimate) anger or simply misled. The essential humanity of the 'host' nation is stressed, through examples where the minority was protected, mercy displayed, and 'secularist' principles were upheld.[73]

---

[71] See *A History of the Freedom Movement. Volume IV. 1936–47* (Pakistan Historical Society, Karachi, 1970; reprinted, Delhi, 1984), pp. 156–7; and Burke and Quraishi, *The British Raj*, pp. 466–7. See also Suranjan Das, *Communal Riots in Bengal*, ch. 6 on the Calcutta killings of 1946, for its more careful, yet extensive use of Tuker's 'evidence'.

[72] The same arguments were made, in reverse, by Hindus and Sikhs about the activities of the Muslim League in Bengal and Punjab.

[73] Apart from the examples cited in this and earlier chapters, see (IOR) Mss. Eur. F200/129, H. S. Suhrawardy's letters to Gandhi, bulletins no. 1–6, (21 and 22 September 1947); (IOR) L/P&J/8/575, Reports on the Disturbances in Bihar and UP, esp. appendix B, Suhrawardy to Firoz Khan Noon (30 November 1946); and reports in *Dawn* (October–November 1946).

In the end, the Indian nationalist historical interpretation of violence has to fit with a representation of India's history of the last century and more as the history of its 'progress'. What stands out in this account is the 'naturalness' of the nation and the heroism of its people in the face of practically impossible odds: and, with this, the extraordinary heritage of tolerance, enlightenment and outstanding leadership, whatever the aberrations or occasional lapses. The little there is of an Indian nationalist commentary on the 'small' affair at Garhmukhteshwar has worked to produce precisely such an effect. Consciously or unconsciously, it has sought to preserve the 'purity' of the people and the land by diminishing the violence that took place at the Garhmukhteshwar fair and town in 1946, by making it (when it is mentioned at all) into a link in a longer chain of conspiratorially inspired events that fed one upon another, and by fixing blame on Hindu and Muslim extremists – but chiefly on the latter.

G. D. Khosla in his *Survey of Events Leading up to and Following the Partition of India* sets out the sequence as follows:

April 1946: open incitement to violence by Muslim League legislators meeting at a special convention in Delhi;
29 July 1946: the Muslim League's 'Direct Action' resolution, which said goodbye to peaceful methods;
16 August: the Calcutta Killings;
October 1946: the Noakhali and Tippera outbreaks; and 'retaliation' in Bihar; 'then for some months there was a lull [Garhmukhteshwar and other widely reported instances of violence are not mentioned here] while a major operation in the north-west was being planned';
March 1947: 'genocide' of non-Muslims begins – 'confined to the Muslim majority areas and the victims were almost invariably Hindus and Sikhs'; May/June 1947: another flare-up in Lahore;
End of July 1947: 'reprisals' by Hindus and Sikhs begin in eastern Punjab;
15 August–30 September 1947: mass killing of Muslims in eastern Punjab and Delhi, when 'the arrival of large numbers of refugees from West Punjab . . . provoked the non-Muslims to retaliate'.[74]

The ongoing series of publications entitled the *Selected Works of Jawaharlal Nehru* illustrate the point equally well. The volumes for 1946 include an important statement Nehru made in the central legislative assembly in New Delhi on 14 November, on the seriousness of recent instances of Hindu–Muslim strife. In the course of this statement, Nehru referred to 'recent events around and near Delhi'. The editors of the volume provide the following footnote in explanation of the reference: 'A communal clash took place at the Ganga Fair at Garhmukhteshwar in

[74] Khosla, *Stern Reckoning*, pp. 297–8.

Meerut district on 6 November. Following this incident, pilgrims returning from the Fair were attacked at various places. Communal clashes were
also reported from Meerut city and Delhi.'[75] This is the sole reference to
Garhmukhteshwar to be found in the *Selected Works* of the man who was
the chief spokesperson of the Congress at this time, the most important
Congress leader of UP, the province in which Garhmukhteshwar lay, and
the head of the interim government then trying to guide the subcontinent
to Independence.

A chapter entitled 'Communal Riots' in a recently published biography
of Mridula Sarabhai, by the senior historian, Aparna Basu, substantiates
my argument further. Here the writing on Garhmukhteshwar appears
even more insidious. 'Twenty days before the Congress session was to be
held in Meerut in 1946', the author writes,

there were communal riots in the city. People believed that the Muslim League
was bent on not allowing the Congress Session to be held peacefully... On
8th November 1946, a special train carrying Hindu pilgrims from the annual
Fair at Garhmukhteshwar was attacked and looted and the passengers manhan-
dled at Dasna railway station... The mob was, however, finally beaten off by the
passengers. Pandit Govind Ballabh Pant and Rafi Ahmed Kidwai [Premier and
Home Minister, respectively, in the Congress Government of UP] arrived on the
scene. A unit of troops came from Meerut and took charge of the wounded, including a number of women suffering from severe burns, stab wounds and effects
of criminal assault.

The writer tells us also that on hearing the news of this attack, 'the
remaining Hindu pilgrims on their way back from Garhmukhteshwar,
who had to pass through Muslim villages', decided to launch revenge
attacks of their own; and so the violence spread.[76]

It should be noted, of course, that the historian's concern here is to trace
the career and activities of an unusual woman and nationalist leader. At
this point in her study, the author wishes to draw attention to Sarabhai's
courageous intervention in attempting to bring back peace to the countryside. Yet, in many reports that Basu should have seen, the story of that
intervention begins with the 'gruesome[ness]' of the 'tragic happenings
in Garhmukhteshwar'. Sarabhai herself refers to them in these words at
the beginning of her statement on 'the Garhmukhteshwar and Meerut
disturbances', issued on 13 November 1946.[77] Basu cites this statement
of Sarabhai's, yet finds it possible to completely overlook the massacre
at Garhmukhteshwar. The violence at this site, which had taken place

[75] *Selected Works of Jawaharlal Nehru*, 2nd series, vol. I (Delhi, 1984), p. 91n.
[76] Aparna Basu, *Mridula Sarabhai: Rebel with a Cause* (Delhi, 1996), p. 92.
[77] AICC papers, G-10/1947; another copy is found in 'non-category file' no. 58/1946.

on the 6 and 7 November, and was not yet over on the 8th – when her account of the communal strife begins – is not so much as mentioned. This is not the result of some design to blame the 'Muslims' as the originators of the trouble, because they threw the first stone (at Dasna, by this account), although Basu's hurried summary could well be read in that way. Nor is it a malicious attempt to deny to Garhmukhteshwar its place in history (might we not all, in the way of some local informants, come forward with our own villages, our districts and our 'riots' that have not been mentioned in an authoritative history?). In my view, the absence of 'Garhmukhteshwar' follows, rather, from a belief in its basic *unimportance* to such an account: more, from the *impossibility* of finding in it a place for this moment of violence – as a 'disturbance', a break in the narrative of our nationalist history. There can be no place for 'riots' in these histories, except in this attenuated form.

'Garhmukhteshwar' emerges here, as do other instances of violence in the work of the nationalist historians cited in the last chapter, as a matter of 'local' detail – a diversion that is of little moment in the overall scheme of 'modern', 'national' (should one say 'universal') history, and one therefore that is best forgotten. The viewpoint is replicated in the Indian Communist, Renu Chakravarthy's account of peasant women's struggles in the decade of Partition and Independence.[78] In the course of a stirring description of women in the great Telengana peasant uprising of 1946–51, 'standing shoulder to shoulder with their menfolk' as they took on the landlords' hirelings and the police and armed forces of the local and the Indian state, Chakravarthy refers to one major campaign to get the local authorities to construct lavatories for women. The author acknowledges that this was one of the 'biggest and most popular campaigns' of the period, and that it 'immensely popularised' the Sangham or peasants' organisation among women. Yet she presents it as an example of 'the small and trifling', 'local' problems – these are her words – that the women organisers of the Communist-led movement had to deal with.

The campaign is taken not as an indication of other, neglected and unresolved contradictions, and new sites of political struggle, as the authors of a more recent feminist study of women in the Telengana uprising note:[79] but as a 'local' problem, something that appears as a bit of a distraction. Here, again, 'history' is equated with the 'national', the 'rational', the 'progressive' – the 'programmed'. This history is recognisable,

---

[78] Renu Chakravarthy, *Communists in Indian Women's Movement, 1940–1950* (Delhi, 1980). The following comments on her work are taken from Stree Shakti Sanghatana, *'We Were Making History . . . ' Life Stories of Women in the Telengana People's Struggle* (Delhi, 1989), ch. 2, 'Writing about Women in People's Struggles'.
[79] *Ibid.*, p. 22.

traceable, and of course *relevant*. It has other names as well, 'Europe' being one of these, as we have noted. In this perspective the national/universal/historical is that which can be narrativised, and theorised, as the road to the future – the Indian variant of the narrative of capital and Enlightenment, so to speak. The 'local' is none of these things: it is, by contrast, of little consequence, mere particularity, and sometimes literally unnameable.

Dipesh Chakrabarty has noticed the procedure in his comments on the ignorance of things non-western, Indian, or 'local' that western scholarship unselfconsciously displays, even in writings on a figure like Salman Rushdie. He quotes a 1989 text on postmodernism which says that Rushdie's 'intertexts for both writing history and writing fiction are doubled: they are, on the one hand, from Indian legends, films, and literature and, on the other, from the West – *The Tin Drum, Tristam Shandy, One Hundred Years of Solitude*, and so on'.[80] A mere reference to the 'Indian' inheritance suffices: the 'West', however, needs to be specified – and, thus, historicised – even in a general statement.

An obituary published in *The Independent* (London) in March 1992 serves to illustrate the point even more dramatically. Written by an obvious admirer of the Austrian Jew turned Muslim and renowned Quranic scholar, Muhammad Asad, the obituary refers briefly to his three wives in the course of its tracing of his extraordinary intellectual and diplomatic career. The references are telling. Asad's first wife, Elsa, was a friend from his Berlin days, we are told, who was with him when he first went to Arabia in the early 1920s. After a quarter of a century spent in the Middle East and India/Pakistan, Asad returned to the West: first Paris, and then New York where he met 'his third wife, Pola Hamida, a Bostonian', whom he married in 1952 and lived with for the next thirty years. Between the first and the third, there had, of course, been a second wife, with whom Asad lived for more than two decades and who was the mother of his only child. We are not told her name. All that the obituary has to say about her is this: 'after Elsa's death, [Asad] married a local Arab woman who bore him his only child – a son'.[81]

The use of the 'local' in this report is by no means exceptional. It signals a minimalist gesture, which is quite sufficient to its purpose. The contrast between the historical ('national') and the 'local' that we encounter in the histories of India produced by Indian historians and political analysts is not radically different. The 'local', I have suggested, has two different connotations. The term refers, on the one hand, to the particular,

---

[80] Dipesh Chakrabarty, 'Postcoloniality and the Artifice of History: Who Speaks for "Indian" Pasts?', *Representations*, 37 (Winter 1992), p. 2.
[81] *The Independent* (23 March 1992).

concrete, detailed and small-scale. It refers, on the other, to that which is not general in a quite different sense: that which is not 'mainstream' or universal, or at one with the 'trend of world history'. It refers, in this meaning, to aspects of our past, and present, that cannot – apparently – be narrativised. They have no beginning, middle and end. They are simply there – awaiting incorporation and transformation by the forces of history and progress. It is in this latter sense that 'India' (and 'the East') are 'local' for the colonialists: self-evident, one-dimensional and unchanging.

It is by 'localising' some occurrences and entities by taking away from them their history, complexity and contested character – by erasing local voices and acts, institutions and programmes – that historians simultaneously produce the 'local' in the second sense and 'history' proper with an identified subject: the Indian nation and its difficult march to Independence, in this instance. It is by so doing that they are able to represent Garhmukhteshwar as a 'riot', and riots generally as part of an unchanging expression of primitive mis-belief, momentary madness or state-inspired manipulation and murder: or, alternatively, the collective suicides of young women (and children and incapacitated men), or their killing at the hands of their own kinsmen, as part of a hallowed tradition of martyrdom in defence of 'purity'.

The 'local' is also an index of power; and the way it is folded into the 'national' has much to tell us about the particularities of a state or nation, and about the course of its history. There are critical moments when the national seems to completely overwhelm the local in our analyses; but equally these can be moments when forceful new constructions of the national work to constitute entirely new kinds of sociality at the local level. An examination of how Partition and Independence came to be played out in the Indian capital city of Delhi serves to illustrate the point very well indeed.

6   Folding the national into the local: Delhi 1947–1948

The declared ground for the Partition of British India was that the Muslims of the subcontinent needed a territory, government and state of their own. The logic of this produced the counter-argument that, if that was the case, the Muslims should have no place in what remained as India. Hence the demand articulated in so many quarters that *everything* be divided into Hindu (or Hindu/Sikh) and Muslim completely and unambiguously – the land, the people, the armed forces, the culture, language and history. Many of the most damaging consequences of 1947 followed from this.

There are moments in history when whole communities come to be refugees, and the members of an entire population (or section of a population, depending on one's point of view) are rendered faceless, undifferentiated, suspect and hunted. This is what happened to the Jews, gypsies and others in Nazi Germany. This is what has happened to the Hututsi in Rwanda, the Serbs in Bosnia and the Albanians in Serbia over the last few years. This is what happened in Delhi and its environs, as of course it did elsewhere in India and Pakistan, for many months in 1947 and afterwards.

Events of this kind work by homogenising and de-classing whole communities. They dehumanise, demonise and de-sex them too,[1] and I say this in spite of the evidence of special atrocities against women that we have noticed in the previous chapters and will encounter again in later ones. Without these moves, one would imagine, the 'nationalising' and 'cleansing' operations of our times would have been harder to initiate.

This chapter examines the new discourses that arose among those who were banished from one part of the subcontinent and transported to

---

[1] In this respect, again, the white man's encounter with the indigenous communities of Australia, New Zealand and the American continent offers obvious parallels; cf., for example, Tzvetan Todorov, *The Conquest of America: the Question of the Other* (New York, 1992); and Gananath Obeyesekere, *The Apotheosis of Captain Cook: European Mythmaking in the Pacific* (Princeton, N.J., 1992); Henry Reynolds, *The Other Side of the Frontier. Aboriginal Resistance to the European Invasion of Australia* (Ringwood, Victoria, 1983).

distant places in another, as well as those who were uprooted even as they stayed in their own habitations – becoming refugees at home, as it were. It reflects also on how one of the most unusual political figures of twentieth-century India responded to what he saw as the vivisection of his land and his people, and how his actions and utterances affected the way in which the national came to be folded into the local at this critical juncture. The chapter focuses on Delhi, because it makes no sense to try and speak of India as a whole in summary fashion, because the focus on one locale may enable us to speak in relatively concrete terms, and because – as India's capital – Delhi reflected, in concentrated form, several tendencies that were at work over a large part of the subcontinent in 1947. After a brief statement on the dislocated condition of the city in 1947–8, it goes on to discuss the actions and accounts of the 'dislocated', Partitioned subject.

Old and new inhabitants

Delhi had a population of perhaps 9.5 lakh (950,000) in 1947 (9.18 lakh at the census of 1941). At Partition, 3.3 lakh Muslims left Delhi, leaving about 6 lakh people (Hindu, Muslim, Sikh and others) behind. Nearly 5 lakh non-Muslim refugees arrived at the same time, making the balance of the new (refugee) inhabitants and the older inhabitants of the city pretty much on par. Even in 1951, by which time the capital had expanded considerably in size (the population of 17.44 lakh marking a 90 per cent increase on the 1941 figure), Partition refugees (not including the local Muslims) still accounted for 28.4 per cent of the total population of the city.[2] In more ways than we generally acknowledge – politically, culturally and even demographically – the Delhi of the 1950s and after was a 'Partition' city.[3]

By the end of the third week of August, rationing authorities estimated that some 130,000 refugees had arrived in Delhi from outside – 30,000 of them during the previous fortnight. Twelve thousand Alwar state refugees (presumably, mostly Meo peasants) were reportedly dispersed in sixteen different relief camps in the city: the biggest of these was on the maidan in front of the Jama Masjid (the great mosque of Shah Jahan's Delhi),

---

[2] See V. N. Datta, 'Panjabi Refugees and the Urban Development of Greater Delhi', pp. 287–96. Mushirul Hasan, *Legacy of a Divided Nation. India's Muslims since Independence* (London, 1997), p. 173 and n., observes that the Muslim population was reduced from 33.22% to 5.71% of Delhi's total between 1941 and 1951.

[3] The 1980s and '90s have seen a rapid transformation of the city. Much of Delhi now gives the appearance of being a city of the upwardly mobile, aggressive commercial bourgeoisie – 'Non-Resident Indians' living in India. At the same time, of course, it remains predominantly a city of less privileged migrants – from Haryana, Punjab, UP, Bihar and elsewhere – seeking a better education or means of livelihood.

where some 5,000 of them were crowded. Other Muslims, from within Delhi and the regions round about, were to join these growing numbers in the following days – as every place which offered any suggestion of security was turned into a refugee camp.

On 3 September 1947, one report notes, violence broke out in some villages neighbouring Delhi on the south-west. From Palam airport, three or four miles away, military officers saw smoke rising from these habitations. As Muslim residents were looted, killed and driven away, 300 of them sought refuge in the airport precincts where a number of troops (including some Muslims) were stationed.[4]

By 7 September, the 'Pak Transfer Office' at 'L' Block in Connaught Place, responsible for organising the transport of Pakistani government officials and property to Pakistan, had 'taken the shape of a refugee camp', as a Muslim officer stationed there put it. By that evening there were about 6,000 Muslims assembled at the site, a majority of them from the privileged Lodi Colony area. By the evening of the 8th, the number of refugees in the 'L' Block camp had increased to 12,000. 'Our own flat had become a small refugee camp', the officer noted, 'as all the women and children of the surrounding flats had come there.'[5]

Around the same time, tens of thousands of other Muslims of Delhi were driven out of their homes to places that provided at least the idea of strength in numbers and a modicum of security – the Jama Masjid area itself, Nizamuddin and Okhla, other graveyards and abandoned Muslim monuments, the houses of cabinet ministers Abul Kalam Azad and Rafi Ahmed Qidwai and other Muslim notables whose dwellings appeared comparatively secure, the Pakistani High Commission – and when these overflowed or (as in the case of the Jama Masjid locality) themselves became insecure, the huge refugee camps that were set up in the Purana Qila (or Old Fort) and Humayun's Tomb.

By mid-September, we are told, there were as many as 121,000 Muslim refugees; and their number was to grow to 164,000 within a short while. In early October, figures of 62,000 and 63,000 Muslim refugees were quoted for the Old Fort and Humayun's Tomb refugee camps respectively, though some put the figure in the Old Fort at 80,000 or even higher.[6] Already, by mid-September, perhaps 60 per cent of the Muslims

---

[4] (IOR) Mss. Eur. F164/21, appendix 7, 'Statement on Delhi Disturbances made by a Military Officer on 21 September 1947', p. xxxviii.

[5] *Ibid.*, pp. xxxviii–xl.

[6] *Ibid.*; (IOR) Mss. Eur. F164/149, D. M. Malik, 'The Tragedy of Delhi (through neutral eyes)', p. 19; (IOR) Mss. Eur. F200/53, minutes of meeting of the emergency committee of the Cabinet (7 October 1947); cf. (IOR) Mss. Eur. D621/14, Wilfrid Russell diaries, entry for 1 October 1947; Anees Qidwai, *Azadi ki chhaon mein*, p. 56; and extract from Ralph Russell's interview with Ebadat Barelvi, published in *Seminar*, 420 (August 1994).

of Old Delhi and 90 per cent of those in New Delhi had fled their homes, seeking refuge where they could. Between 20,000 and 25,000 were said to have been killed. Towards the end of October, about 1.5 lakhs of Delhi's 5 lakh Muslims remained.[7]

Ironically, at this very time, one report put the figure of outside (Hindu and Sikh) refugees in Delhi at 150,000. By January 1948, according to another report, the city had 400,000 refugees from Punjab alone.[8] It is not always clear who is, and who is not, classed as a refugee in these reports, nor what are considered to be the boundaries of Delhi for purposes of enumeration. Figures for the period are in any case unreliable. In addition, the count of refugees sometimes adopts a fairly narrow standard, such as that of people registered at centralised offices and refugee camps. At other times, press reports and private communications reproduce rumours and greatly exaggerated statements. Taken together, however, contemporary and later accounts give us a clear indication of the transformation of Delhi into a 'refugee-istan', with a staggering number of people displaced from elsewhere seeking to find new homes or a safe haven in the city, and an equally staggering number of other – local – refugees imprisoned in their own homes or refugee camps nearby.

Two views of Partition and Independence

Not surprisingly in this context, Partition and Independence had very different meanings for different sections of Delhi's population. 'Independence is . . . an abstract thing', says a senior Indian intellectual whose family migrated to Delhi from Lahore in 1947, 'it didn't give you anything tangible.' On the other hand, Partition was 'in a negative sense a very tangible reality . . . Whenever we met, as a family – for us, it was Partition, not Independence [that counted] . . .'[9] 'Partition changed the course of many lives which would otherwise have run in their familiar channels,' another middle-class migrant from West Punjab wrote.[10]

Partition and Independence are of course both abstractions. One appears more concrete than the other only because of its immediate physical consequences. Indian observers and analysts draw a distinction between them also because, for many of them, Partition diverted Indian politics and society away from 'the normal course of history'. Independence

[7] (IOR) Mss. Eur. F164/21, 'Statement on Delhi Disturbances,' p. xliii; and Malik, 'Tragedy of Delhi', pp. 21, 25.

[8] *The Statesman* (23 August 1947); (IOR) R/3/1/174, G. H. Nicholls' 'Note' to the governor general (27 October 1947); *The Times* (21 January 1948).

[9] Interview (Delhi, 18 March 1995), name withheld at interviewee's request.

[10] Prakash Tandon, *Punjabi Century. 1857–1947* (Berkeley and Los Angeles, 1968), p. 249.

changed lives too, but only by carrying them forward in their 'familiar channels', and only gradually – over time. Partition cut those channels, at one stroke. In that sense, it was more tangible – at least for the middle-class Hindus quoted above, whose families migrated from Lahore to Delhi and Bombay, respectively. Less privileged groups, from the Muslim community of Delhi for instance, articulate the relation between Partition and Independence in a slightly different way.

'*Mere hisse mein azadi aai hi kahan*? [When did I ever receive any share of Independence?]', asks Mohammad Khalid, a bookseller from the Jama Masjid area of Old Delhi. 'Here, there is only Partition and the pain of Partition... Virtually all my relatives are in Pakistan...' 'It was only after the riots started that people began to recognise that Independence had come, Partition had occurred, India and Pakistan had been established', says Rashiduddin Khan, a Muslim whose family had owned a shop in the plush market of Connaught Place in 1947. 'To tell you the truth, it was only in the bloodshed of Partition that ordinary people saw the shape of Independence.'[11] In this perspective, Independence and Partition could hardly be conceived of as separate things: they were the same. The phenomenon that some call Independence was never part of this inheritance: rather, 'it was... in the bloodshed of Partition' that the meaning of Independence was constructed by many 'ordinary people'.

One might even argue that there were two faces of Partition and Independence in evidence in northern India at this time, representing the perceptions of different classes – which could be called, loosely, a 'ruling' (privileged) class celebrating Independence, and a 'refugee' class unable to do so. However, as one would expect, the latter group breaks up immediately into those forced out of their lands and seeking refuge in what is now to be called their nation and their country, on the one hand, and those being forced out of this new state, on the other. The perceptions and actions of the two are polar opposites, as we shall see in the following pages. Nevertheless, the two faces of Partition and Independence, represented by the 'ruling' and the 'refugee' classes respectively – reflected in joy or sorrow, celebration or consternation – are commonly encountered in recollections of the time. They are well represented, for example, in the different answers evoked by the question: 'What were you doing on 15 August 1947?'

---

[11] Interviews with Mohammad Khalid and Rashiduddin Khan, published in *Deshkaal* (August 1996), pp. 21–2. Cf. Mountbatten's remark that he only realised the enormity and extent of Partition violence when it affected his own staff, a number of whom were killed on the night train from Shimla to Delhi, (IOR) R/3/1/172, Mountbatten to Baldev Singh (2 September 1947), and Mountbatten to Prime Minister (2 September 1947).

One response is symbolised by Nehru's well-known, and moving, Independence speech: 'At the stroke of the midnight hour, while the world sleeps, India will awake to life and freedom . . .' Another is captured in the angry rejoinder of a Sikh shopkeeper now living in Bhogal, a small *mohalla* (locality) sandwiched between the refugee colonies of Jangpura, Lajpat Nagar and Ashram in New Delhi. This Sikh shopkeeper came to Bhogal as a child, when large numbers of Hindus and Sikhs fled from their homes in Rawalpindi and Multan districts in March 1947, moving from place to place in search of safety and sustenance. Those who arrived in Bhogal, still a village in 1947, drove out the local Muslims in the process of attrition that ensued. 'What were you doing on 15 August 1947?' I asked. 'What do you think we were doing?' was the shopkeeper's sharp response. 'Wondering where we'd be the next day – whether we'd be able to stay on, even in this place . . . That's what we were doing . . .'[12]

Sometimes, the two faces of Partition and Independence may be found within a single celebratory narrative. Such is the case, for example, with the distinguished Hindi writer, Krishna Sobti's account of her experiences. A college student in Lahore at the time, Sobti had come to Delhi to celebrate her birthday in early 1947. She planned to stay for two days, as she recalls, but in the event never went back. In the months that followed many more people arrived from what would become West Pakistan, and some Muslim neighbours and friends moved away. By August there were forty to fifty refugees in her father's bungalow, many of considerable status and privilege. 'It was a strange feeling', she says. One person arrived with nothing but a bag on his shoulder and 'for two days he didn't say a word'. Women and children came, looking lost and blank.

On the night of 14 August, Krishna Sobti and her younger brother put up an exhibition in the verandah of their house, with photographs of Gandhi, Nehru and other national idols, and extracts from their speeches. 'We were asserting our rights as Delhi-ites and as citizens, so to speak.' At midnight, when the national song was sung over the radio and Nehru made his 'stroke of midnight' speech, the regular inhabitants of the household were in tears. The newcomers, however, still stared vacantly. A servant then brought out a tray laden with sweets, made especially for the occasion in the three colours of the national flag. Sobti says that she can never forget how, as the servant took the tray around, 'everyone who had come from outside, these forty or fifty men and women . . . who were guests in our house, got up one by one and left the verandah . . .'[13]

[12] Interview with Atam Singh (Bhogal, 16 March 1947).
[13] Interview (Delhi, February 1995).

The memoirs of G. D. Khosla, the judge of the Punjab high court who moved from Lahore to Mussoorie for the summer vacation of 1947 (once again, never to return), provide another striking example of the divided soul of Delhi. Khosla and his wife travelled to Delhi from Shimla specifically to witness the transfer-of-power ceremony on 14–15 August 1947. 'Never have I been so moved and for so long as on that unforgettable occasion', he recalls in his autobiography.

There was an atmosphere of quiet, purposeful expectation [inside Parliament House]... Total strangers greeted me with quiet, benign smiles, and though I was wearing clothes of western style, I felt myself a portion of the khadi clad assembly. In a few moments, I would be a free citizen of India... I kept saying to myself that we were free, free, free...

Khosla goes on to describe the government of India's official flag-hoisting function at India Gate the next morning as 'a happy, uninhibited exhibition of fun... The memory of the natural and spontaneous jubilation manifested by the crowd around me on that memorable day gives me a warm, delicious glow of joy and of pride.'[14]

Four months later, the author was appointed to enquire into the workings of the Custodian of Evacuee Property in Delhi and to settle the opposing claims of Delhi's Muslims (large numbers of whom were in refugee camps at the Old Fort and in Humayun's Tomb by this time) on the one hand, and Hindu and Sikh refugees who had migrated from West Pakistan on the other. Overcome by the immensity of his task, Khosla went to see Gandhi late in January 1948, a few days before Gandhi was assassinated, and began to tell him of his difficulties. This is how he reports the conversation:

Khosla: 'The Muslims in the Old Fort camp have no wish to stay in this country. They told me, when I visited them, that they would like to go to Pakistan as soon as possible. Our own people are without houses or shelter. It breaks my heart to see them suffering like this, exposed to the elements. Tell me, Bapuji, what should I do?'
Gandhi: 'When I go there, they [the Muslims] do not say they want to go to Pakistan... They are also our people. You should bring them back and protect them.'

'I mentioned other facts, other difficulties', says Khosla. 'He pointed out the flaws in my argument... When I left him after having spent thirty minutes in his company, I knew what I had to do...'[15]

---

[14] G. D. Khosla, *Memory's Gay Chariot. An Autobiographical Narrative* (Delhi, 1985), pp. 159–61.
[15] *Ibid.*, pp. 175–6.

The divided city

The response of the Sikh shopkeeper from Bhogal – 'wondering where we'd be the next day . . . that's what we were doing' – speaks not only of the condition of Sikh (or Hindu) refugees in Delhi in 1947. It also speaks of the condition of all of those who lived outside the circle of 'ruling class' Delhi, in what we might call 'refugee' Delhi. It reflects the state of Muslim refugees all over northern India (and in some parts of southern India too), and that of other communities now designated minorities or foreigners in other parts of the subcontinent. Consider the Muslims of Delhi.

Abul Kalam Azad, Shahid Ahmad Dehlavi, Ebadat Barelvi, Anees Qidwai and Ishtiaq Husain Qureshi are only some of those who have written about those tortured days when 'murder stalked the town' and Muslims found it hard to move out of their homes (and then, at some point, to remain in their homes too), when 'men and women of all kinds and condition – rich and poor, young and old – huddled together in sheer fear of life' and 'no Muslim householder could go to sleep at night with the confidence that he [sic] would wake up alive the next morning'.[16]

'September, 1947 will be remembered by Delhi residents as a period of horror', wrote a British resident at the beginning of October.[17] 'Moslems were being systematically hunted down and butchered', wrote another.

Thousands of them were herded into camps . . . The dead lay rotting in the streets, because there was no one to collect and bury them. The hospitals were choked with dying and wounded, and in imminent danger of attack because of the presence of Moslem staff and Moslem patients . . . Appeals for protection poured in from every side . . . [18]

On 4 September, reports a Muslim military officer who was attached to the quarter master general's branch at army headquarters in connection with the movement of Pakistani government officials and materials to Karachi, the whole of Delhi had been under curfew for eighty-eight hours. Nevertheless, Sikhs could be seen moving about in jeeps, 'armed with swords and possibly other weapons' (the Sikhs were now 'so strong and confident in themselves', another observer noted a little later, that they could only be dealt with by a combination of force and diplomacy) and

---

[16] The quotations are from Abul Kalam Azad, *India Wins Freedom: the Complete Version* (Madras, 1988), pp. 228–30.
[17] *The Statesman* (7 October 1947).
[18] (IOR) Mss. Eur. F200/165, 'The Indian Situation. A Personal Note', by Lord Ismay (5 October 1947).

there was a widespread rumour that violence would occur on a large scale on or about 5 September.[19]

The background to this rumour is provided perhaps by the planned evacuation of Pakistani government personnel who were stranded in Delhi. Approximately 8,000 officials who had opted for Pakistan had already left for Karachi by special trains. Another 6,000 or so still waited in Delhi owing to the suddenly much increased insecurity of rail travel.[20] 'Operation Pakistan', which aimed to take these officials out by air, was to be launched at Palam airport on 4 September. It is alleged that a directive went out in the meantime from underground anti-Pakistani quarters stating that 'Pakistan personnel and property' were not to be allowed to escape.[21]

A mere listing of a few instances of violence that occurred in Delhi in September 1947 conveys something of the terror that Muslims had to live through. On 5 September, widespread and concerted attacks upon Muslims occurred in several areas. The attacks in Qarol Bagh included one upon a high school where students were sitting their matriculation examination. 'The mob called on the boys of one community to stand and they were butchered [outside the examination hall],' the *News Chronicle* reported.[22] Other reports suggested that the Muslim examinees were separated from the start, and asked by the invigilators to write the examination in another room – where they were massacred.[23]

On 7 and 8 September, the attacks spread to some of the best guarded areas of New Delhi and, to quote a Muslim military officer's 'Statement on [the] Delhi Disturbances' once again, 'the Muslims of Delhi lost their morale, and the will to resist, because they had not only to resist the well-armed Sikhs but also found the Police and Military against them.'[24] A European witness reported seeing 'car loads and lorry loads of armed Sikhs freely going around'; and the *Daily Mirror* of 9 September reported that the Paharganj area was 'like a battle-field with blazing houses, hordes of refugees, dead cattle and horses and the rattle of automatic weapons'.[25]

[19] (IOR) Mss. Eur. F164/21, 'Statement on Delhi Disturbances', pp. xxxvii–xxxviii. The quotation in brackets comes from Mss. Eur. F200/165, Ismay's note on 'The Indian Situation'. See also *ibid.*, vol. 141, draft *aide mémoire* on 'The Sikhs' [in East Punjab], prepared for the governor general on 24 February 1948.

[20] *Dawn* (27 August 1947).

[21] (IOR) Mss. Eur. F164/21, 'Statement on Delhi Disturbances', p. xxxviii.

[22] *News Chronicle* (6 September 1947), cited in Malik, 'Tragedy of Delhi', p. 5.

[23] Shahid Ahmad Dehlavi, *Dilli ki bipta* (*Naya Daur*, 1948), reprinted in Mumtaz Shirin, ed., *Zulmat-i-nimroz*, (Karachi, 1990), p. 152. I am grateful to Alok Bhalla for drawing my attention to this important memoir and for kindly providing me with a photocopy of the reprinted version. Page references provided in the text below refer to this reprint.

[24] (IOR) Mss. Eur. F164/21, 'Statement on Delhi Disturbances', p. xxxix–xl.

[25] See Malik, 'Tragedy of Delhi', p. 7; and *Daily Mirror* (9 September 1947).

Some incidents reported from New Delhi on 7 September help to drive the point home. In the posh shopping centre of Connaught Place, an enraged Prime Minister Nehru stopped his passing car, grabbed a baton from police personnel who were standing by idly, and personally dispersed some looters near the Odeon cinema.[26] Outside the Regal cinema, 500 yards away, two Muslim servants were struck down with a sword. Five people were killed outside the Roman Catholic cathedral while the morning service was in progress. At the same time, a crowd coming from the Lodi Road area stopped cars that were passing in the vicinity of Willingdon airport, and dragged out and killed a number of Muslims travelling in them.[27]

At the end of the month, some 200 raiders from nearby villages attacked the Refugee Hospital at Safdarjang in south Delhi. They appear to have scaled the wall together at a pre-arranged signal, and although the police guard opened fire, three Muslim patients were done to death and several injured in an attack that lasted perhaps five minutes. On the same day, a man was stoned to death in front of a travellers' *sarai* (or inn) at the New Delhi railway station. 'The victim was held down by two men while another hit him on the head with a big stone', an eyewitness reported.[28]

Towards the end of September when the mayhem had decreased somewhat, there were rumours of a likely recrudescence of attacks in early October. Hindu militants threatened the Hindu residents of *mohalla* Jatan, Pahari Dhiraj, Sadar Bazaar, with grave consequences if they continued to provide protection to scavengers and other low-caste Muslims who lived in their streets. About the same time, Indian and European volunteers working in Muslim refugee camps received similar threats from small groups of Sikhs.[29]

Cases of stabbing and looting and clashes between Hindus, Muslims and Sikhs had, of course, started in Delhi a long time before September. The violence was provoked not only by the extremist propaganda and activities of different parties in the months leading up to August. It was fuelled by uncertainty and calculations about the future, not least among

---

[26] Nehru did this so frequently during these days that people around him were greatly concerned about his safety, interview, Azim Husain, ICS (London, 12 October 1995); *People's Age* (19 October 1947); *Daily Telegraph* (21 January 1948); and Dehlavi, *Dilli ki bipta*, p. 157.

[27] This paragraph is based on reports in *The Statesman* (8 September 1947).

[28] *Ibid.* (1 October 1947).

[29] (NMML) CID records, 5th instalment, file 136/1947, Casual Source Report (27 September 1947); (IOR) Mss. Eur. F200/52, minutes of meeting of emergency committee of the Cabinet (24 September 1947).

government employees, of whom there were large numbers in Delhi;[30] by
news of riots and killings elsewhere (Calcutta, Noakhali, Bihar, and then
on the very doorstep of Delhi, in Garhmukhteshwar and Gurgaon); and
by the arrival of bodies of Hindu and Sikh refugees from West Punjab, the
North West Frontier Province and Sindh in the months after March – a
stream that became a veritable flood in late August.

Contemporary records as well as later recollections give us a picture
of how – as protective gates went up at the boundaries of the *mohallas*,
and preparations for 'defence' were made all around, among Hindus and
Sikhs as well as Muslims, and as the police and the army came to stand
guard at the *mohalla* gates, on rooftops and at mosques, targeting mainly
the Muslims – a whole community came to feel defenceless, isolated and
increasingly suffocated.[31] An escape to Pakistan, or temporarily to the
large refugee camps that now sprang up, often became the only option
available to the Muslims.

Anees Qidwai put the number of people in the Purana Qila in the month
of September at 80,000 to 100,000. When she got there in October,
the numbers had declined to perhaps 60,000. Even so, there was 'as
far as the eye could see' nothing but 'disorganised tents and heaps of
tin roofs' amidst which 'naked children, unkempt women, girls without
their heads covered and men overcome with anger wandered up and down
endlessly'.[32] The conditions in the Purana Qila 'defied description', wrote
one senior British official: 'no food, no water, no sanitary arrangements,
not even assured security'.[33] Dr Zakir Husain put it more searingly in

---

[30] For such propaganda and activities in Lodi Colony, see, for example, CID records, 5th
instalment, file 78; (NAI) Home Poll 5/6/46, Home Poll (I) 33/26/46, Home Poll (I)
5/7/47, etc.; and letters to the editor of *Dawn* through late 1946 and 1947.

[31] There are numerous reports of Muslim policemen being disarmed in Amritsar,
Hoshiarpur, Gurdaspur, Ferozepur, Jullunder and other places in East Punjab in August
1947, and of the same thing being done to Hindu and Sikh policemen in West Punjab,
Rees coll., PBF bundles, 'Report of the Punjab Boundary Force' by T. W. Rees
(15 November 1947), and File, 'Communal Subjects and Incidents'; (IOR) R/3/1/171,
telegraphic message from Generals Messervy and Rees (13 August 1947); R/3/1/172,
memo by R. N. Banerjee, secretary, home dept, government of India (10 September
1947); and N. N. Vohra's memoir, '91, Garden Town', in Geeti Sen, ed., *Crossing Boundaries* (Delhi, 1997), p. 51. It is likely that similar steps were taken in Delhi to neutralise
any Muslim police or military presence, although I have not come across any direct
reference to this in the records I have seen. Contemporary reports on Delhi make it
clear, however, that Hindus and Sikhs were never restricted in their movements to quite
the same extent as the Muslims, even during curfews and in the worst affected areas.
Lamentably, the practice has continued over much of northern India into recent years,
cf. Vibhuti Narain Rai, *Shahar mein curfew* (Delhi, 1987).

[32] Anees Qidwai, *Azadi ki chhaon mein*, pp. 38–9, 56.

[33] (IOR) Mss. Eur. F200/165, Ismay's note, 'The Indian Situation'; cf. his *The Memoirs of
General the Lord Ismay* (London, 1960), p. 438.

his evidence before the Delhi government's emergency committee: those who had made it to the camp had escaped from 'sudden death', he said, to be 'buried in a living grave'.[34]

Religious affiliation as national affiliation

It is perhaps necessary to reiterate that much the same condition prevailed over large tracts of territory on the other side of the international border. In many parts of the new domains of India and Pakistan, being a Sikh or a Hindu (on the one side) or a Muslim (on the other) had become virtually synonymous with being a refugee and a foreign national. Those who had long adhered somewhat loosely to the label of Muslim, Hindu or Sikh were now categorically named as one or the other. The Meos of Mewat, the Momins of UP and Bihar, the Mapillas of Malabar – all became simply Muslims and, for a while, nothing else. And whole religious communities came to be suspect.

Individual recollections and memoirs are replete with examples of the disbelief experienced by one person after another at discovering their own acquaintances and peers, many of them from fairly privileged and protected backgrounds, among the hunted. Krishna Sobti recalls the tears of humiliation in the eyes of a middle-class Muslim neighbour when people from her home went to see him in the Purana Qila camp, and speaks of the touchiness of the Hindu and Sikh refugees from West Punjab in her father's bungalow, for the change from privileged and proud – even haughty – backgrounds to the status of 'refugees' was not easy to accept.[35] Shahid Ahmad Dehlavi writes of his and his family's shock and sorrow, when, on the evening of their arrival at the Purana Qila refugee camp, they found the families of both his elder brother and a younger brother occupying equally cramped and rain-sodden spots but fifty yards away. The two brothers shared a large bungalow in the well-protected, predominantly official and elite Civil Lines area of Delhi, while Dehlavi lived with his family in the overwhelmingly Muslim Jama Masjid locality. When they met each other at the camp their outcry was simultaneous: 'But I thought your locality was safe?'[36]

The business of marking everything as Hindu (or Hindu/Sikh) and Muslim – and hence privileged, or unwanted – went even further. Clearly

---

[34] Cited in Azad, *India Wins Freedom*, p. 233.
[35] Interview (Delhi, February 1995).
[36] Dehlavi, *Dilli*, p. 166. Consider too Nehru's shock, when he visited Sheikhupura on 31 August, at finding 'old colleagues . . . (now) bereft of everything . . . trudging along with the rest in the long caravan [of destitute wanderers]', (IOR) R/3/1/172, Nehru to Mountbatten, camp Lahore (31 August 1947).

the body manages to signal such attributes even at 'normal' times. In the claustrophobic circumstances of 1947, the semioticity of these markers was considerably intensified. The very clothes that people wore were now read as being unambiguously 'Hindu' or 'Muslim'. As Ishtiaq Husain Qureshi, a professor of history in Delhi University put it in his account of his and his family's escape from the university campus in September 1947, the women 'put on Hindu caste marks on their foreheads and put on Hindu clothes'.[37] Not Punjabi or Bengali, even though that too could be misleading, or middle class, or other such classification, but Hindu. The caste marks and the clothes referred to are, presumably, the *bindi* and the saree, neither an exclusively Hindu attribute then or now; the women leaders of both Bangladesh and Sri Lanka continue to wear the saree as a national dress, as other women from these countries and from Pakistan have done.

In 1947–8, no doubt drawing from the actual socialisation of the body even before this, a person's very demeanour came to be read as Hindu or Muslim. How else can we understand the actions of officials and workers who rounded up a number of Hindu women in the course of operations to recover abducted Muslim women for repatriation to Pakistan, or of 'some Muslims ... being mixed up' in vehicles bringing non-Muslim evacuees from West Punjab to India?[38] The frantic effort to divide up everything into Hindu and Muslim, Indian and Pakistani, also provides the context for the troubled statement of Josh Malihabadi and other Urdu writers belonging to the Progressive Writers' Movement that Urdu (the common heritage of urbanised Hindus and Muslims, at least in the Delhi, Agra, Lahore, Lucknow and Hyderabad regions) could not be partitioned:[39] a prediction that seems to have been belied by the paths charted out by official policies in both India and Pakistan – and, I should add, by some of the longer-term tendencies of Hindu and Muslim nationalism in undivided India.[40]

[37] I. H. Qureshi, 'A Case Study of the Social Relations Between the Muslims and the Hindus, 1935–47', in Philips and Wainright, eds., *Partition of India*, p. 368.
[38] (IOR) Mss. Eur. F200/129, meeting of the Punjab emergency committee (13 September 1947). For further discussion on the rounding up of 'abducted' women, see next chapter.
[39] *People's Age* (7 September 1947).
[40] All India Radio's Hindi and Pakistan Radio's Urdu have become mutually incomprehensible, and among the younger generation in India, Urdu seems to have become a language of the Muslims alone. On this, see David Lelyveld, 'The Fate of Hindustani. Colonial Knowledge and the Project of a National Language', in Carol Breckenridge and Peter van der Veer, eds., *Orientalism and the Postcolonial Predicament: Perspectives on South Asia* (Philadelphia, 1993); and on the longer-term struggle by Hindu and Muslim propagandists to adopt and promote Hindi and Urdu respectively, Amrit Rai, *A House Divided: the Origin and Development of Hindi/Hindavi* (Delhi, 1984); Christopher R. King, *One Language, Two Scripts. The Hindi Movement in Nineteenth Century North India* (Bombay, 1994).

This was the context for the serious debate that now took place on the appropriate composition of the population of Delhi – and of India. G. D. Khosla's reported conversation with Gandhi, cited earlier in this chapter, was symptomatic of this debate. 'The Muslims...', Khosla had said, 'have no wish to stay in this country.' What would Delhi be like, Gandhi asked in speech after speech in September 1947 and afterwards, if the Jama Masjid (or Great Mosque) were no longer there?[41] What would it be like without its 'Muslim' heritage and its Muslim inhabitants? 'Delhi has a long history behind it', he said in one of his prayer speeches in October 1947. 'It would be madness even to try to erase that history.'[42] What would be left, then, of its mosaic of buildings, its complex of cultures, and its claims of uniqueness? Jawaharlal Nehru agonised over the same question: what would happen to India if Pakistan became an 'all-Muslim State' and India, in consequence, an 'all-Hindu/Sikh' one?[43]

The events of late 1947 and early 1948 in Delhi marked a crucial moment in this debate: indeed, they were a primary mode in which that debate was conducted. The changing responses of different sections of Delhi's populations – political leaders and their followers, Muslims, Hindus and Sikhs – indicate the grave contention that took place over the questions asked by Nehru and Gandhi. They reveal a great deal too about the different ways in which the new national – Indian and Pakistani – was being conceived, and what this did to reconstitute local forms of sociality.

September 1947

A brief report that appeared in *The Statesman* points to the many layers that went to make up the Delhi of 1947, and the contemporary struggle to add new layers while attempting to obliterate older ones – an exercise that is far from finished even today. The remains of a Mughal house, apparently dating back to the eighteenth century had been unearthed in the Dhobiwara area of Dariba Kalan in Old Delhi. A mosque had at some point been constructed on a part of the foundations of the old house, the newspaper said. Presumably the debris at the site came from the collapse (or destruction) of the mosque. When local inhabitants (almost certainly Hindu) cleared the debris they allegedly found two stone images

---

[41] *The Collected Works of Mahatma Gandhi* (hereafter *CWMG*), vol. LXXXIX (Delhi, 1983), pp. 181, 201, 206, 223 and *passim*. I am suggesting that this was a question about India's future. Gandhi spoke a more religious language, however, arguing that it would spell the end of Hinduism or Sikhism if the Jama Masjid was ever converted into a Hindu or Sikh temple, *ibid.*, p. 201.

[42] *CWMG*, vol. LXXXIX, p. 393

[43] (IOR) R/3/1/172, 'Top Secret Note' on Mountbatten's interview with Nehru (8 September 1947), 4.30–5.30 p. m.

of Parvati and Nandi, wife and vehicle respectively of the great god, Shiva. 'The house has been converted into a little Shiva shrine [sic]', the report concluded.[44]

As the conflict over this site indicates, there is a great deal that is – almost necessarily – covered up in the history of Delhi, a great deal that needs to be carefully unearthed. One representation of the city is found in Ahmed Ali's summary of its history in his novel, *Twilight in Delhi*:

[Delhi] was built after the great battle of Mahabharat by Raja Yudhishtra [*sic*] in 1453 B.C., and has been the cause of many a great and historic battle. Destruction is in its foundations and blood is in its soil. It has seen the fall of many a glorious kingdom, and listened to the groans of birth. It is the symbol of Life and Death, and revenge is in its nature.[45]

However, this and other Muslim memoirs, fictional and non-fictional, have more to say about the particular, not to say exceptional, character of a more recent and all too well remembered Delhi.

'*Dilli Musalmanon ka shahar tha*', wrote Ebadat Barelvi.[46] Delhi was a city of the Muslims, a Muslim city – unparalleled in the subtlety and beauty of its culture or the grandeur of its public displays. The streets of Old Delhi were so busy and crowded that it was difficult to walk on them, '*Yahan khoye se khoa chhilta tha . . .*' 'From morning to night, there was such gaiety at the Jama Masjid that it brought to mind the age of Akbar and Shah Jahan.'[47] That world was not likely to survive in the face of colonial capitalism, the spread of possessive individualism and of modern science and, accompanying these, new ideas of nationalism and democracy. *Twilight in Delhi*, written in the late 1930s, laments the fate of the city as it comes under the sway of a corrosive, corrupting, commercialised and aggressive colonial culture. Muslim writings after 1947 linked the collapse of that old world in Delhi specifically to Partition and, more particularly, to the violence of September 1947.

Consider Shahid Ahmad Dehlavi's *Dilli ki bipta* ('The misfortune [or calamity] of Delhi'), a hastily written, detailed, moving and bitter account of how he was forced to leave a city he had never contemplated leaving.[48] The title of this memoir itself has much to tell us. The word *bipta* or *bipda* is of course from the Sanskrit *vipatti*, transformed, popularised and incorporated into the common speech of Hindustani – the Urdu/Hindi of

---

[44] *The Statesman* (23 October 1947).
[45] Ahmed Ali, *Twilight in Delhi* (1940; Delhi, 1991), p. 4.
[46] Ebadat Barelvi, *Azadi ke saaye mein* (Lahore, 1988), p. 18.
[47] *Ibid.*, p. 13. Since the construction of a new capital city by the British called New Delhi, just to the south of the older habitation, the city built up since the time of the Mughals has come to be known as Old Delhi.
[48] Dehlavi, *Dilli*. Cf. n. 23 above.

the great Indo-Muslim cities of northern India – Delhi, Agra, Lucknow and so on. This common tongue of urban north India accepts Sanskrit loan words only after they have been 'corrupted', vernacularised and thereby distanced from their classical roots. Here there would appear to be a notable difference from, say, Bengali where the *sadhu bhasha* ('pure', literary or elite language) takes over Sanskrit loan words in a form where the 'corruptions' of popular speech are largely removed. The choice of the vernacularised *bipta*, then, contains in it a whole history – of the making of a new *lingua franca* for northern (and pockets of southern) India, of a new Indo-Muslim culture, of a new 'Delhi', and a new 'India', over the eighteenth and nineteenth centuries. *Dilli ki bipta* is perhaps, from this point of view, not the calamity of Delhi alone: it is the calamity of India's Muslims, the calamity of Shahid Ahmad's family – the calamity of India?[49]

'Who can tell what evil spell the city came under as the sun of independence dawned upon its horizon? Such great storms arose that they shook this city of unparalleled grace to its foundations, destroying its prosperity and reducing its gaiety to nought': these are the words of Ebadat Barelvi.[50] 'We had heard accounts of the [1857] Mutiny from our elders, and also read the stories about that time written by Khwaja Hasan Nizami,' recalls Shahid Ahmad Dehlavi. 'And we thought that such destruction had never before been visited upon Delhi, nor ever again would be. But [even] the devastation of [18]57 paled before the ravages of September . . .'[51]

September 1947 is a crucial month in the recollections of many Delhi Muslims. Ebadat Barelvi, then a teacher in the famous Delhi College (once known as the Anglo-Arabic College, and since renamed Zakir Husain College), described the events as follows in an interview done in the 1960s:

Until about 2 or 3 September 1947 nothing much happened in (the vicinity of our college) . . . That area had a mixed population. Hindus were on one side, but at the time there were also a good number of Muslims. On 4 September I remember well that there was (major) trouble in Qarol Bagh . . . about a mile and a half from our college . . .[52]

The dates vary – 4, 5, 6 September – but we know from contemporary records and later accounts that the situation in the capital deteriorated sharply about that time. 'Qarol Bagh' marked a new stage in the violence

---

[49] I owe the reflections in this paragraph to the prodding of that other Shahid (or witness), my colleague and comrade for over thirty years now – Shahid Amin.
[50] Barelvi, *Azadi*, p. 19.
[51] Dehlavi, *Dilli*, p. 145.
[52] Barelvi's interview, in *Seminar*, 420 (August 1994), pp. 36–7.

in Delhi, moving beyond individual stabbings and looting to the systematic marking out of 'enemy' houses and shops and concerted attempts
to drive out Muslims from every part of the city. The police too became
openly partisan. Barelvi and his colleagues and students stayed on in their
college for another few days, amidst sounds of incessant firing, rumours
of large-scale violence and killing in one area and another, and increasing
fears for their own safety.

Finally, on 7 or 8 September, they escaped to the Pakistani High Commissioner's residence – for, as Barelvi records it, the High Commission,
with which telephone contact had been established by chance as some
members of the staff tried to get through to a senior Muslim minister of
the Indian government, had information of an attack on Delhi College
planned for that very night.

> The next day the trouble escalated. We were . . . [in the compound of the High
> Commissioner's house] and we heard that there had been trouble in Delhi Univer-
> sity and that [the] Dean of the Faculty of Arts, Dr. Ishtiaq Husain Qureshi . . . and
> the Registrar, Akhtar Husain, were coming too and they were in a very bad state –
> just a pair of trousers and a shirt, no shoes even . . .[53]

Qureshi's own recollections of the period match Barelvi's. In July and
August, he says in a memoir written in the 1960s, a 'feverish collection of
arms' began in the Old City. 'The fortified mohallas . . . developed into ar-
senals. One could see that an undeclared and unofficial civil war was in the
offing . . . At night the house tops began to bristle with armed men . . .'[54]
Qureshi lived on the campus of Delhi University, several miles north of
the Old City, but close to several new camps opened for refugees from
West Pakistan, which were also areas of active recruitment for the Hindu
right-wing organisation, the RSS. The arrival of Hindu and Sikh refugees
in such numbers aroused a wave of sympathy for them and embittered
Hindu/Sikh feelings towards the Muslims, writes Qureshi. 'Soon after
armed Sikhs and others were seen roaming in and around the campus.'

'At last [in September] the inevitable happened.' Muslim inhabitants
of Timarpur, about a mile from the campus, were attacked. As Qureshi
recalls it, a Muslim recluse living in a deserted mosque near the university
was killed, and the keepers of other mosques in the area fled. Very soon,

---

[53] *Ibid.*
[54] Qureshi, 'Social Relations', in Philips and Wainright, eds., *Partition of India*, p. 366. The
Daily Mail of 29 August 1947 reported that 'thousands' of leaflets and pamphlets were
being openly distributed and stuck on the walls of Delhi calling on Hindus and Sikhs
to avenge the murder of their co-religionists in West Punjab. One pamphlet depicted
a Muslim slashing a Hindu woman with a sword, and said: 'If you wish to make your
country prosperous and peaceful, eliminate your opponents . . . Remember August 30 is
Martyrs' Day! The day should begin with the mass murder of all Moslems, including
women and children . . .'

Muslims who worked in the orchards that stretched for miles around the university began pouring in to seek asylum in the campus; many of them had been attacked and killed in the orchards.

That night was full of terror for us. We could hear screams of men, women and children who were intermittently being killed in their homes. Next morning the campus was attacked. There was no loss of life, but all Muslim houses were looted, one by one. Muslim students and teachers were evacuated with difficulty. We escaped in our car. Women hastily put on Hindu caste marks on their foreheads and put on Hindu clothes. I took them to the Pakistan High Commission . . .[55]

'September' stands out also in the recollections of some who initially observed Delhi from the sidelines. A striking example is provided by Begum Anees Qidwai of Lucknow, whose husband Shafi Ahmed Qidwai (a respected government official, and younger brother of the Congress leader and central cabinet minister, Rafi Ahmed Qidwai) was murdered while walking to his office in Mussoorie one day in early October. Anees Qidwai went to Delhi shortly afterwards and began to work in the Muslim refugee camps at the bidding of Gandhi. Before that happened, however, and before her husband was killed, she had followed events in Mussoorie and Dehradun, Delhi and Punjab, from 'faraway' Lucknow: and she had had to answer many anxious queries from other Muslims of Lucknow and places in the vicinity who knew that she had well-placed contacts in Delhi and elsewhere.

Qidwai's memoir, based on a journal she kept from the time she began work in Delhi, has the same title as Ebadat Barelvi's – *Azadi ki chhaon mein* ('In the Shadow of Independence').[56] She begins it with these words: '*Sitambar shuru hua aur apne saath beesiyon balayen aur pareshaniyan lekar aaya* [September came bringing with it unnumbered troubles and misfortunes]' (1). This in an opening chapter tellingly entitled '*Karta hun jama phir jigar-i-lakht-lakht ko*' ('I gather together [or 'seek to gather together'] the scattered pieces of my heart'). 'And then September came', she writes a few pages later. 'India had not been independent for fifteen days when violence and killing began in Delhi' (6). 'It all began in Delhi. The killing did not begin from anywhere else', recalls another high-status Muslim woman who lived through the terror of Partition in a distant, and relatively safe, part of eastern UP.[57]

[55] Qureshi, 'Social Relations', in Philips and Wainright, eds., *Partition of India*, pp. 367–8.
[56] I should add that the title of Qidwai's original Urdu publication and the Hindi translation is the same, and that Qidwai's *chhaon* and Barelvi's *saaye* are different versions of the same word, for 'shadow'. Page numbers given in the text after this refer to the Hindi edition (1990).
[57] Interview with Ruqaiya Begum (Allahabad, 4 October 1994). Ruqaiya Begum still lives in Allahabad. Her brother, a senior government official, who was stuck in Delhi in 1947, migrated to Pakistan.

The longer-term residents of Delhi were persuaded, however, that these troubles would pass. Delhi was, after all, the seat of the national government. The government would maintain peace here at any cost. They were not entirely mistaken: the government did try (though governments are made up of many parts that do not always pull together). In early September, when the crisis threatened to blow everything apart in both East Punjab and Delhi, Indian political leaders summoned Mountbatten back from Shimla to help with his military experience in what was nothing short of a war situation. An 'emergency committee' of the Cabinet was set up on 6 September, with parallel emergency committees for Delhi and East Punjab: and Mountbatten's comment in one of the early meetings, 'If we go down in Delhi, we are finished',[58] sums up the urgency felt by the government. In any case, these streamlined agencies at the centre of government ensured that decisions were taken quickly and their implementation continuously monitored; and they contributed substantially to containing the violence.[59]

Conceiving the new political community

With the unfortunate equations that were being made between Muslim and Pakistan, Hindu and Indian, it seemed at one point in 1947 that the Delhi administration, if not the government of India, had given up responsibility for the Muslims of the Delhi region. Several ministers in the emergency committee meetings of the Indian Cabinet in September claimed, as Khosla had claimed, that nearly all the Muslims in the refugee camps of Delhi wanted to go to Pakistan. And, while this view was challenged by other members of the same Cabinet, and by Gandhi, there is evidence to suggest that the giant Muslim refugee camps at Purana Qila and Humayun's Tomb were, for a significant length of time, treated by Indian officials as being the responsibility of the Pakistani government.

Several reports indicate a considerable imbalance in the conditions in Hindu/Sikh camps, on the one hand, and Muslim camps on the other, and in the treatment meted out to refugees in the two. This is not to say that conditions in the former were satisfactory: far from it. Nevertheless, as Anees Qidwai pointed out to Gandhi in the winter of 1947–8, while the government distributed thousands of blankets and quilts in other refugee camps, those housing Muslim refugees received no official aid. Many months later, in September 1948, when Gandhi was no longer alive,

---

[58] Pyarelal, *Mahatma Gandhi. The Last Phase*, vol. II (Ahmedabad, 1958), p. 433. Cf. the front page headline in the Communist party paper, *People's Age* (21 September 1947), 'Defend Delhi! Defend India!!'
[59] (IOR) Mss. Eur. F200/165, Ismay's 'The Indian Situation'.

Qidwai visited the large Hindu/Sikh refugee camp in the old Kingsway (now a locality officially called Kingsway Camp) and was again struck by the difference that marked Hindu/Sikh and Muslim refugee conditions. Seeing a large quantity of cloth brought for distribution in the camp, she noted in her diary that even a whole year's effort had not enabled her to obtain from the government one set of clothes for distribution to a single one of those refugees who lay around, in tattered clothes and in fear, in Muslim refugee camps.[60]

Muslim memorialists have stated too that it was some time after the emergence of a huge Muslim refugee population that any official camp was opened for them. When the Purana Qila camp was finally established, allegedly after an appeal by the Pakistani High Commissioner, a Pakistani army contingent was deputed for the defence of the camp. The government of Pakistan sent out hundreds of tents to accommodate at least some of the refugees. Some amount of food for the refugees was apparently flown in from Pakistan, in British civil airline planes that were being used to transport Pakistani government officials to Karachi and returning empty on the flight to Delhi.[61]

Qidwai, who worked extensively in the countryside around Delhi in 1948, noted that many local Hindus had fled along with the Muslims when fighting broke out in their localities. Hindu and Sikh refugees from Pakistan occupied many of the deserted lands, and a major conflict arose when the local Hindus and Muslims sought to return on the re-establishment of peace. Dalit ('Untouchable') cultivators, who had been among the chief tenants of local Muslims, especially suffered, since the immigrants – themselves cultivators – had no need of tenants on their newly occupied lands. The official Relief Committee in Delhi had apparently been instructed that its task was to look after Hindu and Sikh refugees from Pakistan. Unofficial peace committees tried to take care of Muslim refugees in August–September 1948. An official department was responsible for the relief and rehabilitation of Hindus and Sikhs from across the border. However, there was no one to look after the local Hindus: 'No Department had been opened for them', Qidwai observed.[62]

It was only after Gandhi had visited the Purana Qila camp on 13 September 1947 that the Indian government sent out the message clearly that these camps of Muslim refugees were also *our* camps, and these refugees *our* citizens if they wished to stay – unambiguously the

---

[60] Qidwai, *Azadi*, pp. 64, 282. Qidwai adds in a footnote that the large numbers of Muslims from the Delhi countryside and from Punjab who lay around in the lanes and by-lanes of the city had never been to Pakistan nor, in her words, 'thought of going', p. 282n.
[61] Dehlavi, *Dilli*, p. 168. See also Barelvi, *Azadi*, pp. 80–1, and Qidwai, *Azadi*, p. 38.
[62] *Ibid.*, p. 275.

charge of the government of India. And it was after this, it seems, that Indian officials took over full responsibility for the supply of rations as well as for security at these camps.[63] It is a telling comment on the place assigned to the Muslims in the early days of independent India, and on the struggle that had to be waged to establish a nation which declared plurality and secularism, and a sociality consonant with those principles, to be its goals.

Perhaps Gandhi's arrival in Delhi was the turning point; perhaps his intervention gave to secular nationalist elements the moral strength they needed to renew the fight for the composite and tolerant India that so many had dreamed of; perhaps his very presence stunned the government and an army of stupefied Congress workers into action. Local officials and activists now moved quickly to hold neighbourhood meetings, establish peace committees, and look more generally to the restoration of peace and normalcy. Aided by the work of the government's emergency committees, already meeting daily to monitor developments, the transfer of large numbers of displaced Muslims to Pakistan, and the deployment of south Indian troops (who took a more neutral stand in the battle between Hindus and Muslims – whether because this was a largely north Indian affair, or because of the different signals emanating from the government), these efforts helped gradually to change the situation on the ground.

At the end of October 1947 – by which time, however, only one and a half lakhs of Delhi's five lakh Muslims were thought to still be in the city – those still there were reportedly disinclined to leave. In mid-October, hundreds of Muslims were returning to the Old City from the refugee camps; others seem to have waited until after the passing of the Hindu and Muslim festivals of Dasehra and Baqr Id (on 23/24 October) before they moved back.[64] By 31 October, the number of Muslim refugees at the Humayun's Tomb camp was down to 4,000 from its high point of 63,000 or more a few weeks earlier, and the camp at Purana Qila had been closed. There were, however, still 1,000 or so Muslim refugees in Tihar village (now the site of Delhi's largest prison), some 6,000 at Chhattarpur, and others scattered through the shadows and ruins of Muslim monuments, mosques and graveyards from the Jama Masjid to Nizamuddin, Arab Sarai, Safdarjang's Tomb and beyond: and new refugees came in

---

[63] Dehlavi, *Dilli*, p. 166. The observation that these were Indian citizens of course became even less doubtful after the Pakistani government declared in late September that Pakistan would not accept any more Muslims from Delhi or Uttar Pradesh.

[64] (IOR) Mss. Eur. F200/190, summary for week ending 17 October 1947. In the event the festivals passed off quite peacefully in most parts of India, with unusual public fraternisation between Hindus and Muslims being reported from cities like Pune.

periodically from the countryside, moving from place to place in search of food, greater security or the hope of getting on a train to Pakistan.[65] In November, again with Gandhi's active intervention, and not without some expression of dissent, the All India Congress Committee reiterated its commitment to building a non-sectarian, democratic India in which there would be place for people of all faiths. 'India is a land of many religions and many races, and must remain so...' The Congress aim was unchanged, the Committee declared: to build a 'democratic secular State where all citizens enjoy full rights and are equally entitled to the protection of the State, irrespective of the religion to which they belong'.[66] But it was perhaps not till after the assassination of Gandhi that the Muslims of Delhi were accorded anything like full rights as Indian citizens, and the equation between 'Muslim' and 'refugee'/'alien' was seriously challenged.

A leader refuses his consent

One Delhi Muslim has likened Gandhi's arrival in Delhi on 9 September 1947 to the arrival of the rains after a particularly long and harsh summer. '*Sukhe dhanon mein pani pad gaya.*'[67] The Mahatma had had exceptional success in maintaining the peace between Hindus and Muslims in Calcutta, where a year earlier 4,000 or more people had been butchered on the city's streets within three days. Now many of Delhi's inhabitants looked to him to perform another miracle. 'Delhi will now be saved', 'the Muslims will now be saved', Muslims said to one another in the Old City, Shahid Ahmad Dehlavi records. The speeches that Gandhi made at his daily prayer meetings were broadcast on the radio. And – so we are told – from the day that Gandhi arrived in Delhi, no further instance of major rioting occurred, although stabbings continued and Muslim houses and shops continued to be raided.[68]

On 28 November 1947, on the occasion of Guru Nanak's birthday, when Gandhi went to address a meeting of Sikhs at Sisganj Gurdwara, he saw not one single Muslim on the road in Chandni Chowk, the heart of Old (Muslim) Delhi. 'What could be more shameful for us', he asked in his after prayer speech that evening, 'than the fact that not a single Muslim could be found in Chandni Chowk?' The only Muslim to be seen was

---

[65] (IOR) Mss. Eur. F200/52, minutes of meeting of the emergency committee of the Cabinet (31 October 1947); Mss. Eur. F200/190, summary for week ending 14 November 1947; Qidwai, *Azadi*, p. 277.
[66] *CWMG*, vol. XC (New Delhi, 1984), pp. 537–8.
[67] Dehlavi, *Dilli*, p. 156.
[68] *Ibid.*, pp. 156, 159.

Sheikh Abdullah, the leader of the popular movement in Kashmir, and he was sitting beside Gandhi in the car.[69] In December, Gandhi spoke out against the continued attempts of Hindu and Sikh refugees to occupy Muslim houses.[70] The police were now more active in seeking to protect Muslims and their property, but this was not the 'heart unity' that Gandhi spoke of and longed for.

'If there is comparative peace in Delhi...', the *Times* correspondent in Delhi wrote in early October, 'it is a peace based upon an intolerance which has succeeded in killing or driving out the minority almost to a man.'[71] It was good that because of the strong action taken by the government of India, people were no longer cutting each other's throats, Gandhi observed a fortnight later, 'but what of that?' 'There is [still] storm within the breast', he wrote two months later. 'I hear that even today [6 January 1948] people have been trying to get into the Muslim houses.' 'If it is our wish that Muslims should leave India [this on 20 December 1947], we should say so clearly or the government may declare that it will not be safe for Muslims to continue to live in India.'[72]

This was the context for the fast-unto-death that Gandhi commenced on 13 January 1948: 'I have no answer to return to the Muslim friends who see me from day to day as to what they should do.'[73] In the event, the fast, and Gandhi's subsequent martyrdom, did work something like a miracle. The demand for continued Partition, for the driving of every Muslim out of every part of Delhi, lost its immediate appeal; many Muslims were able to return to their homes and *mohallas*, and perhaps for the first time since late 1946, the people of Delhi began to return to the business of living and of rebuilding their lives, their uprooted city and their future.

The effect of Gandhi's fast was 'electric', wrote Azad. 'Groups which had till recently openly opposed Gandhiji came forward and said they would be prepared to do anything in order to save Gandhiji's precious life...' Qidwai in her turn writes of the 'contrition written on people's faces, a stoop in their walk, tears in their eyes': everywhere, she says, 'conversation was about Bapu's fast'.[74]

Jawaharlal Nehru, Arthur Moore (a former editor of *The Statesman*) and thousands of others, including a number of Hindu and Sikh refugees from Pakistan, decided to fast along with Gandhi, and broke their fasts

[69] *CWMG*, vol. XC, p. 127.
[70] *Ibid.*, pp. 358, 373.
[71] *The Times* (6 October 1947).
[72] *CWMG*, vol. LXXXIX, p. 366; vol. XC, pp. 408, 373, 266.
[73] *Ibid.*, p. 408.
[74] Azad, *India Wins Freedom*, p. 236; Qidwai, *Azadi*, p. 107.

only after Gandhi had given up his.[75] Outside Delhi too, the fast had a considerable impact: there were anxious enquiries about Gandhi's health even from across the border, and officers and ministers in the Pakistani government sought for ways to offer him support at this critical juncture.[76]

On the fifth day of the fast, 100,000 government employees, who had been to the fore in both pro-Pakistani and anti-Pakistani propaganda in Delhi since 1946, signed a pledge promising to work for peace and appealing to Gandhi to break his fast. The police signed a separate pledge.[77] Among others who had more or less openly opposed Gandhi up to this point, representatives of the RSS and the Hindu Mahasabha arrived with leaders of various Sikh and Muslim organisations, the Pakistani High Commissioner, and the chief commissioner and deputy commissioner of Delhi (who signed on behalf of the administration) to pledge their acceptance of the basic demands set out by Gandhi and to urge him to now break his fast.[78]

M. S. Randhawa, the deputy commissioner, who in the view of many observers had played a less than honourable part in the preceding weeks of violence, took a group of Hindu and Sikh leaders to begin repairs to the shrine of the Sufi saint Khwaja Qutubuddin Bakhtiar Chishti, near Mehrauli, which had been desecrated in September. Other local societies and peace committees took up the task of repairing damaged relations in their own areas, and a central peace committee was formed to coordinate moves to implement the written pledges given to Gandhi.[79] In the circumstances, Gandhi felt able to abandon his fast.

Twelve days later, he was assassinated. There had been another assassination attempt just a few days earlier – both the unsuccessful and successful attempts being the work of Hindu extremists, angered (like many other Hindus and Sikhs) at Gandhi's supposed 'concessions' to the Muslims and to Pakistan. However, the assassination had the contrary effect to what many observers – Indian and British, Muslim and Hindu and Sikh – had hoped or feared, which was a weakening of secular elements in the government and outside. Instead, the state moved quickly to take more direct and purposeful action against Hindu communalist forces and associations. The RSS was banned, at least for a while; many of its leaders were arrested; the rajas of Alwar, Bharatpur and other states which had aided and abetted, if not organised, the killing and persecution

---

[75] Azad, *India Wins Freedom*, p. 240; *CWMG*, vol. XC, pp. 449, 453.
[76] *Ibid.*, pp. 424, 447, 461.
[77] Qidwai, *Azadi*, p. 115.
[78] *CWMG*, vol. 90, pp. 444–5.
[79] *Ibid.*, p. 462n.; Azad, *India Wins Freedom*, p. 238.

of Muslims, were pulled into line.[80] Hindi newspapers and other sections of the Indian press that had been conspicuously silent about attacks
against Muslims on the Indian side of the border – in Punjab, Delhi,
Rajputana – now began to report the incidence of such violence much
more fully.[81]

Thus Gandhi achieved through his death even more than he had achieved through his fast. His success at this juncture conveys an unusual
message about the meaning of politics and the possibility of a new kind
of political community. It is an improbable story of how a certain kind of
bodily sacrifice in the public sphere – and a refusal by one outstanding
leader to give his consent to the particular conception of the political
community that was emerging – changed the nature of sociality at the
local level. Muslim recollections of the effect of Gandhi's martyrdom are
indeed extraordinary. '*Duniya hi badal gayi*', more than one Muslim who
was in Delhi at the time recalls. The assassination of Gandhi wiped out the
blaze of Hindu–Muslim violence in such a way that 'the world veritably
changed'. 'The fire of sectarian strife that had raged for months, or rather
years, died down as if such strife had never occurred . . . Overnight, such
calm was established, such a peace that one could not have dreamed
of even a few days earlier.' The Muslims of Delhi felt secure now and
'returned to their normal occupations and routines'.[82]

'*Musalmaan ab azadi se ghumne phirne lage the* [The Muslims were
now able to go around freely].' '*Sab kuch kho kar logon ko hosh aa raha
tha* [People returned to their senses when they had lost everything].'
'It was not only the administration and the atmosphere of Delhi that
changed – for [public] workers and for the ordinary people the world
itself changed.' 'Gandhiji made it possible for Muslims to continue to
live in India.'[83]

This was the context for the letters and messages that many of Delhi's
Muslims now sent to relatives and friends who had fled to Pakistan. 'There
is peace now, and no danger of riots . . . You should come back.'[84] The
assassination of Gandhi and the widespread reaction that it precipitated
against the cycle of senseless violence that the subcontinent had seen in

[80] (IOR) Mss. Eur. F200/2; *People's Age* (15 February 1948).
[81] (IOR) Mss. Eur. F164/31, Syed Azhar Husain Zaidi, 'The New Nazis' (n.p., n.d.).
[82] Barelvi, *Azadi*, p. 119.
[83] Qidwai, *Azadi*, pp. 162, 163, 278; interview with Qazi Jalil Abbasi, who made the last
quoted comment with tears in his eyes (Delhi, 31 January 1995). For other tributes,
from opponents as well as well-wishers, see (IOR) Mss. Eur. D621/15, Russell diaries,
entry for 31 January 1948; (IOR) Mss. Eur. D833/43, diary of Vincent Ellis Davies,
ICS (Bihar), entry for 31 January 1948; I. H. Qureshi, 'Social Relations', in Philips and
Wainright, eds., *Partition of India*, p. 368; and Pakistan Historical Society, *History of the
Freedom Movement*, vol. IV, p. 184.
[84] Dehlavi, *Dilli*, pp. 180, 147.

the preceding months, thus marked a turning point in the demand to carry Partition further and make Delhi – and by extension, India – an exclusively Hindu/Sikh territory.

Yet these developments could hardly make for a final resolution of the Muslim question in India.[85] On the contrary, the ghettoisation of Muslims was carried further, even as many Muslims returned to their homes in urban as well as rural areas. Numbers of Hindus and Sikhs continued to express their resentment at the Indian government's encouragement to Muslims to return to their homes and villages, even from Pakistan, when the fate of the lives and properties of the non-Muslims who remained in Pakistan was still uncertain. And there is evidence to suggest that for a long time after January 1948, many of Delhi's Muslims remained estranged, sitting ready to escape to Pakistan at the first recrudescence of trouble.[86]

Exile – at home or abroad

In spite of the fondness with which some of Delhi's Muslims recalled the community that was once Delhi, great numbers – indeed nearly all of the city's Muslim community – were a besieged, demoralised and terrified lot by August–September 1947. Curfews, which had begun to be imposed much earlier, now seemed interminable. When curfew was lifted for a few hours, there was a desperate rush for supplies. Food and other necessities soon ran out. Black-marketing and cheating increased. People began selling whatever they had in their possession and searched for alternative sources of sustenance. Poorer Muslims even began to sell, and to eat, their pet sheep, goats and ponies. Muslims discovered too, as we have noticed, that the local police had turned against them, or were at best indifferent. We have one account of the anguished rethinking that flowed from these experiences in Shahid Ahmad Dehlavi's *Dilli ki bipta*.[87]

Hindu neighbours had reassured Muslims in the Old City that, come what may, they would defend their Muslim brothers and sisters to the last. In many instances they did. Dehlavi provides a touching example of

---

[85] The history of the 1980s and '90s would give the lie to that, if nothing else did.

[86] Every Muslim who could afford it wanted to get away to Pakistan somehow, Anees Qidwai noted in July 1948; Qidwai, *Azadi*, p. 268. For the special 'Muslim zones' informally established in Delhi in 1948, so that Muslims might feel relatively more secure, see *ibid.*, pp. 200, 209–10; for Muslims returning to their villages, *ibid.*, pp. 169, 192, and Hasan, *Legacy*, p. 171. The change in Muslim dreams in subsequent years is stressed in my interviews with Mohammad Asif Usmani and Syed Mahmud 'Ramz' (Allahabad, 15 October 1994).

[87] The preceding paragraph draws heavily from Dehlavi's account. Page references for the quotations that follow are provided in the text.

this in his description of events in Khari Baoli, a predominantly Hindu *mohalla*, where his mother lived with a handful of other Muslims. In the late 1930s, Dehlavi had bought a house near the Jama Masjid and moved into it. But his family still owned two houses in Khari Baoli. His mother lived in one (the *zanana ghar*), and Dehlavi maintained his press and office in the other, two doors away.

'*Jab Dilli mein hangama hua . . .*': when the disturbances broke out in the Old City on 5 September,[88] a bomb was thrown at the Fatehpuri Mosque, crowds gathered, the police opened fire, one or two people were killed and several injured in the exchange, local militias formed on both sides, slogans were raised and people ran helter-skelter, Dehlavi was caught in his office in Khari Baoli. Amidst rising tension, he and his co-workers managed to escape through back-ways and alleys that they knew well. But they breathed freely again only when they reached the point from where Muslim habitation started. '*Bas us din se aaj tak dobara Khari Baoli jaana naseeb nahin hua.*' Dehlavi had hoped to return to his office within a day or two, at least to sort out some urgent papers, but 'from that day to this, I have never had the fortune of going back to Khari Baoli'.[89]

When Dehlavi and his colleagues fled from the Hindu locality of Khari Baoli on 5 September, his mother refused to leave. Conditions worsened in the following days, however, and relatives forcibly took her away to the nearby Muslim area of Farash Khana. The very next day, Hindu elders of Khari Baoli went to Farash Khana and pleaded with the old lady to return to her home; for her departure amounted to a slur upon them and upon the whole *mohalla*. No one would be allowed to touch a hair of her head as long as they lived, they declared. '*Jab tak hamari jaan mein jaan hai, aap par anch nahin aa sakti*' (147). Upon this, Dehlavi's mother returned to Khari Baoli. She was still living there, along with his younger brothers and sisters, when he wrote his memoir some time after he and his immediate family had moved to Pakistan.

This indeed was part of the context for Dehlavi's bitter reflections on how he left his native city. His mother and his siblings, the family property, his work, his home, all were in Delhi. '*Dilli mujhse bhala kaise chhoot sakegi?*' 'How would I ever be able to leave Delhi?' he had asked himself. Through the frightening weeks of July and August 1947, Dehlavi exhorted the people of his locality to stay put, in spite of news and rumours of impending adversity, reassuring them in whatever way he could. But then, as the curfews lengthened, the shouts of arsonists and looters drew nearer, food and water became scarce, the streets and houses grew smaller, and

---

[88] The details here are taken from Dehlavi, *Dilli*; and (NAI) Home Poll (I), file 5/26/47.
[89] Dehlavi, *Dilli*, p. 151.

the sense of suffocation reduced the possibility of rest or sleep, people of the *mohalla* began to slip away quietly, making their way to the Old Fort or wherever else they might find security.

One day, not long afterwards, Dehlavi and his family left too – with whatever belongings they could quickly pile onto a truck. People in the *mohalla* remarked, '*Babuji bhi chale*'; and 'I walked with my head bowed, guiltily, like a criminal'(164). They went to the Old Fort refugee camp where conditions were, if anything, worse than where they had come from: 60,000 or more people crowded into the grounds, with a handful of tents to accommodate a few lucky ones; one tap with running water, as the writer describes it; no provision for lights, lavatories or bathrooms, and heavy rains to compound the conditions of dirt and disorder (165).

It is noteworthy that Ebadat Barelvi and Ishtiaq Husain Qureshi, writing their memoirs in two different tongues, Urdu and English respectively, should use exactly the same metaphor for the Delhi they left behind in 1947–8. The penultimate chapter of Barelvi's *Azadi ke saaye mein* is titled '*Rukhsat-i-Zindaan*' ('Liberation from the Prison House'). The city of Delhi had become 'a prison for the Muslims', writes Qureshi.

Qidwai personalises the city with another metaphor of devastation. '*Aktubar–Navambar ki Dilli ek khoon mein lithdi hui laash thi . . .* [The Delhi of October–November [1947] was a corpse bathed in blood, over which hundreds of vultures and kites continued to hover . . .]'. '*Purana Qila hashr ka maidan bana hua tha* [At the Old Fort, it was as if Judgement Day was at hand],' wrote Dehlavi.[90]

Liberation from this place of incarceration and death became the primary concern of very large numbers of Muslims. Many who could leave the city or the country did so – among them, Ebadat Barelvi, Ishtiaq Husain Qureshi and Shahid Ahmad Dehlavi. But the mortification of being hounded out, hunted and humiliated remained, for them as for those who did not have the resources or the connections to take them very far.

Indeed, the man whom Dehlavi likens at one point to the coming of the rains on a parched field – '*sukhe dhanon mein pani pad gaya*' – appears in a far less favourable light in his more detailed ruminations. When Gandhi visited the Jama Masjid on 12 September, the news of his impending visit spread among the Muslims like wildfire. Thousands of them assembled to see him, and there was no chance of offering prayers in the mosque. There was a great commotion as soon as Gandhi arrived. The assembled Muslims cried themselves hoarse, shouting 'Mahatma Gandhi *zindabad!*'

---

[90] Qureshi, 'Social Relations', in Philips and Wainright, eds., *Partition of India*, p. 367; Qidwai, *Azadi*, p. 22; Dehlavi, *Dilli*, p. 165.

'At that moment', writes Dehlavi, people even forgot Allah: 'They looked on Gandhiji himself as the Omnipotent (*Qadir-i-mutlaq*)' (160). Such were the straits to which Delhi's Muslims had been reduced.

Gandhi himself stayed but a few minutes and said only a few words, because of the disorganisation, Dehlavi's sarcastic account states further. However, his post-prayer speeches were broadcast on the radio every day. In these he repeatedly pronounced the Muslims guilty of atrocities in West Punjab, of abducting Hindu and Sikh women, and much more. Having said this, he asked Hindus and Sikhs in Delhi to show their moral strength by not seeking revenge and urged the Muslims to 'surrender all their weapons' and live as loyal Indian citizens (159–60).[91] 'For all that, the coming of Gandhiji did restore some calm among the Muslims', the writer observes, adding caustically, 'he even provided them some support. For example, he inspected their camps and advised them to construct and clean their own lavatories...' (160). The bitterness revealed here was, of course, accentuated by everything that Dehlavi and his fellow Muslims went through at the refugee camp in Delhi, and afterwards.

Within days of their arrival at the Purana Qila, as soon as they were able to obtain seats on a train to Pakistan, Dehlavi and his family escaped from the refugee camp, from Delhi, and from India. The details of that train journey to Pakistan are no less harrowing than Dehlavi's account of the conditions they had left behind: 125 passengers crowded into a compartment meant to seat thirty-two; no lighting or water; practically no chance of replenishing any supplies at stations on the way; attacks at one point; panic and terror and suffocation; what should have been an overnight journey taking all of forty-eight hours, which seemed to stretch endlessly.

The train ran the gauntlet, as the writer recalls it, from Nizamuddin station in Delhi to Meerut and Muzaffarnagar, Deoband and Rajpura, Ludhiana, Jalandhar, Amritsar and a couple of smaller stations before they reached Pakistan. Hindus and Sikhs were milling around at every stop, but there were practically no Muslims to be seen. At Meerut, the military guard did not let anyone disembark to get water, saying that it could well have been poisoned. At Amritsar and Beas stations, water was gushing out at full force from taps on the platform. However, the passengers were kept inside the train; there were thousands of Sikh and Hindu refugees at these stations, and a Sikh guard said sternly (if wisely), '*Yeh Amritsar hai* [This is Amritsar].'

Just before Ludhiana the train had screeched to a halt: and the passengers were locked in for over an hour, with all the doors and windows

---

[91] Gandhi's speeches, as reported in his *Collected Works* and other accounts, in fact appear to me more cautious and anguished, but this is how Dehlavi recalls them.

shut, while the troops guarding the train – and reinforcements apparently rushed from Ludhiana – fought off an attack by 'thousands' of armed men. In the course of the attack, three carriages were almost completely emptied: they arrived in Ludhiana laden only with corpses and a few grievously injured people. Hundreds had attempted to flee from the train, Dehlavi adds: they should also be counted among the dead.

The Muslims on the train breathed again only when they reached Jatto, the first station in Pakistani territory. '*Murdon mein jaan aa gayi.*' Hundreds of people were waiting here, to greet them with slogans of 'Pakistan *zindabad*' and generous supplies of drinking water and food – *roti, dal* and *achar.*[92]

Six months after his journey to Lahore, Dehlavi was to return to his native Delhi, with curiously mixed feelings of happiness and sorrow ('*Ajeeb tarah ki khushi aur ajeeb tarah ka gham tha*') (185). Many of Delhi's Muslims were by this time returning to Delhi from Pakistan, having heard of the restoration of peace, he recalls. But there were no houses left for them. The streets and the markets had been captured by refugee Hindus and Sikhs; and a Muslim seemed out of place even in the act of withdrawing money from a bank (182).

The Muslims of Delhi lived in fear, he observed. They trusted no one and spoke in whispers, constantly on the lookout for informers. Muslims were considered anti-national, which is to say, anti-Indian. Large numbers had been, and were being, arrested. Seeking to hide their Muslimness, some – especially younger – men had shaved off their beards. The few Muslim shopkeepers still in business tried to protect themselves by hiring Hindu and Sikh agents and workers (188–9). It was difficult to breathe freely.

Dehlavi's experience – of breathing freely for the first time, and tasting their first morsel of food for days, on reaching the safety of their own people – is recounted by many other Partition migrants, Muslim, Hindu and Sikh, travelling both east and west.[93] The feeling of security, and the revival of spirits that came with the thought that they were now on their own 'national' soil, is a common theme in the migrants' recollections. So is the memory of an all-engulfing aggression and counter-aggression. 'In those two and a half hours when we first heard that Dinanagar had become part of Pakistan, the Muslims began to kill the Hindus', as Maya Rani, a Dalit woman, recalls. 'And then two and a half hours later there was a phone call which said that no, Dinanagar hadn't gone to Pakistan, it

---

[92] The above account is based on *Dilli*, pp. 169–78.
[93] This feeling was expressed in numerous interviews I had with Partition migrants. See also Ebadat Barelvi's recollections cited in n. 52 above.

was part of Hindustan. And in this time the tide was reversed and Hindus began to kill Musalmaans . . . '[94]

The Sikh military guard's warning to Dehlavi and his Muslim co-passengers, '*Yeh Amritsar hai*', is matched by Bhishma Sahni's physically unimpressive Hindu *babu* fleeing the other way, who is transformed into a marauding wolf as soon as his train nears Amritsar: '*Amritsar aa gaya*.'[95] The same kind of account of immediate vengeance is provided by other refugees travelling in either direction – towards Pakistan or towards India. Dehlavi's train journey ends at Lahore where, he recounts, sections of the waiting crowd proceeded at once to determine whether the train had been attacked and how many had been killed or wounded. They then promised summary justice. 'Wait!' they said, according to Dehlavi, 'we shall settle scores right now, in your presence': and, stopping a refugee special going the other way at Baghbanpura station just outside Lahore, they paid back the killers of eastern Punjab in their own coin – 'with interest'.[96]

Millions of people became 'refugees' in the subcontinent in 1947–8 and the years that followed, some moving to another country, some not moving very far or indeed leaving their homes at all. The point of arrival for many of the latter was, in a physical sense, no different from the point of departure: but in a physical sense alone. Thousands of others were abducted and had to wipe out all signs of an earlier life to survive in a new one. The Muslims who stayed on in India, like the Hindus who stayed on in Pakistan (large numbers of them in its eastern wing), now constituted a 'minority' problem. The abducted persons who remained on the ' wrong' side of the international border constituted a different sort of problem – conceived of as impurity, or theft, or both. What would be the place of these people in the new dispensations of India and Pakistan (and, after 1971, Bangladesh)?

---

[94] See Butalia, *Other Side of Silence*, pp. 257–8.
[95] See Bhishma Sahni's '*Amritsar aa gaya*', in *Kitne toba Tek Singh. Bharat vibhajan ki das kahaniyan* (Delhi, 1987).
[96] Dehlavi, *Dilli*, pp. 176–7.

7   Disciplining difference

A nation is constructed not only as a bureaucratic, state-oriented community, but also as a moral one. That is what gives nationalisms their
greater or lesser appeal and staying power. What constitutes this moral
community? What gives us the right to call ourselves 'Indians'? 'Are we
entitled to claim the status of true citizens, who have sacrificed family,
caste, community and religion in the name of the nation?' as one newspaper asked in September 1947.[1]

The point I want to begin with here is the simple one of the unrealisable
quality of the nationalist search for clarity and 'purity' in the midst of the
blurring, mixing and uncertainty that is the actually existing condition
of all nations and nationalisms. Nations everywhere have claimed to be
defined by well-marked cultural–political boundaries. Yet, such boundaries are never easily drawn. Nationalist thought, therefore, commonly
proceeds to carve out a core or 'mainstream' – the unhyphenated national, the real, obvious, 'natural' citizen (Indian, Nigerian, Australian,
American, British, whatever). Alongside this core, there emerge notions
of the hyphenated 'national' (Indian Muslims, Indian Christians, Indian
Jews, or African-Americans, Mexican Americans and Indigenous Americans): minorities and marginal groups that might be part of the nation,
but 'never quite'.[2]

How do nationalists set out to cleanse the sacred space of the nation –
of Pakistan (the 'Pure Land') or 'Mother India'? How are 'impure'
elements to be dealt with? How do we contain, or discipline, difference? The question was posed sharply in the case of the Muslim

---

[1] *Vartman* (14 September 1947), editorial. (I am grateful to Saumya Gupta for giving me
access to her photocopies of the files of this newspaper.)
[2] Brackette F. Williams makes the point as follows in her discussion of ethnicity in the
context of territorial and cultural nationalism. Like tribe, race, or barbarian, she notes,
the label ethnicity identifies those who are at the borders of empire or nation. 'Within
putatively homogenous nation-states, this border is an ideologically produced boundary
between "mainstream" and peripheral categorical units of this kind of "imagined" social
order'; Williams, 'A Class Act', p. 439.

'minority' in India, as well as in that of 'abducted persons', at the time of Partition.[3]

The search for a one-nation nation

August 1947 was the date of establishment of two new nation-states, India and Pakistan. But it was also, as we have seen (and here the date is distinctly less clear-cut), the moment of the congealing of new identities, relations and histories, or of their being thrown into question once again. What made Partition and Independence particularly bitter was that neither of the two new states turned out to be what its proponents had hoped for. Pakistan has perhaps had the more anguished history in this respect. It had been proposed as a Muslim homeland, the country of the Muslim nation of the subcontinent. There was always going to be some doubt about the ethnic and even territorial basis of this religiously defined nation. For there was never any suggestion that the ninety million Muslims of undivided India – spread out all over that territory, with Muslim-majority regions existing in north-western and north-eastern India and in pockets (towns and sub-districts) elsewhere – could all be accommodated, or even wish to migrate, to the areas that became Pakistan.

When Mohammad Ali Jinnah articulated his conception of a secular, multi-religious Pakistan in his famous speech at the inaugural session of the Constituent Assembly of Pakistan, on 11 August 1947, the proposition produced bewilderment among many of his followers. 'How could Muslims cease to be Muslims and Hindus cease to be Hindus in the political sense when the religions... were, in Jinnah's passionately held belief, so utterly different from one another? Was Jinnah giving up the two-nation theory...?' one Pakistani commentator was to ask later.[4] On 21 October 1947, in a letter to the *Civil and Military Gazette*, Muhammad Sa'adat Ali of Lahore protested against a minister's statement that Pakistan was 'a secular, democratic and not a theocratic state'. Such a statement 'has absolutely no support of the Muslims', he wrote.

Ever since Mr. Jinnah undertook to fight our case, he has on occasions without number, proclaimed emphatically that Muslims were determined to set up a

---

[3] For a discussion of the terms 'majority' and 'minority', especially in their Indian usage, see my 'Can a Muslim be an Indian?'

[4] Burki, *Pakistan. A Nation in the Making*, p. 42; cf. Stanley Wolpert, *Jinnah of Pakistan* (New York, 1984), pp. 339–40. To confuse matters even further, Jinnah's speech referred to a 'nation of 400 million souls', implying that all of British India's 400 million people belonged to one nation, among whom the question had been one of the appropriate distribution of power – see A. G. Noorani, 'The Cabinet Mission and its Aftermath', in Philips and Wainright, eds., *Partition of India*, p. 105.

state organised and run in accordance with the irresistible dictates of the Islamic *Shariat*...If secularisation were our sole aim, India need not have been partitioned...We raised this storm for partition because we wanted to live as free Muslims and organise a state on Islamic principles...[5]

On the Indian side, too, Partition and Independence gave rise to an intense debate about what the character of the new nation-state should be: secular (which was to say multi-community, with equal rights for all)? socialist? Hindu? Pakistan emerged, after the long drawn-out moment of Partition, with its communal holocaust and forced migrations, as an overwhelmingly Muslim country, especially in its western half. As they saw this happening, sections of the Hindu nationalist press in India observed that Pakistan was on its way to establishing an '*ekjatiya rashtra*' (literally, a 'one-nation nation', or a homogenous, one-people nation), and lamented that India might never be able to achieve the same kind of unity (or homogeneity). Substantial sections of the north Indian population – especially Hindu and Sikh refugees from West Pakistan and those most directly affected by their influx – and sections of the political leadership – especially the Hindu right wing and leaders of the Sikh community – also demanded that India (or at least some parts of it, like East Punjab, Delhi and the neighbouring districts of western UP where Hindu and Sikh refugees had flooded in the weeks before and after 15 August 1947), should be cleared of Muslims: the latter should be sent to Pakistan, and the territory handed over to the Sikhs and Hindus.

Nationalism necessarily raises the question of who belongs and by what criterion. In India, in 1947, this took the peculiar form of the 'Muslim question': can a Muslim be an Indian?

The natural nation

The figure of the 'nationalist Muslim' will serve as a useful starting point for our discussion of this question. The first point to be made is that there is no equivalent category for the Hindus or, for that matter, any of the other religious groupings in India. Interestingly, in speaking of the politics of Hindus, the term is frequently reversed to read 'Hindu nationalists'. The reversal is of course not coincidental. What does the term 'Hindu nationalists' signify? It does not refer simply to nationalists who happen to be Hindus. It is, rather, an indication of their brand of nationalism, a brand in which the 'Hindu' moment has considerable weight. It is a nationalism in which Hindu culture, Hindu traditions and the Hindu community are given pride of place.

---

[5] *Civil and Military Gazette* (21 October 1947).

Alongside the rise of this Hindu nationalism, and much more emphatically in the course of time, another more inclusive kind of nationalism
had developed, which emphasised the composite character of Indian society and refused to give the same sort of primacy to the Hindu element in India's history and self-consciousness. This is what would later
come to be termed 'secular' nationalism, 'real' or 'Indian' nationalism as
Jawaharlal Nehru called it, 'something quite apart from . . . [the] religious
and communal varieties of nationalism and strictly speaking . . . the only
form which can be called nationalism in the modern sense of the word'.[6]
This was the 'nationalism' of the Indian constitution – 'nationalism', pure
and simple, in Nehru's phrase. Given the existence of both these brands of
nationalism from the late nineteenth century onwards, and so evidently
in the 1940s and again in the 1980s and 1990s, politically conscious
Hindus have readily been divided into 'Hindu nationalists' and 'secular
(or Indian) nationalists'.

There were of course signs of a growing 'Muslim' nationalism over the
same period. Like Hindu nationalism, this Muslim variant developed side
by side with the broader 'Indian' nationalist movement, in which large
numbers of Muslims were also involved (including leading figures like
Badruddin Tyabji and Maulana Mohamed Ali; Mohammad Ali Jinnah
and Fazl-ul-Haq; Mukhtar Ahmad Ansari, Abul Kalam Azad, Zakir
Husain and Sheikh Abdullah). However, politically active Muslims were
not divided into 'Muslim nationalists' and 'secular nationalists'. They
were divided instead into 'nationalist Muslims' and 'Muslims' – and here
the proposition extended of course to more than just those who were
politically involved.

The Hindus – or the majority of politically conscious Hindus, for there
were in this view many who formed part of a large inert mass, and at
least a few who were loyalists – were, in other words, nationalists first and
foremost. Whether they were Hindu nationalists or secular nationalists
was a subsidiary question. All Muslims were, however, Muslims. And
the matter of political inactivity or inertia made little difference in this instance. Some Muslims were advocates of 'Indian' nationalism, and hence
'nationalist Muslims'. The remainder of that community, however – in
town and country, north and south, handloom workshop or sugarcane
field, modest hut or railway quarters – were not likely to be supporters
of Indian nationalism, on account of their being Muslim. The peculiar
history of Hindu–Muslim political differences from the later nineteenth
century onwards, and British efforts to keep the Muslims on their side
against the rising tide of what they saw as *babu*, Hindu nationalism, had

[6] J. Nehru, *Glimpses of World History*, vol. II (1934; 2nd edn, Bombay, 1961), pp. 1129–30.

contributed to the development of this view. But the years immediately preceding Partition and Independence, Partition itself, and the very fact of agitation for separate Muslim rights, clearly had more than a little to do with its wide acceptance as an axiomatic truth.

An editorial published in the Kanpur Hindi daily, *Vartman*, in October 1947, provides a very good illustration of 'majoritarian' nationalist thinking on this issue.[7] 'Whose country is this?' the editors ask in their opening line; and answer: 'All those who can call India their native land (*swadesh*) in the real sense of the term, this country is theirs.' They then proceed to spell out how the Buddhists and Jains, Sikhs, Christians, Anglo-Indians, and Parsis all belong in India, because they think of it as their native land. Persecuted in early times, some Hindus became Buddhist and Jains. 'However, they did not change their nationality [*sic*]. They did not leave the country. They did not start calling themselves Chinese or Japanese.' Similarly, a Sikh *panth* (community or tradition) arose. 'This Sikh community also recognizes India as their *janmabhumi* [land of their birth] and therefore their country.'

The analysis so far is simple. The Buddhists (even though they have practically disappeared from the land of the Buddha), Jains and Sikhs treated India as the land of their birth because this is where they and their religious traditions were born. They are, in that sense, 'original', 'natural' Indians. The argument shifts in the case of the other small religious (and racial) groupings – the Christians, Anglo-Indians and Parsis. Many of the lowest castes and classes had embraced Christianity in recent times, the editorial noted, to escape the worst oppressions of untouchability, as much as anything else. 'Yet they did not forget that they could never go and settle in Europe; [they knew that] India would always be their country.'

The Anglo-Indians had, on the other hand, remained ambivalent for some time. They were, after all, Eurasian, both English and Indian by blood, and many of them had sought to migrate (as they would continue to do during the 1950s and to some extent later). But there were two points that went in their favour, as *Vartman* saw it. First, their numbers were never very great. Secondly, the departing British had left them to fend for themselves: '. . . they came to their senses as soon as the British left' and recognised India as their native land.

These propositions are both patronising and contradictory. The Indian Christians could not dream of settling in Europe. The Anglo-Indians did dream of it, but were left high and dry by the departing colonial rulers. In any case, the two communities were numerically small and quite widely

---

[7] *Vartman* (12 October 1947).

dispersed. They had no other country to go to and they constituted no threat to the nation or its culture. India could therefore be treated as their native land.

The logic is different in the case of the Parsis. They came to the country from Iran, but as refugees fleeing to save their lives, not as aggressors or missionaries. Nor did they give up their religion, culture or 'language' on settling here. 'Nevertheless, many of them have contributed to the economic, intellectual, social and political development of India like true citizens.' This is a line of reasoning with which we are not unfamiliar. Wealthy Japanese business people and Arab sheikhs are welcome in England, the United States and Australia because they contribute to the 'economic' and 'intellectual' development of these areas: not so the Bradford Muslims or Sikhs of Southall, the Mexican casual labourers or Vietnamese boat-people. That was what went in favour of the Parsis in India: they were a small, almost a microscopic minority, and because of the fairly privileged economic and social position they enjoyed in places like Bombay, many of them had – 'like true citizens', as it was said – contributed to the economic, intellectual, social and political development of India.

The situation of the Muslims of India was another matter altogether. Over the centuries, the immigration of small groups of Muslims had been supplemented by conversion to Islam on a fairly large scale, so that there were now ninety million Muslims in the subcontinent, 25 per cent of the total population of undivided India. The majority of these Muslims had come from the depressed classes of the Hindu population, the paper acknowledged: they had become Muslims to escape from the extreme sanctions and disabilities of the caste system. However, resisting the oppressiveness of the Hindu caste system was one thing, and shedding one's 'national' culture, religion, language and dress another.

Flesh and blood of the Hindus though they were, these Hindavi Muslims came to think of themselves as belonging to the Arab and Mughal communities [or nations, since the term *jati* can refer to either] . . . Rulers like Aurangzeb, and later on the British, never tired of preaching that they [the Muslims] have been the governors of this country, and that their direct links are with Arabia, Persia, and Turkey. Their language, appearance, religion, and practices are all different from those of the Hindus.

The *Vartman* editorial refers to the tyranny and destructiveness of the Muslim invaders. It adds that the local converts had been no less fanatical, attacking Hindu temples, images and religious processions, and making a point of sacrificing the cow at the Baqr Id precisely because the cow was sacred to the Hindus. But these sweeping generalisations are by way of a rhetorical flourish: well-known propositions that serve only to underline the basic argument that the Muslims of India are (or may be suspected of being) alien, because 'when they changed their religion, they also dreamt up schemes of changing their country'. 'They did not think of the [other] people living in India as their own. They thought of the local language [as if there were only one!] as foreign. They cut themselves off from Indian civilization and culture . . . '

In the course of the anti-colonial struggle, the argument goes on, when people of every other community joined in a common fight for freedom, the Muslims stood in the way. They made separatist demands, played into the hands of the British and were rewarded, finally, with the prize of Pakistan – from where Hindus were now being driven out. Many Indian Muslims had earlier tried to migrate to Persia, Arabia, Mesopotamia and Turkey, only to return disappointed. Today, 'if there was place in Pakistan, if there were agricultural lands, jobs, and if they had their way, [these Muslims] would undoubtedly go and settle there'. On other occasions, the editors of *Vartman* had declared that Pakistan was like Mecca, like paradise even, for every Indian Muslim, and Jinnah was like their Prophet.

Now, on 12 October 1947, the editorial continued: large numbers of Muslims had already gone to settle in Pakistan, and many more were waiting to go. As for the rest, who had decided to stay back, did they show signs of willingness to live in peace with the other communities of India – 'Sikh, Jain, Buddhists, Christians, Parsis and Anglo-Indians'? 'These machine-guns, mortars, rifles, pistols, bombs, dynamite, swords, spears and daggers, that are being discovered daily [in Muslim houses and localities], are all these being collected for the defense of India?' There was simply not enough place for all of these Muslims in Pakistan; and the fact that many stayed on in India was no reason to think of them automatically as Indian.

It would be a waste of time to point out all the errors of fact and the blatant half-truths that pepper *Vartman*'s analysis of the Muslim condition.[8] There is one feature of the statement, however, that requires specific noting. At some stage in this articulation of the conditions of citizenship, an

---

[8] In connection with the proposition that the 'language, appearance, religion and practices' of the Muslims were 'all different' from those of the Hindus, I might note only that all the Indian Muslims I know or have heard of speak the Bengali, Gujarati, Marathi, Malayalam, Punjabi, Hindi, Urdu (or to break the vernaculars down further, the Awadhi, Bhojpuri, Magahi) of their regions. I should add that Urdu – designated the language of the Indian Muslims, which is also my language and the language of very large numbers of Hindus and Sikhs of my parents' and grandparents' generation – whatever else it might be, is not a foreign language, but distinctively Indian (or, now, subcontinental). And just as Indian intellectuals claim, with considerable justification, that English too is now one of the languages of India, one would also have to assert that Islam is now (and has long been) one of the religions of India.

argument about culture gives way almost imperceptibly to an argument about politics — or, more precisely, about political power. The Anglo-Indians, unable to attain the numerical strength of the Muslims, never constituted a threat. The Parsis remained different in religion, culture and language too, according to the paper, but they had contributed significantly to our political, economic, intellectual and social development. The Muslims had, on the other hand, put forward their own, separatist demands and had stood in the way of the united struggle against the British. They had not accepted our conception of India: they were therefore not Indians.

There is another important aspect of this articulation. It is noteworthy that in the entire analysis, the Hindus appear only a couple of times, in passing, as the people from whom the Muslims sought to differentiate themselves. An editorial that elaborates the character and place of the different religious communities of India in answer to the question, 'Whose country is this?', does not even feel the need to mention the Hindu community as a separate constituent of the nation. For the Hindus are not a constituent. They *are* the nation, the 'we' who demand cooperation from the minorities, the 'us' that the Muslims have to learn to live with.

There was a touching moment in the Constituent Assembly debates on the question of minority rights when Frank Anthony, the leader of the assembly's Anglo-Indians, referred to a comment sometimes made to him that, if he was as strongly committed to India as he claimed to be, he should drop the prefix 'Anglo' from the name of his community. Anthony's response was that, 'good or bad', 'rightly or wrongly', the word 'Anglo-Indian' 'connotes to me many things which I hold dear'. He went further, however: 'I will drop it readily, as soon as you drop your label . . . The day you drop the label of "Hindu", the day you forget that you are a Hindu, that day – no, two days before that – I will drop by deed poll, by beat of drum if necessary, the prefix Anglo . . . ' That day, he added, 'will be welcome first and foremost to the minorities of India'.[9]

The Anglo-Indian leader's argument was logical, but misplaced. It would have appeared meaningless to many Hindus, who did not have to use the designation 'Hindu' in any case. At Partition and for a long time afterwards, they were the silent majority. They did not need to advertise the fact that they were Hindus: for some time after the assassination of Gandhi by a Hindu extremist, it was even a little difficult for the more militant among them to do so. Inasmuch as they were Hindu, they were automatically Indian. It was enough in this age of high nationalism to claim the latter designation. The question of what it meant to be a

---

[9] *Constituent Assembly Debates, Official Report*, vol. VIII (16 May to 16 June 1949), p. 271.

Hindu, what advantages such a classification brought to the lower castes and classes, and whether the Hindus as a whole were disprivileged, was not to be taken up in a sustained way until the 1980s or '90s.[10]

To have given greater political visibility to the category of the 'Hindus' at the moment of nationalist triumph in the 1940s would have meant running the risk of differentiating and problematising it, and of having to recognise that history and culture and naturalness are not uncontested. To present an argument about *belonging* as a political argument would be to concede that the nation was a *political* project, first and foremost, and to acknowledge its historicity. The progress of the nation could not mean exactly the same thing to all parts of that imagined community. To acknowledge this, however, would be to foreground the question of political power and to what end that power should be used – which in turn would defeat the nationalist claim that the nation was a natural moral community.

The needs of a modern state

For all that, even 'natural' nations must have their own states, and the needs of modern statehood must not be compromised. In this respect, too, the non-natural citizen could be a problem. The disciplining of difference was a necessity.

Everywhere, we would argue, the nation/people has historically come into being through struggles to define and advance a national interest. Everywhere, however, there is a simultaneous – and it seems almost necessary – desire to present the nation as given, an already formed totality, even a spirit or essence. Everywhere, moreover, once the nation comes to have a state of its own or (in nationalist parlance) to be realised in the nation-state, this essence, this totality, comes to be concretised in the state and its territory. The national interest comes to be equated with the integrity of the state and its boundaries; and the preservation of the latter comes to be proclaimed the primary concern of the nation.

The governance of the modern state is rooted in knowledge practices that enable the state to produce new technologies of order through technologies of objectification – statistics, budgetary models, a strong army – that embody certain rationalities and produce ever-expanding horizons for regulation.[11] These techniques of government provide vital inputs to the political imagination of 'nationalist' parties and pressure groups.

[10] Ambedkar and other Dalit leaders had of course already initiated a significant debate about the relevance of the category 'Hindu' for their followers; and similar questions had been raised in connection with the *adivasis* (literally 'original inhabitants', used for various tribal peasant groups in India) in the work of anthropologists like G. S. Ghurye and Verrier Elwin.

[11] For a fuller discussion of this point, see my *Construction of Communalism*, ch. 3 and *passim*.

'Non-violence is of no use under the present circumstances in India', as Major-General K. M. Cariappa, deputy chief of the Indian army staff, declared in October 1947; only a strong army could make India 'one of the greatest nations in the world'.[12] Durga Das, a young correspondent of the pro-Congress *Hindustan Times*, went further, demanding the building of a strong state (through the liquidation of 'enemy pockets') and a strong army on the Nazi model.[13] Nathuram Godse, Gandhi's assassin, put it no less plainly in explaining his opposition to Gandhi: India needed to become a modern nation, 'practical, able to retaliate, and ... powerful with the armed forces'.[14] For this purpose Gandhian notions of non-violence and turning the other cheek were simply of no use.

It was in the midst of this growing statist militancy that Sampurnanand, then education minister in the Congress government of UP, wrote of the needs of the new India, two weeks before official Partition and Independence. If, 'God forbid', there was ever a war between India and Pakistan, 'our worries will be greatly increased, for it is not impossible that the sympathies of our Muslim population will veer towards Pakistan'.[15] The fear expressed here grew in strength in the weeks and months that followed, as Partition worked itself out and large numbers of Indian Muslims were pushed into a corner. Indeed the political history of India for some time afterwards, and some might say until today, has in no small part been the history of a struggle to control this fear.

In the later months of 1947, a wide range of India's nationalist leaders began to focus on the issues that Sampurnanand had raised – war, and loyalty in war. The renowned Socialist leader, Dr Ram Manohar Lohia, speaking at a public meeting in Delhi on 11 October 1947, urged the people to 'rally round the Nehru Government and make it strong enough to take, when necessary, effective measures against the Pakistan Government'. This was an appeal to all communal forces, Hindu, Muslim and Sikh, and to those who harboured doubts about the government's declared secular platform. But three days earlier, at another rally in Delhi, Lohia pointedly asked India's Muslims to 'surrender arms and ... be loyal citizens of India, ready to fight, if need be, against Pakistan or any other country'.[16]

---

12 *The Statesman* (29 October 1947).
13 *The Hindustan Times* (28 September 1947), cited in *People's Age* (12 October 1947).
14 Cited in Ashish Nandy, *At the Edge of Psychology. Essays in Politics and Culture* (Delhi, 1980), p. 91.
15 *Vartman* (30 July 1947).
16 *The Statesman* (9 and 12 October 1947). At the end of September, at a public meeting of prominent citizens addressed by Gandhi, one person declared that 'the citizens of Delhi [*sic*] were ready to live in peace with the Muslims provided they were loyal to the Union and surrendered all arms and ammunition which they possessed without a license', *ibid.* (2 October 1947).

At the same time, Govind Ballabh Pant, Congress chief minister of Uttar Pradesh – accomplished parliamentarian, able administrator and a man of large, secular, human sympathies – was driving home the same point in Allahabad. Indian Muslims should 'realize clearly' what loyalty to the nation would mean if Pakistan invaded India, he declared. 'Every Muslim in India would be required to shed his blood fighting the Pakistani hordes [*sic*], and each one should search his heart now, and decide whether he should migrate to Pakistan or not.'[17]

Muslim leaders who stayed on in India were under some pressure to express themselves in the same kinds of terms. The Raja of Mahmud-abad, Secretary of the All-India Muslim League and Jinnah's right-hand man for much of the decade before 1947, provides a striking illustration. As with so many other Muslim League leaders of UP and Bihar, Mahmudabad had never contemplated leaving his native land. Broken by the experience that Partition turned out to be, he resigned from the Muslim League in September 1947. The party had committed hara-kiri, he said. To keep it alive in India now was a cruel joke. Most of its leaders – Mahmudabad actually said 'all' – had run away from India, leaving the Indian Muslims to their fate. These opportunists should now be clear in their minds that they would never be able to mislead the Muslim masses again. 'All Indian Muslims would go to war for India, even if they had to go to war against Pakistan.'[18] Taking a similar tack, M. A. Salam, a member of the Madras Legislative Assembly and the All-India Muslim League Council, declared that his community of Andhra Muslims was loyal to the Indian Union and 'shall defend it against anybody to the last drop of their blood'.[19] That last contention had become a password to citizenship, as it were: it is a password that has been demanded of Muslims in India, in one form or another, ever since.

Partition produced a plethora of statements on the question of what would constitute an adequate proof of loyalty on the part of Indian Muslims. Many called for the disbanding of the Muslim League and the giving up of any demand that smacked even remotely of 'separatism' – such as appeals for separate electorates or an assured quota of legislative seats for Muslims. As Vallabhbhai Patel, the deputy prime minister of India and acclaimed 'strong man' of the Congress party, put it in the Constituent Assembly debate on 'minority rights', these were the measures that had resulted in 'the separation of the country': 'Those who want that kind of thing have a place in Pakistan, not here (*Applause*) . . . we are laying the foundations of One Nation, and those who choose to divide

---

[17] *Ibid.*; see *Aj* (22 September 1947) for report of another, very similar speech by Pant.
[18] *Aj* (7 October 1947).
[19] *Pakistan Times* (8 October 1947).

again [*sic*] and sow the seeds of disruption will have no place, no quarter here... (*Hear, Hear*).[20]

Others declared that Muslims alone could stop the killings in Punjab and the neighbouring states. All those who had any links with the Muslim League should urge 'their Pakistani brethren' to put an end to the violence. Leaguers must make an unqualified denunciation of the two-nation theory and campaign actively for reunification. Muslims generally must step forward to help Hindu and Sikh refugees, and thereby demonstrate their patriotism. They should report fellow Muslims who collected arms or otherwise created trouble. They should be prepared to go to West Punjab and 'take up the cudgels against their Pakistani brothers for their misdeeds'.[21] Indian Muslims would of course have to be prepared to lay down their lives for the country, as already noted, but even before war broke out, they could prove their loyalty by taking up arms against 'their Pakistani brothers'!

Two comments made during the debate on minority rights in the Constituent Assembly sum up the position of the Indian Muslims in the aftermath of Partition. One came from Mahavir Tyagi, a prominent Congressman of western UP, when the debate was being wound up on 26 May 1949:

The Muslims already know that they will not be returned [in elections to the various legislatures] for some time to come, so long as they do not rehabilitate themselves among the masses and assure the rest of the people that they are one with them. They have been separate in every matter for a long time past and in a day you can't switch over from Communalism to Nationalism.[22]

The other was a blunt statement from Vallabhbhai Patel to the Muslims, made in the course of the speech quoted earlier: '*You* must change your attitude, adapt yourself to the changed conditions... don't pretend to say "Oh, our affection is great for you". We have seen your affection... Let us forget the affection. Let us face the realities. Ask yourself whether you really want to stand here and cooperate with *us* or you want to play disruptive tactics...'[23]

Here, Hindu nationalism and secular nationalism come to be imbricated in the discourse of the new 'India'. From the late nineteenth century on, the politics of the middle-class Hindu had written the Indian people into existence by developing the modern discourse of 'the

---

[20] *Constituent Assembly Debates*, vol. VIII (16 May to 16 June 1949), p. 271.
[21] See the comments of the UP Congress leaders, A. P. Jain and Charan Singh, as reported in *Aj* (26 September) and *Pakistan Times* (11 October 1947), respectively; also other reports in *Aj* (7 October) and *Vartman* (27 September 1947).
[22] *Constituent Assembly Debates*, vol. VIII, p. 346.
[23] *Ibid.*, p. 271 (emphasis added).

people' – imagined, on the one hand, as an ignorant, uneducated mass to be dignified through nationalism, and on the other as a 'people/nation', embodying an authentic cultural spirit. This 'people' was an empty signifier, to be filled in by political contingency. From the Hindu nationalist perspective, the violence of Partition could be seen as a kind of patriotic baptism. From the secular nationalist too, it necessitated cooperation with 'us', and with 'our' cultural/political project.

The return of the native

Like the land and the trees, rivers and mountains, the 'Hindus' were the natural core – the 'us' of the Indian nation. In July 1947, Patel had written to an anxious Hindu correspondent from West Punjab that while the matter of citizenship was at that moment under the consideration of the Indian Constituent Assembly, 'whatever the definition may be, you can rest assured that the Hindus and Sikhs of Pakistan cannot be considered as aliens in India [*sic*]'.[24] In other words, the Hindu and Sikh communities were *natural* citizens of India, wherever they might live and whatever the constitutional definitions of citizenship might turn out to be in the two new nation-states.

If Hindus and Sikhs were 'naturally' ours, and Muslims 'naturally' theirs, as in the circumstances of Partition they were commonly declared to be, the hostile conditions of the time also raised the demand that these natural possessions be restored to their natural homes. The poignant history of abducted women caught on the wrong side of the new international border illustrates some of the tragic consequences of this curious collapsing of religious community into natural nation.

In earlier chapters, I have drawn attention to what amounted to an open declaration of war on the men, women and children of the 'enemy' community. This was signalled very clearly indeed in a letter from the 'front', written by a non-commissioned officer in the erstwhile Punjab regiment of the British Indian army, two weeks after the official Partition of India. The letter reports his platoon's 'destruction' of Hindus and Sikhs in the villages of the Gurdaspur region:

Whosoever from the Hindus and Sikhs came in front of us, were killed. Not only that, we got them to come out of their houses and ruthlessly killed them and disgraced their womenfolk. Many women agreed to come with us and wished us to take them, but we were out for revenge . . . This Indian government cannot last

---

[24] Letter to Parmanand Trehan, 16 July 1947, in Durga Das, ed., *Sardar Patel's Correspondence, 1945–50*, vol. v (Ahmedabad, 1973), p. 289.

much longer. We will very soon conquer this and on the whole of India the flag of Pakistan will fly.[25]

Others were equally ready to take away the women, before or after 'disgracing' them. 'We took away the women. That was the system', a retired captain of the Alwar army declared, in his recollections of the 'Meo-Jat war' of May to November 1947 in the region south and west of Delhi. 'Women do not have any religion after all (... *auraton ka to koi dharam hi nahin hota)'.*[26] This is in line with the misogynist north Indian proverb, '*beeran ki kai jaat*' ('what caste [or nationality] can a woman have?') – for she 'belongs' to someone else, and therefore to *his* caste, nationality and religion. Yet, the evidence from 1947 seems at times to suggest almost the exact opposite: not that 'women [had] no religion (or community or nation)', but that they came for a moment to stand for nothing else.

When the worst phase of that violence was over by November–December 1947, the question of the recovery of 'our' women, and the restoration of 'theirs', became an urgent one.[27] At the initiative of a number of women social workers, supported by some of India's most important political leaders, a programme for the 'recovery of abducted persons' was drawn up towards the end of 1947. This was to remain in operation, in one form or another, until the middle of the 1950s. Represented as nothing but the possessions of their men, their communities and their nations, however, many of the women and children who were the victims identified by this programme became mere pawns in the crossfire of nationalist demands that came to mark it.

Gandhi pronounced it to be the foremost responsibility of the two governments, of India and Pakistan, to bring these abducted women back to their native lands. So important was the question for him that he called for intervention at the highest levels, in terms of government-to-government action – a significant departure from his normal advocacy of minimal government, self-help and people's initiative. 'Yes, a team of women workers could be sent to East Punjab and another team to West Punjab', he now declared, 'but I do not think that would be effective... This is a task for the Governments to tackle... There is only one way of saving these women and that is that the Governments should even now wake up to their responsibility, *give this task the first priority and all*

---

[25] (IOR) R/3/1/173, translation of intercepted letter from Fateh Khan, Jamadar to 'brother Malik Sher Mohd Khanji' (31 August 1947).

[26] Shail Mayaram, *Resisting Regimes*, p. 191.

[27] What follows is a summary of important research findings that have been published over the last few years, supplemented by my own archival and other research.

their time and accomplish it *even at the cost of their lives*.'[28] Moreover, he felt that the women concerned had no real hope of considered judgement or choice in this matter. 'It is said that the [Sikh and Hindu] women concerned do not now want to return', he said in one of his prayer meetings, '*but still they have to be brought back* . . . I do not admit that they are not willing to return. Similar is the case of Muslim women in India.'[29]

Others put the case for restoration – and, indeed, 'reparations' – much more sharply. 'You will remember, Sir', declared a member of the Constituent Assembly of India, debating the question of recovery of abducted persons in December 1949,

> how when one [Mrs] Ellis was kidnapped by some Pathans the whole of Britain shook with anger and indignation and until she was returned Englishmen did not come to their senses. And we all know our own history, of what happened in the time of Shri Ram when Sita was abducted. Here, where thousands of girls are concerned, we cannot forget this. We can forget all the properties, we can forget every other thing, but this cannot be forgotten.

And another, in the course of the same debate: 'You are not prepared to go to war over this matter. I do not know why. If you are prepared to do so for a few inches of land in Kashmir, why not over the honour of our women?'[30]

Within months of official Partition and Independence, even Prime Minister Nehru had come to be caught up in this rhetoric to some extent. 'Please remember', he said in a speech inaugurating the 'rehabilitation of women and children week' in January 1948, 'we may gradually forget any other hardship which we have undergone but this matter concerning our women will not be forgotten, either by our country or the world, and the longer it continues, the deeper will be our sense of shame. It will sow seeds for future bitterness and wars . . .'[31]

That considerable force was used in the recovery programme is now well documented. It is implicit in the 'Abducted Persons (Recovery and Restoration) Act' which replaced an existing ordinance of the government of India in December 1949: if any police officer of the rank of assistant sub-inspector or higher, or any other police official authorised by the provincial government, had 'reason to believe that an abducted person resides or is found in any place, he may . . . without warrant, enter

---

[28] *CWMG*, vol. xc, p. 194 (emphasis added).

[29] *Ibid.*, p. 193 (emphasis added).

[30] *Constituent Assembly of India (Legislative) Debates. Official Reports*, vol. vi, no. 14 (15 December 1949), p. 642 (speech by Pandit Thakurdas Bhargava); and vol. vii, no. 1 (19 December 1949), p. 799 (speech by Sardar Bhopinar Singh Man). Extracts from these speeches are also quoted in Veena Das, *Critical Events*, p. 70, and Menon and Bhasin, *Borders and Boundaries*, p. 111.

[31] *Selected Works of Jawaharlal Nehru*, 2nd series, vol. v (Delhi, 1987), p. 116.

and search the place and take into custody any person found therein who, in his opinion, is an abducted person...'³² One officer recalled that 'the operation was a raid in every sense of the word – we did many irregular things, like dipping a police officer under water and keeping him there till he told us where the women were... sometimes I would slap the women and tell them that I would shoot them if they didn't inform us...'³³

It is scarcely surprising that 'mistakes' occurred in the process. 'Hindu women are sometimes arrested [sic] and taken to the camp for Muslim recovered women', a leading woman social worker observed. Sardarni Santokh Singh, the Delhi Provincial Organiser of these 'recovery' operations noted that six such cases of 'wrongful arrest' had taken place within a two-month period in the Delhi region alone. Premvati Thapar and other workers also reported several examples of such 'mistakes'.³⁴ If a woman was young, and pregnant, or nursing an infant, and at the same time afraid, while living in a Hindu or Sikh area, she was (in this view) likely to be a 'Muslim'. By that 'fact' alone, she could be taken for a 'Pakistani', an abducted person from Pakistan: and the logic of the new nationalisms demanded her immediate 'repatriation'.

As it happened, many abducted women were hesitant about returning to their original families and countries – for fear of ostracism; because they felt they had been 'soiled'; because they could not bear the thought of being uprooted yet again and exposed (possibly) to new levels of poverty and uncertainty; or simply because they were grateful to their new husbands and families for having rescued them from (further?) assault and afforded them some protection. The governments of the two dominions decided, however, that in such cases 'they should be forcibly evacuated'.³⁵

Modern technologies of government were very much in evidence: and the gathering of statistics was a central part of the exercise. One widely quoted estimate of the total number of abducted persons detained in 'foreign' territory was 50,000 Muslim women and children in India and 33,000 Hindu and Sikh women in Pakistan, although some social

³² For the text of the Abducted Persons (Recovery and Restoration) Act of 1949, see Menon and Bhasin, *Borders and Boundaries*, appendix 1, pp. 261–3.
³³ Quoted in *ibid.*, pp. 117–18. Another commentator noted that 'the opinion of the Assistant Sub-Inspector [of police] determines the fate of the lad[ies]', see speech by Thakurdas Bhargava in *Constituent Assembly (Legislative) Debates*, vol. VII, no. 1, pp. 800 and 802.
³⁴ Rameshwari Nehru Papers, 'Reports', no. 1, 'Memorandum on the Recovery of Women. Review of the position since October, 1948' (by Rameshwari Nehru, 20 June 1949). See also *Constituent Assembly (Legislative) Debates*, vol. VII, no. 1, p. 800.
³⁵ And again, at a later meeting, that abducted persons were to be recovered 'without any concession', Qidwai, *Azadi*, p. 314; Butalia, *Other Side of Silence*, p. 120. See also the debate on the taking away of the women's right to habeas corpus, *Constituent Assembly (Legislative) Debates*, vol. VII, no. 1, pp. 799–802.

workers felt that the actual numbers were far greater. Of this number 12,552 women and children were said to have been 'recovered' from India, and 6,272 from Pakistan, by December 1949. By 1955, the figures had increased to 20,728 and 9,032 respectively.[36]

As several writers on the subject have noted, this disparity in the numbers of abducted persons recovered on the two sides produced new recriminations. Rameshwari Nehru wrote of the growing resentment and expressions of dissatisfaction in Delhi at the fact that, between November 1948 and June 1949, the number of abducted women recovered in India was four times that in Pakistan.[37] Pakistan, the 'abductor nation', had not kept its part of the bargain, it was said. There was, therefore, no reason why India should not keep recovered Muslim women as hostages at least for some time.[38] The abducted women themselves were in an unenviable position – not free to stay if the nation wanted them to go, nor free to go if it wished them to stay.

The illusion of choice

All nations, all nationalisms and nationalist discourses, are made in exceptional (that is to say, particular, if not unique) historical circumstances. It was in the particular context of 1947 – building on more than a century of colonial governance premised on the division between Hindus and Muslims, and on an extended (and oft-retold) history of Muslim adventurers raiding the land, settling and setting up towns and kingdoms in which the question of religious and ethnic identities allegedly became the central determinants of privilege – that the 'we' of Indian nationalism came to be elaborated and the Muslims came to be marked out as a suspect minority.

It was whiteness that came to be constructed as the core of American, or Australian, nationhood, and Englishness that became the core of the British nation, in spite of the substantial presence of the Scots and the Welsh and the Irish – though, in all of these cases, the demographic and political changes brought by a more recent history of substantial coloured immigration (at times actively encouraged for purposes of production,

[36] Menon and Bhasin, *Borders and Boundaries*, pp. 70 and 99.
[37] Rameshwari Nehru Papers, 'Reports', no. 1, 'Memorandum' of 20 June 1949. Not only was there a demand for the recovery of an equal number of women on both sides, it was also necessary, as Veena Das notes, that women in their reproductive years especially be brought back; for 'this interest in women was not premised upon their definition as citizens, but as sexual and reproductive beings', *Critical Events*, pp. 68–9 and *passim*; also *Constituent Assembly (Legislative) Debates*, vol. VII, no. 1, pp. 796, 803. On the question of national honour, see also Butalia, *Other Side of Silence*, chs. 5 and 6; and Menon and Bhasin, *Borders and Boundaries*, pp. 110–13 and *passim*.
[38] Menon and Bhasin, *Borders and Boundaries*, pp. 113–14, see also pp. 76, 78.

at other times severely discouraged) have pushed the 'mainstream' into other channels or, at least, different debates. In other circumstances – such as those of the subcontinent, where diverse regions and groups have fought to retain a greater degree of autonomy and political power – national cores have crystallised very differently. Indeed, even within a given set of historical circumstances, there remains the distinct possibility of national identities, boundaries and mainstreams coming together in various ways. Surely the India of 1947 provides striking testimony to this.

The process of Partition had claimed large numbers of lives and destroyed the peace and well-being of innumerable individuals and families, even before official Partition and Independence occurred. Within weeks, it would destroy many more, and uproot practically a whole countryside in Punjab and neighbouring areas, as people fled in both directions in search of minimal safety and security. In Bengal, the movement of minorities did not assume quite the same proportions as in the north-west. The migrations were far from being insubstantial, but they occurred on a smaller scale than in Punjab, and were more spread out in time, coming in waves that were observable in East Bengal in 1948, the 1950s and even later. For all that, the minorities lived in fear all over the partitioned subcontinent in 1947–8. There was simply too much evidence of families and fortunes destroyed on account of nothing but their religious affiliation; and far too many reports and rumours of rape, abduction and forced religious conversion – from near and far.

Towards the end of September 1947, the prime minister of India remarked that, Hindus or Muslims, only those men and women were welcome to live in the country who considered it their own nation, gave it their undivided loyalty and refused to look to any outside agency for help. Removed from the confusion, suspicions and violence of the time, this was an unexceptionable statement. But as the Calcutta daily, *The Statesman*, commented editorially on 5 October, how were the Muslims of India to prove their loyalty when the very act of fleeing in fear from their homes was interpreted as a sign of disloyalty and extra-territorial attachment?

Everywhere, refugees struggled to find new homes and means of survival; and in places where they had some breathing space, the minorities made desperate attempts to articulate a new sense of belonging. I have referred to leaders of the erstwhile Muslim League who called upon Indian Muslims to be prepared to shed every last drop of their blood for the Indian motherland. Consider the parallel response of the Anglo-Indian Association of Hazaribagh in Bihar on the attainment of Indian (and Pakistani) independence: 'In this new India..., the role of the Anglo-Indian Community in the land of their birth will be to join in co-operating with all her other children towards India attaining true and lasting greatness.' The resolution went on to say that 'an Anglo-Indian father in West Bengal with a son employed in East Bengal cannot treat one another as aliens, and the community *naturally desires a reunited India*'. At the same time the Hazaribagh Anglo-Indians noted, however, that the Congress 'has not been ungenerous and the Muslim League has shown a realistic appreciation of our position, and the Anglo-Indians hope that by loyal, ungrudging service in whatever part of the Sub-continent they happen to be, they will vindicate the *national and non-partisan* character of the Anglo-Indian community'.[39]

Or consider the course followed by Lala Murlidhar Shad, owner of Lyallpur Cotton Mills, 'the only cloth mill in Western Pakistan' as the *Pakistan Times* reported, who returned to Pakistan from Delhi as late as June 1949, 'to stay here permanently'. He was 'proud to be a Pakistani', the mill owner declared in an interview to the Press; 'that is why he had brought his family back to the land of his birth'.[40]

The choices were no easier for Muslims living in India than they were for Murlidhar Shad. The consequences of Partition were hard even for the most privileged among them. In October 1947, Choudhry Khaliquzzaman – high-profile leader of the Muslim League in the Indian Constituent Assembly, long-time ally of Nehru and other Congress leaders in UP and, subsequently, a vocal champion of the rights of India's Muslims – unexpectedly and abruptly migrated to Pakistan, leaving a bewildered Muslim League party behind. No one knew quite why he had suddenly made this decision, and his own explanations – that he wanted to make way for younger blood, that he could not reconcile himself to learning Hindi which had been made the official language of UP, and (in his autobiography, ten years later) that he felt someone who had Jinnah's continued confidence should replace him and serve as the leader of the Indian Muslims – did not set the controversy at rest.

Somewhat later, in 1949, Z. H. Lari, the deputy leader of the Muslim League in the UP legislature, also left for Pakistan, although he had by then spoken out strongly against the two-nation theory, separate electorates, reservations and the accompanying baggage. It was, as many who lived through those times recall, primarily a question of where one could live in relative mental, and physical, peace.

Ustad Bade Ghulam Ali Khan, the doyen of the Patiala *gharana* (school) of Hindustani music, moved to Pakistan, where he lived in relative obscurity for some time, before returning to India – and to a successful

[39] AICC papers, File G4/1947, F. M. Holland, honorary secretary, Hazaribagh Anglo-Indian Association, to 'Secretary, Congress High Command, Delhi' (21 August 1947), forwarding a copy of the Association's resolution (emphasis added).
[40] *Pakistan Times* (14 June 1949).

revitalisation of his musical career – many years before his death. Josh Maiihabadi, the great Urdu poet from Malihabad, near Lucknow, who had declared along with a host of other progressive writers that 'we cannot partition Urdu',[41] went and came and went again several times over, unhappy in that he had no nation, no home now, and probably unclear to the end whether Urdu had been partitioned and what its fate would be in the two countries.

The fact is that the choice between India and Pakistan was a practically impossible one for Muslims living in what were called the 'Muslim-minority provinces' of British India, especially in the immediate aftermath of Partition and Independence. The individuals mentioned in the preceding paragraphs were part of an elite, and possessed the resources as well as the bureaucratic and political contacts that enabled them to move to and fro, at least for a time. There were innumerable others who did not have the luxury of such trial periods – or the chance of an appeal to Jawaharlal Nehru – yet moved one way and then the other in search of security and peace.

The divisions at the borders were already being replicated at the level of localities. In November 1947, it was reported that nearly 5,000 Muslim railwaymen who had earlier opted for service in Pakistan, had now 'set the authorities a serious problem' by withdrawing their preference for Pakistan and refusing to leave India. They were of course, by this change of heart, laying themselves open to the charge of being Pakistani agents engaged in a conspiracy, although their motives were almost certainly more mundane, the result of news of troubles on that side of the border too, and of the fact that working in Pakistan would create its own set of problems. However, even their co-workers in UP were not inclined to be so generous in their response to this change. Hindu railwaymen in Lucknow threatened to go on strike if the 'Pakistan personnel' were allowed to stay, and the railway authorities insisted that those who had opted for service in Pakistan must now go.[42]

A letter from one such railway worker, and the Indian government's response to it, provides another illustration of the hopelessness of many choices. The letter was written in September 1947 by Safdar Ali Khan,

---

[41] *People's Age* (7 September 1947).
[42] *The Statesman* (23 November 1947). Cf. AICC papers, File G-18, KW I (Pt. I)/1947–48, complaint by Harikrishna Dua, 'Refugee', against Muslim postal employees who had changed their 'option' from Pakistan to India, and had been allowed to stay on, as he alleged, 'owing to [Rafi Ahmad] Kidwaiji's favour'. Note also the report in *The Statesman* (15 October 1947), that 'By an interesting unanimity of purpose, backed, no doubt, by a firm administration of law and order, [the Muslims of UP who, it notes, form the largest concentration of Muslims outside the 'Pakistan areas'] have been determined hitherto to stay put.'

'Guard, Moradabad', to the Secretary, 'Partition Department', government of India. Headed 'Permission to revise my decision "to serve in India"', it said:

I had submitted my final choice to serve in Pakistan... The persuasions of my fellow-workers and friends favoured [forced?] me to come to this decision at which I am rubbing my hands now [*sic*].

... My old mother is lying very seriously ill and she is not in a mood to allow me to go to Pakistan as she has no hope to survive her illness.

... I have blundered in favour of Pakistan. Really speaking, as I have stated above, the decision was not my own but... made under compulsion. I am an Indian first and an Indian last. I want to live in India and die in India...

Hence I humbly request your honour to permit me to revise my decision and allow me to serve in India.[43]

Maulana Abul Kalam Azad, the education minister of India, forwarded this letter to the home minister, Vallabhbhai Patel, who responded briefly: 'The Partition Council decision has been that once a final choice is made it should be adhered to. I [can] see no prospect, therefore, of the gentleman, whose application you have sent me, being allowed to change his option now.'[44]

There is a bureaucratic imperative at work here. Two new state administrations are being set up, rules have to be made and followed. But there is a moral imperative as well. People simply have to decide where they stand and who they are, once and for all. This was a demand that was made insistently of *one* part of the new India's inhabitants, as the preceding pages should have shown. The modern state insists on a separation between the public and the private. Yet Partition produced a situation in which one part of the private (the 'Hindu' in India, and the 'Muslim' in Pakistan) articulated itself as the public, while denying that possibility to the 'other'. There were perhaps two voices of nationalism that could be heard in the above exchange between Patel and Azad; but it was the second that won out, as it has so often done in our times, asserting certainty even in the midst of the wholly uncertain.

The same clarity of choice was demanded of abducted, then recovered women, as we have observed. Evidence of the reluctance of many women to return to what others saw as their 'natural' homes was brought up by concerned social workers at a number of conferences in India during the later stages of the recovery programme. Following from this, it was agreed 'as a compromise', to quote Rameshwari Nehru, that 'such unwilling women should be sent to Pakistan in the first instance for one month only. At the end of this period, they should be given the option of returning

---

[43] Durga Das, *Patel's Correspondence*, vol. IV, p. 421.
[44] *Ibid.*, p. 422.

to India.' This incredible solution speaks of how a whole section of the population, now classified as victims, had become unconsulted objects in an unthinking game of boundary marking. It is no surprise to find that, in Nehru's words again, 'as far as I know, no woman has come back'.[45]

At another stage, an order was issued whereby children born in circumstances of 'abduction' would have to be left behind in the countries where they were born. Once again, the protests of several women workers led to further consideration of the question. Out of this came the desperate resolution that Muslim women being repatriated from India to Pakistan, who insisted on keeping their children, would be allowed to take the children with them to the transit camp in Jalandhar where, after fifteen days, they would decide whether they wanted to keep them or not.[46] This was surely little better than the solution of sending 'unwilling women' to Pakistan for a month only 'in the first instance'.

By 1949, there was a good deal of opposition to the 'abducted women's recovery programme'. Anees Qidwai recalls people asking:

Why are these girls being tortured in this way?... What is the advantage of uprooting them once again? If making them homeless again is not idiocy, what is it? To take a woman who has become a respected housewife and mother in her [new] home, and force her to return to her old home and [or] her parents, is not charity but a crime. Forget this business: those [women] who are left in Hindustan and those left in Pakistan are happy where they are...

Rameshwari Nehru was overcome by some of the same misgivings. Viewed from the human angle, she wrote,

I am convinced that we have not achieved our purpose, and that it is inadvisable to continue the work of recovery any longer. Two years have elapsed since the original crimes were committed, and though there may still be a considerable number of unrecovered women, to remove them at this stage from the homes, in which they have settled, would result in untold misery and suffering.[47]

The question of restoring abducted women to their respective nations, which admitted of no easy solution in any case, also generated new kinds of self-censorship and fear. Individuals who had almost gone berserk in the first phase of the violence and migrations, searching high and low for sisters, daughters and wives they had lost, making anxious enquiries of friends and acquaintances from their original homes, combing refugee camps and hospitals, railway stations and bazaars, sometimes preferred

[45] Rameshwari Nehru Papers, 'Reports', no. 1, 'Memorandum' of 20 June 1949.
[46] See Menon and Bhasin, *Borders and Boundaries*, pp. 84, 101; and Svati Joshi, 'Torn Up by the Roots' (a review and commentary on Kamlabehn Patel's *Mool sota ukhadela*, Bombay and Ahmedabad, 1985), *Manushi*, 48 (1988), p. 16.
[47] Qidwai, *Azadi*, p. 313; Rameshwari Nehru Papers, 'Reports', no. 1, 'Memorandum' of 20 June 1949.

to withdraw and draw a blind over the subject once the recovery of abducted persons had become a public issue and a matter for settlement between two governments. Thus the government of East Punjab was unable to publicise a list of abducted persons that had been compiled under its orders because a number of ministers' families were named in it. As the compiler of a two-volume *List of Non-Muslim Abducted Women and Children*, put it, 'The publication of this volume was not undertaken earlier out of deference to the feelings of the victims and their relations.'[48] When the list was published, it was in a small number of copies, for limited administrative circulation.

Where family members were abducted or otherwise taken away, and this threatened to become public knowledge, a common response was to refuse to acknowledge the fact. The honour of the local community, household, father, husband, necessitated such suppression. At the same time, while the raped and abducted women might not be recognised by many relatives and families, the 'nation' demanded that all 'our' women must be returned – 'at any cost', as Gandhi had it. On both sides of the border, the abducted women – 'recovered' or not – have lived on as shadows from 1947 until today. Some have survived as quiet housewives and mothers in new lives, in which the 'past' has simply had to be buried;[49] others in so-called women's 'homes' – charities funded by the state and certain private organisations, with strict disciplinary regimes and minimal resources. Family, community and nation take their toll in different ways.

---

[48] *List of Non-Muslim Abducted Women and Children, Part I and Part II* (1,414 pages; copy in Haryana Secretariat Library, Chandigarh), 'Preface', p. i. The document gave the total number of Hindus and Sikhs abducted as 21,809 (p. ii of 'Preface', dated 24 May 1954, by A. J. Fletcher, commissioner, Ambala and Jullunder divisions and 'high-powered officer for recovery of abducted women and children, India').

[49] Consider the example of Lajwanti in Rajinder Singh Bedi's eponymous story: 'Sundar Lal stopped her saying, "Let's just forget the past." . . . And Lajwanti couldn't get it all out. It remained buried inside her. She withdrew into herself and stared at her body for the longest time, a body which, after the partition of the country, was no longer hers, but that of a goddess,' Rajinder Singh Bedi, 'Lajwanti', tr. from the Urdu by Muhammad Umar Memon, in Memon, ed., *An Epic Unwritten*, p. 28.

8   Constructing community

How is life and community to be reconstructed out of the contradictory and difficult 'memories' described in these pages? One possibility, widely enforced by individuals and communities, is to maintain individual silence, to leave the pain of events like Partition unspoken, to suppress it in the body.[1] Alongside that, however, there is also the need for a public forgetting, that goes hand in hand with a recitation of past deeds.

There are two familiar procedures in such forgetting that readers will have encountered repeatedly in the preceding chapters. One is to transform such moments of violence and suffering into moments in a war (of liberation); the other, to represent it as part of someone else's history – what *others* did, or were responsible for. While the second move is observable very commonly indeed in the accounts of Partition survivors, it comes at times with an implicit recognition that the disorder is somehow part of *our* history too. These reconstructions of violence in the past are frequently forced to grapple with the question of the meaning of this violence for the community – past and present. In other words, they are compelled to pose the question of what constitutes the community, the subject of history, 'us' and 'them'. Here, in the handling of the relationship between violence and community, I submit, Partition – and accounts of Partition – have something unusual to tell us.

The morality of memory-history

Ultimately, the question of collective violence, and of writing (and speaking) about it, is a question that has both moral and political consequences. What kinds of political community do we see as possible, what kind do we wish to construct? The moral issue is related to this, and it is obviously of importance. I have maintained that there is a pressing need to

---

[1] On the question of how communities and individuals have coped with traumatic moments of violence and the more insidious forms of social suffering that flowed from them, cf. Veena Das and Arthur Kleinman, *Violence and Subjectivity*, and Das's own forthcoming book on violence.

recognise the enormity of the event called Partition, and the universality, the obscenity and the unacceptability of its violence. It is a need that certainly comes out in survivors' accounts. In a very large number of these recollections, as in many of the other reports cited, the detail seems to put on record the awful suffering that people went through, as also, perhaps, the fact that the violence is in all of us. Given the same kinds of circumstances, how many of us would turn away from this unacceptable political community, and yet turn towards the task of imagining other communities out of the same human material – as Gandhi did?

This leads us to the more tangible *political* consequences. It is my contention that the accounts of violence discussed here contribute significantly to the making of new subjectivities, new versions of self and other, new communities and new histories. The Partitioned subject – individual, community, nation, humanity – is a nationalised, but also a historical subject: historically produced and subject to the continuing contentions of society and politics. At the level of nations/peoples, and myths about nations/peoples, Partition, coming at the end of colonial rule in South Asia, seems to have established as 'truth' an illusion that colonialism had long believed in and fostered – that the people(s) of the subcontinent were a zealously, not to say uniquely, religious people[2] – at the very time, ironically, when all fear of God or of the consequences of karma seemed to disappear from their behaviour.

In the subcontinent, it has served to naturalise pre-existing notions of fundamentally opposed Hindu, Sikh and Muslim communities. Since then, the nation-states of South Asia, as well as ethnic communities that aspire to nation status, have continued to construct, commemorate and consolidate themselves through a constant retailing of tales of sacrifice and war. The tendentious and interested character of these accounts needs to be critiqued. However, it needs to be noted too that what is suspect here is not the historical character of a particular nation-state called India (or Pakistan), but the historical character of nationalist thought in general. The point bears a little elaboration.

Michael Billig has drawn attention to the qualities of innocence and intolerance built into 'an ideology [until recently called 'nationalism'] which is so familiar that it hardly seems noticeable'.[3] A nationalist intolerance that is daily reinforced by school textbook and media stories, by

---

[2] Notice the representation of Indians and Pakistanis in the western media, as opposed, say, to that of the Chinese, Japanese and now Malaysians. Compared to India and Pakistan, again, Bangladesh emerges as a land of less religious zeal – because the periodic havoc wrought by cyclones and other such phenomena make it a 'disaster zone' of a different kind.

[3] Michael Billig, *Banal Nationalism* (London, 1995), p. 12 and *passim*. This paragraph owes much to the arguments and examples presented in this book.

box-office hits and the no longer noticed vocabulary of everyday national politics, shared by the left and the right alike. This is the way in which national communities have long been reproduced, national 'memories' kept alive – and nations frequently incited to violence. This is what sustains the regular demand for conformity with the national (the 'American', the 'Indian', the 'Australian') way, the ever-present assumptions of uniqueness, the touting of political and military glory in the past and the continued aim of political, industrial and military glory in the future. This is what has made for the incredibly quick mobilisation of nationwide chauvinism and calls for murder in Nazi Germany and at the mosque in Ayodhya (northern India), in Buddhist Sri Lanka as well as in the United States of the Gulf War and the Britain of the Falklands adventure. Surely, these mobilisations and the violence they sanction raise major doubts about our contemporary understanding of civilisation and our justifications for war.

Nations, and communities that would be nations, seem to deal with the moment of violence in their past (and present) by the relatively simple stratagem of drawing a neat boundary around themselves, distinguishing sharply between 'us' and 'them', and pronouncing the act of violence an act of the other or an act necessitated by a threat to the self. As it happens, however, just as there are far more fluid and uncertain boundaries than the claimed 'natural' boundaries of nations and nation-states, there are also less sharply delimited histories than the self-fulfilling autobiographical accounts of these 'natural' and 'permanent' entities.

Face-to-face local communities have to live with disturbing memories of this kind more uncertainly, and continuously, than nations and states. This is, in part, simply a consequence of scale. In part, the difference arises because nations and states are able to insulate themselves behind grand, rhetorical propositions about 'national' interests and 'national' agendas. How do these local communities, by contrast, and their non-disciplinary 'histories', deal with the painful moment of violence? In part, at least, by acknowledging the violence, even as they seek to dismiss it. I wish to explore this point at some length in this concluding chapter. In order to do this, it will help to begin with a closer examination of a number of 'impromptu' local accounts of the violence of 1947.

Violence 'out there'

Let us consider, first, a set of accounts of 'revenge attacks' in a small part of the erstwhile Patiala state in East Punjab. The stories of these attacks and the events surrounding them, which I have collected in the main from the inhabitants of one village, Gharuan (some twenty kilometres from Chandigarh), employ a variety of techniques to elide the violence or consign it – often against their own testimony – to happenings somewhere else ('out there'). The most detailed statements I have come from a male civil servant and distinguished Sikh scholar, now retired from the bureaucracy, who was a college student in Amritsar in 1947; from his mother; and from his mother's brother, who is seven years senior to the civil servant and was at the time a student in Lahore.[4]

Forced to flee from West Punjab, where the future civil servant had gone to be with his parents for the length of the 1947 summer vacation, mother and son arrived in the mother's natal village, Dhamot, where the uncle (mother's brother) had already gone from Lahore for his summer break. Here and in Gharuan, the village from which the civil servant's father came and where mother and son went a week or so after their arrival in Dhamot, these respondents were surrounded by, and to some extent caught up in, the situation of vicious attacks and counter-attacks against Muslims that had begun in East Punjab by August 1947.

The civil servant tells the tale of these attacks with shame, embarrassment and self-questioning. His is a well-constructed, reflective statement about revenge-killings, brutality, complicity, the abduction of Muslim girls and women, his uncle's role in the attacks, his mother's upbraiding of his uncle for that role, and the incomprehensibility of it all. The scholar in him asks what in the Sikh polity allowed the Sikhs to act in this way, and to feel no compunction for it even now; and seems to imply that the question may be unanswerable.

The civil servant's uncle, a robust farmer as he appears even now in his seventies, and a retired inspector of police, in his turn, provides me, as interviewer, with a clear-cut and confident account, which suggests nothing about any personal involvement in the attacks against Muslims. He is brought to tears when his nephew reminds him of one such incident, and informs him that I already know of it – through the nephew. 'Don't talk of these things', the uncle says, almost to himself, 'they are too painful to recall.' For the rest, his story is one of attacks launched by the Muslims upon an unsuspecting and innocent Sikh and Hindu population (in Lahore, where he was studying, as elsewhere); of subsequent preparations by the Hindus and Sikhs; of counter-attacks and revenge, especially in the eastern part of Punjab where Hindus and Sikhs were present in strength; of his own status as one of the most well-educated youths in his village; and his consequent leadership of 'defence' squads and 'defence' statements (in front of investigating officials) when the village and its surroundings came to be caught up in the violence.

---

[4] Interviews with S. S. Dhanoa, Balwant Singh and Dalip Kaur in Chandigarh, Mohali and Gharuan (20 February and 10 March 1995).

The civil servant's mother speaks all too briefly. In part because such an interview is somewhat unusual for her, in part because I cannot altogether escape the historian's agenda of asking about 'grand' subjects like 'Partition', and 'Jinnah', and 'Patel' and 'Gandhi', she responds repeatedly with the proposition that she has nothing to tell, that she knows nothing about 'politics', that her son can answer all these questions and if he has already spoken to me, then surely there is little left to say. She informs me also that 'nothing happened in our village', that all the attacks (against the Muslims) occurred 'outside', that she herself never left her home and therefore knew nothing of what was going on outside, and that, no, there was no discussion of these things amongst the women inside the homes.

It is only on being specifically reminded of this by her son, the civil servant, and indeed needing to be reminded twice over, that she recalls having stopped her brother from killing a poor Muslim family whom they found hiding in the fields as they walked from the railway station to the village of Dhamot, on the last leg of their journey from West Punjab. 'Have you gone mad?' she now remembers having said, 'is this a demonstration of your Sikhi [Sikh *dharma*]?'

The civil servant had told me the story of two young Muslim girls, one perhaps in her late teens, the other even younger, who had been abducted and kept in a house neighbouring his father's in Gharuan; and of how, when he had been asked to take some food over for them, they had mistaken him (a college student) for a buyer; and also how, from the little he saw of them, the older girl did what she could to protect the younger from their abductors. To this, the mother added the story of a *badmash* of the village (a known 'bad character', here referring to someone with a 'police record') who had brought and kept with him seven young women and girls. She mentioned the case also of a little girl (her recollection of the girl's age was six, the civil servant thought it was more like ten) who had been abducted and brought to their own house by a relative of theirs. The civil servant told me that the latter was a mentally handicapped man, who had remained unmarried and seems to have found in the Partition 'disturbances' the opportunity to overcome his problem of finding a 'wife'.

The mother went on to say that, when she found this little Muslim girl in the house on her arrival in Gharuan, she kept her by her side 'day and night': 'I didn't let her out of my sight . . . she became part of the family.' Many months later, when the 'recovery' officials came (to recover abducted persons being held in wrongful confinement), and 'we pointed out all the houses' in which abducted women were being kept, the little girl too went away ('cheerfully', as this recollection has it).

There are other people of Gharuan, however, who tell the story of Partition violence very differently. I shall cite two examples. One is that of Babu Khan,[5] who became 'Babu Singh' during Partition but has since reverted to his Muslim denomination, along with the majority of the small group of Muslims who stayed on in the village rather than migrate to Pakistan. 'Call me "Babu Khan", "Babu Singh", whatever you like, what difference does it make?' he announced, when I pressed him for his full name, and others sitting around prompted him to specify, 'Khan' or 'Singh'?

'They told us to eat "meat"', he went on to say, using the euphemism for pork that other villagers had also used. 'We ate it. We had to, to save our lives.' 'I still get scared thinking about it all', he adds with an embarrassed laugh. 'You asked me – so I'm telling you.' Unlike that of the Sikhs of the village, his account refers to 'rivers of blood' and 'thousands of corpses', and to the consternation, fear and uncertainty that prevailed for a very long time. The hyperbole is evident but it is a different hyperbole from that employed by other informants from the area.

My last example from Gharuan is that of a person who was of school-going age in Calcutta in the 1940s, lost his uncle in the 'Calcutta riots' (of 1946 or '47), returned with his father to Gharuan in August or September 1947 but then had to escape again to Calcutta – which seemed the comparatively safer place.[6] Several people from the village had asked me to meet him because of his unusual personal history: he had been a Muslim, who was converted to Sikhism in the 'dreadful' days of 1946–7 (as he himself described them) and who had – unlike many others – stayed on with the new religious affiliation even when circumstances improved. Now the owner of a fleet of taxis, a local Congress leader and a municipal corporator in a town not far from this village, he spoke of the 'huge', 'terrible' slaughter of the time. 'Why does it always happen in Punjab?' he asked, pointing out that the same kind of violence had broken out in the region again in the 1980s. It is the Sikhs who take arms, he went on, elaborating this last point: they go out in *jathas* (gangs) and they kill.

This 'Sikh' spoke in the most fundamental terms about love, religiosity and the need for universal humanity. He declared all religions to be the same essentially; condemned them all for their narrowness and for their excessive expenditure on temples, gurdwaras and the like; but singled out Christianity, and its notion of charity, for praise, citing the example of Mother Theresa's work in Calcutta.

With all that, and through a longish interview in which I asked many questions that were guided by what I had been told about him, he refused in any way to acknowledge that he had once been a Muslim, later

[5] Interview (Gharuan, 9 April 1995).
[6] Interview (12 March 1995).

'converted' to Sikhism. In the course of the conversation, I scribbled in my note-pad: 'This is just like [the reporting of] rape.' How does the rapist, or the raped, talk about the experience of rape? And how does the interviewer ask about it?[7] Here is a past which the victim denies – through his subsequent success in business and the political world, through a barely concealed sense of shame, and through suppression of that that was in his own reckoning most shaming.

A denial may occur in several different ways, however. The standard story I heard in Gharuan was that of the exceptional peace and harmony of this large Sikh village. 'Nothing happened in the village'; 'our Muslims were unharmed'; 'not a single woman or child was touched [abducted or raped] here'. Whatever violence occurred, occurred outside the village, I was repeatedly told. Yet it is from the very same Sikh respondents' accounts that I learnt of the many women and children abducted from surrounding villages and kept by local Sikh men: and there is considerable agreement on the large numbers and extreme youth of many of the women and girls involved. I was told also of forty to fifty (or twenty to thirty – the figure varied with different respondents) Muslim women who were captured in some 'raid' by local squads, brought to the village, kept at the village gurdwara for a night or more, and then killed in the compound of the gurdwara on the outskirts of the village.

The location of the site of violence 'outside' the village – even the precincts of the gurdwara, which appears to have been the shared property of several villages, might technically be considered 'outside' – seems to be a matter of some importance to the informants. Not a single Muslim of the village was harmed, the point is made again and again in the recollections; they were only made to eat 'meat' (i.e. pork, the eating of which symbolised the Muslims' conversion to Sikhism) for their own safety. It is asserted, indeed, that Muslims were safe wherever they were a minority in a village: they were attacked only where they lived in hamlets or villages separated from the rest of the population. So, 'our Muslims' were untouched. However, numbers of male villagers, younger and older, went out in squads to settle scores with Muslims elsewhere: they killed large numbers of them in the surrounding countryside, in a nearby camp where they had been herded together, in the fields where they hid, and on the roads along which they fled, not to mention the score or more of Muslim women and girls killed at the village gurdwara.

There is an acknowledgement here that bears reflection. It suggests a will to truth which we perhaps need to recognise, and even underline – a part of the struggle, waged by every one of us, to come to terms with our

---

[7] On the difficulty of speech in such situations, cf. Butalia's remarkable chapter on her uncle, 'Blood', ch. 2 in her *Other Side of Silence*.

pasts. There are of course different nuances in the different stories that I heard. Yet traces of this 'will to truth' may be found in all of them. They are present in the uncle's tears – why dwell on things 'so painful to recall' – and in Babu Khan's parallel suppression: 'You asked me, so I am telling you. I still get scared thinking about it all.' The civil servant/scholar's narrative is unusual because of its reflectiveness, but also because of its specific acknowledgement of forced conversion (however symbolic), and the retention of abducted girls in the village. His mother's account is different too from the majority of the men's accounts, in its reticence and repeated avowal of a lack of knowledge, but also in its sensitivity to the fate of abducted women and children. She provides many details of the number of abducted women, where they were kept in the village, and how they were treated (to the extent that she knew about this).

However, the will to truth is commonly accompanied by the need to forget. In the mother's denial of any discussion amongst the women, or any knowledge of what was going on in the way of 'revenge'; in her statement that it was a *badmash* who abducted and kept seven girls or women; as in the civil servant's generalised account of men from the village going 'out' to attack Muslims; and in his explanation that it was a demented relative who had taken a little Muslim girl and held her captive in their house, there is a complicity with the collective statement that 'our village' was something of an exception, that the violence did not take place here and, when it did, it was 'outsiders' who were responsible.

The mother's story of the little girl who was kept in her house and 'became a part of the family', and of other abducted persons kept in the village, going away 'cheerfully' when the 'recovery' people came to take them, achieves the same effect – of 'normalising' the experience – in another way. A good deal of evidence has come to light which shows that in instance after instance, women and girls had been repeatedly raped, passed on from hand to hand, sold, auctioned, cheered, petted, used, thrown away, before some of them were lucky enough to be 'taken in', to find a home, perhaps be married, and in time even have children and raise a family. Many abducted women, separated from their husbands, fathers, brothers, and other male and female relatives, for a few days, or weeks or months, found it difficult to gain acceptance back in their original families and communities. Consequently those among them who had found something of a home and a minimally settled existence in these troubled times were often reluctant to risk everything again, and to expose themselves to the same uncertainties and insecurities and pressures, when the 'recovery' operations began.[8]

[8] See ch. 7 and references cited there.

The bland suggestion that the abducted persons held in Gharuan went away to Pakistan 'cheerfully' when the 'recovery' officials arrived to take them several months after their abduction – and even though some, like the little girl, had got fairly well integrated into their new households – sounds, in this context, like another effort to wish away the violence of the times and the terror that so many had to negotiate. It is something more than guilt, I would like to suggest, that leads to such recollection and such forgetfulness.

It did not matter in those days whether you had killed someone or not...

Before discussing this point more fully, let me introduce another account of 1947 that emphasises the incomprehensibility of the situation and the meaninglessness of moral codes in the face of such total disorder. This particular recital comes from a Hindu businessman and social worker who escaped from Baluchistan in September 1947, and took several days to reach Delhi after a harrowing journey by a tortuous route.[9] The businessman's family had been separated from him, and news had reached him of the massacre of all passengers on the train by which they were supposedly travelling to the safety of India. 'I was a dead man for one month', he says, speaking of the time when he believed his whole family had been killed. His is a deeply moving, even literary statement of personal and family losses, and the delirium and death that were the mark of the time. Yet there is a different tenor when he comes to speaking of scenes of loot and murder in Delhi.

On his arrival in the city, this man first stayed in an area of Old Delhi with the brother of a Sikh who had accompanied him on the long journey from Baluchistan. There was rioting in several parts of Old Delhi, such as Sabzi Mandi, he recalls: 'We also went to see the area. . . . so many people were killed.' He then goes on to recount an incident involving rape and murder in a matter of fact way, almost without a change of tone. It is this manner of telling that captures something of the extraordinary character of Partition violence: a violence that takes place outside the context of recognised, or recognisable, community.

In those early days of his time in Delhi, when 'riots' were still going on, the businessman recalled, the Sikh they were staying with went out with two friends to 'some Muslim house . . . and there was only one girl left [there], of the age of 16 or 17 . . . They brought that girl. And now, they kept her for three or four days in the house, and [then they were]

---

[9] Interview Mr Gulati (26 July 1994).

perplexed to think what to do with her – either to kill her . . . or__? [the sentence was left hanging]. Ultimately they took her in a *tanga* (a horse-drawn carriage) or a jeep . . . and killed her at the road that goes to Qarol Bagh; from Panchkuian to Qarol Bagh on the way there is a jungle . . . After four days . . . In those days nobody was troubled about such matters, that have they killed her or not killed her (*kisi ko yeh takleef nahin hoti thi, ki usko mara hai ke nahin mara hai*)?'[10]

One may easily multiply examples of such incomprehensibility as a consequence of the breakdown of all inherited senses of community. It will suffice for my purposes here if we return for a moment to the civil servant with whom I began my account of Gharuan. The scholar/civil servant explains away many of his own actions of that time – such as his trailing behind some groups of men and boys who had gone out to attack Muslims, or along with other boys from the village ('just for fun') chasing some 'miserable', 'starved' Muslim women who had strayed from their refugee camp in search of a few vegetables or edible leaves – as a result of 'youthfulness' and 'lack of understanding'. Much of it still remains a puzzle for him. Indeed a striking motif in the civil servant's narrative – one that surfaces again and again – is that of 'sleeping through it all', even through the roughest and most dangerous moments of the journey from West to East Punjab.[11] This is not so far removed from the experience of former soldiers that Jonathan Glover writes about, who see their actions in war as 'coming from a different identity . . . "the person in me that fought the war" ',[12] 'Sleeping through it all' is perhaps another comment on the disintegration of given notions of community and the incomprehensibility that supervenes while the struggle for a new order takes place in the mind.

A life that has gone

Both recollection and forgetting have something to do with the question of the collapse of lived community – of rendering the incomprehensible comprehensible, in other words. The point is well illustrated by the Muslim recollections of Delhi in 1947, which I have discussed in an earlier

---

[10] The major part of the businessman's account was in English. The last sentence quoted here was spoken in Hindi.

[11] As he recalls it, he slept right through when the train in which he and his mother were fleeing was rained with bullets from a train going in the opposite direction and all other passengers in their coach took cover under the seats; and again when his mother tried to keep him awake, for fear of what marauders might do to them or take from their luggage, when they were stranded for a night at a wayside station full of armed Sikhs, discussing the attacks they had successfully carried out during the day, the numbers they had killed, the goods they had looted, and the tasks that remained for the next day.

[12] Glover, *Humanity*, p. 51.

chapter, and which we may now put by the side of the Gharuan story. Several of these are written accounts that differ in numerous respects from oral accounts generated through interviews, yet resemble them in their emotion, their vivid and detailed description of the 'everyday' terror of the time, and – not least – in what they tell us about the communities of everyday life.

It is clear that the Muslims of Delhi constituted a bewildered, demoralised and terrified population by the date of official Partition and Independence. Curfews were frequent, especially in Muslim localities, and now became longer. Supplies of food and other necessities grew scarce, corruption and looting increased and, as we have noted, poorer Muslims had to sell, as well as eat, their domesticated animals. Forced out of their *mohallas* and their homes, Muslims like Shahid Ahmad Dehlavi and many who were far less privileged than him and his family, fled to the torrid 'safety' of the refugee camps – where, however, conditions were, if safer, not less deadly (*'Purana Qila hashr ka maidan bana hua tha'*, as Dehlavi wrote)[13] – and from there, if they were lucky, to the torrid conditions of the trains to Pakistan.

And yet, Delhi was home, 'our' city, 'our' *vatan*. How could he ever leave this home, Dehlavi asked himself: 'The scars of this forced separation will never disappear.' It was torture, like one's nails being pulled out of one's flesh (*'Dilli ka Dilli-valon se juda hona gosht se nakhun ka juda hona hai'*). 'Delhi which had now become like a witch *(dayan)*... even though she had become a *dayan*, she still remained a mother.'[14]

In chapter 4, I quoted Ebadat Barelvi's view that Delhi was a 'Muslim' city: *'Dilli Musalmanon ka shahar tha.'*[15] The proposition bears some further consideration. When its older Muslim residents refer to 'Delhi', they refer by and large to the walled city of Old Delhi, Shahjahanabad, which had been a centre of commercial and cultural activity ever since Shah Jahan built the spectacular palace complex called the Red Fort along with the Jama Masjid and other public buildings nearby, and laid out the great market complex around Chandni Chowk, in the seventeenth century. This was a 'Muslim' city in a quite tangible sense – built by Muslim rulers, full of grand Mughal monuments, and dominated by the Muslim aristocracy (even one in decline). It is noteworthy that the city so lovingly conjured up in *Twilight in Delhi* has virtually no non-Muslims in it: the only 'Hindus' who live in the city of Ahmed Ali's imagination, it seems, are men and women from the lowly Dalit castes, whose menial services are required for sundry purposes on sundry occasions, and

[13] Dehlavi, *Dilli*, p. 165.
[14] *Ibid.*, pp. 179–80.
[15] Barelvi, *Azadi*, p. 18.

a modern medical practitioner – predictably, a Bengali – who makes his appearance towards the end of the novel.

A sense of power and exclusion is certainly built into the claim over the city's past. Delhi was a 'Muslim' city in another sense too: and in that sense not a city of Muslims alone or of Muslims in general, but of the cream of Muslim society. More precisely it was a city of elite Muslim culture – for non-Muslims and even sections of the non-elite might (and did) share that culture. In asserting that 'Delhi was a Muslim city', Barelvi immediately adds the rider that Hindus also lived here in large numbers: they were people providing numerous services, businesses and capital, they were also moneylenders, bankers and landlords. However, he says, most of the Hindus shared the culture of the Muslims. 'They [dressed and] spoke like Muslims'; they shared the same festivities and etiquette, and they thought of Urdu as their own tongue.[16]

This nostalgia for the Delhi that was – 'ek Musalmanon ka shahar' – finds its parallel in the Bengali bhadralok's sense of Bengal as a quintessentially Hindu bhadralok (respectable, upper-caste Hindu) province, not in numbers (at least not since the censuses of 1872 and 1881) but in terms of culture and history. It was a culture and a history that, in the reckoning of the older elites of Delhi and Bengal, they had built. In Delhi, the distinguishing marks of that culture were to be seen in a leisured pace, self-respect and hospitality, shared poetry and subtle conversation, innocent diversions like kite-flying and pigeon keeping, and – with all that – in inherited status and breeding, and clear hierarchies: between man and woman, father and child, master and servant, high-born and low.

A common tendency in the two sets of recollections, from Gharuan and from Delhi, may be noted here. In the first set, from Gharuan, there is an almost self-conscious attempt to promote the idea of a composite community – which had survived at least in part – and with which the respondents had to continue to live. In the second lot of memories, from Delhi, we see the nostalgic construction of a community that was in the process of disintegrating 'right before our eyes'[17] – as the narrators struggle to define a new home and a new community.

Dehlavi's fiercest diatribe, in his account of Delhi in 1947, is reserved for those Hindu and Sikh refugees who had flooded into the city from outside. That Delhi was a 'Muslim city' is another way of saying, as these accounts do over and over again, that Delhi was a *cultured* city.

---

[16] *Ibid.*, p. 18.
[17] The phrase, used in reference to the erosion of Delhi's culture under the impact of colonialism, is Ahmed Ali's, see his *Twilight in Delhi*, p. viii.

The memorialist notes that, for 700 years before 1947, the people of Delhi (Hindus and Muslims) had never had to experience the vulgarity that was now rampant. The refugees, especially the Sikhs, seemed to be everywhere. They had taken over the streets and the footpaths, the deserted buildings, the mosques and the graveyards.

'*Behayai aam hai.*' Meat was now sold out in the open, women bathed in the streets, even the older Hindu women had altogether stopped going out into the markets because of the obvious decline of manners. '*Dilli ab bhi baqi hai, aur vahan Musalman bhi baste hain, lekin ab woh Dilli kahan?* [Delhi still exists, and Muslims live there too, but where is that Delhi of yore?]'[18] 'Nothing remained of that speech and that etiquette', as Dehlavi's fellow Delhi-wala, Ebadat Barelvi, put it, 'that generosity and that humanity, that warmth and that colour by which Delhi once used to be recognized.'[19]

The newcomers were prepared to do anything to make a buck, we are told, and resorted to violence on the slightest pretext. The 'Hindus of Delhi' and the 'Muslims of Delhi' both suffered at their hands, writes Dehlavi: and 'in the riots that followed, the Hindus of Delhi took no part'. At the insistence of the Hindus of her locality, as we noted in Chapter 6, Dehlavi's mother had returned to Khari Baoli. She was still living there, along with his younger brothers and sisters, when he wrote his memoir sometime after he and his immediate family had moved to Pakistan. 'Not a single Muslim was killed in Khari Baoli', declares the memorialist. 'And my mother is still there.' Indeed, once relative calm had been restored, his mother urged him to come back. 'She writes to us saying that all of us fled unnecessarily: "you should come back now" . . . *This is but a trifling example of how Delhi's Hindus behaved towards Delhi's Muslims.*'[20]

Not all of the writer's own evidence supports this conclusion, however. He writes at other points of how even the lowest caste Hindus joined in the looting and terrorising of Delhi's long-standing Muslim residents, and of how the latter rarely felt secure in areas where they were not the majority – and, later on, not even there. Given this undeniable evidence, Dehlavi has to attach a significant rider to his claim about the non-participation of the Hindus of Delhi in the violence against the Muslims: 'Except for those who were carried away by a religious [read 'communal'] madness'[21] – and, one might add, those who were carried away by the desire for loot and property, and political advancement, too.

---

[18] Dehlavi, *Dilli*, pp. 179 and 189 for the quotations, and *passim*.
[19] Barelvi, *Azadi*, p. 150.
[20] Dehlavi, *Dilli*, pp. 146–7, 180 (emphasis added).
[21] *Ibid.*, p. 146.

The community lives on

I have suggested elsewhere that the breakdown – or threatened break-down – of community leads to a categorisation of violent events as 'history' in non-official, local narratives.[22] What is happening in all the above accounts, it seems to me, is a constitution of community through a discourse of violence 'out there'. Violence happens – and can only happen – at the boundaries of community. It marks those boundaries. It is the denial of any violence 'in our midst', the attribution of harmony *within* and the consignment of violence to the *outside*, that establishes 'community'. Violence and community constitute each other, as it were. It is important to reiterate, however, that they do so in many different ways; that slippages occur in the very accounts that signal such a mutual constitution; and that the communities thus constructed are necessarily fragile and open to question, however much they come to be invoked in the wake of social and political turbulence.

Disciplinary history, I have argued, is still based largely on the assumption of a pre-constituted subject (usually a community, nation or state) and a known, hence predictable, course of evolution or change. The category of 'violence' is reserved in this genre of writing for 'exceptional', disorderly actions, and not for events for which there is a ready political name, such as insurrection, uprising, repression, counter-insurgency or war. The former kind of violence is generally taken to be historically inconsequential. When it does enter the historical record – say, because it occurs on a massive scale – it is often represented as being so overwhelming, and so palpable and obvious, that it practically disappears from the analysis. It is sometimes reduced in these circumstances to a set of grand statistics, which allow but one inference: that the violence was extraordinary, not to say aberrational. The worst kinds of violence in our pasts – Holocaust, Partition – come to be represented in this way, as the 'limits' of history.

Non-professional reconstructions of the past mark those 'limits' quite differently – because they conceive of 'history' quite differently. Here, the example of Partition is instructive. Disciplinary histories, on the one hand, and memoirs and other survivors' accounts, on the other, yield up almost opposing assessments (and conceptualisations) of 1947, in spite of the fact that individual and collective recollections form the basis of many of the sources that historians use (if they are not classified as 'sources' themselves). The 'Partition' that historians describe in careful constitutional detail, and seek to explain in terms of political machinations, comes across very differently indeed in the non-disciplinary accounts.

---

[22] See my *Construction of Communalism*, ch. 4.

As already indicated, no clear-cut distinction is made in the majority of these non-professional 'histories' between something called 'Partition' and something else called 'violence'. Partition *is* the violence. Indeed, the English word 'partition' is often used interchangeably with terms like *raula* (disturbance), *maar-kaat* (mass killing), *maashal-la* (martial law), and *miyan-maari* (the killing of Muslims, this last being used specifically in Bihar), 'migration', and other descriptions signifying other conceptualisations of the event. Even the date for Partition in the non-academic account sometimes differs from the official date adhered to by historians, for it relates to the time of local attacks, killings, abductions and banishment, events that seriously threatened or destroyed particular senses of community.

Although they employ their own means of distancing the subject from a history of 'violence', the conditions and procedures of memoirs and non-disciplinary accounts of the past are, moreover, very different from those of historians' history. Whereas the latter's historical narrative leads up to the 'event' – 'explaining why it happened, and why it happened at the time it did'[23] – non-disciplinary practices of reconstructing the past appear to move in another way. The event (say, the 'partition' of British India) is not the object of explanation in these accounts. They do not lead up to it. Indeed, because that is the temporal structure of collective memory, they deny its 'pastness', suggesting rather its 'continuing presence'.[24] By contrast with historians' history, these 'non-historical' practices of recollection use the event to describe a set of other relations and constituencies – which I have labelled 'community'.

In the end, what comes across most forcefully in the recollections of survivors is a struggle to assert a heroic sense of community in the face of the breakdown of all inherited senses of belonging and home. This may be seen in a theme that recurs very commonly indeed in the local account of 1947: the undying valour of the community. The tales that are told of the heroism and sacrifice of the community and its members rely heavily upon silencing evidence of disagreement, denying lapses in solidarity, and asserting that the entire community acted together to overcome the 'enemy', whether through 'suicide' or through 'revenge attacks'.

[23] Dipesh Chakrabarty, 'Remembered Villages. Representation of Hindu-Bengali Memories in the Aftermath of the Partition', *Economic and Political Weekly* (10 August 1996) p. 2143. Cf. Novick: 'Historical consciousness . . . focuses on the historicity of events – that they took place then and not now, [and] that they grew out of circumstances different from those that now obtain', *Holocaust*, p. 4 (emphasis Novick's).

[24] Novick, *Holocaust*, p. 4. See also Chakrabarty, 'Remembered Villages'; and Nora, 'Memory is a perpetually actual phenomenon, a bond tying us to the eternal present; history is a representation of the past', 'Between Memory and History', p. 8.

The Rawalpindi Sikhs' reconstruction of the violence of March 1947 illustrates the proposition very well indeed.[25] One account after another stresses how *our* people preferred death to conversion and humiliation: not a single Sikh was converted in any of our villages, it is said again and again, although a few may have given in elsewhere. Several people from Thoa Khalsa pointed out to me that the first person to be killed by Sant Gulab Singh on that fateful day of 12 March 1947, was a crippled Sikh. Poor and unemployed, this cripple, whom everyone had until then thought of as a worthless character, came up to Gulab Singh and appealed to him to kill him first: for, as he is reported to have said, the rest were all fit and could run away or otherwise take care of themselves, whereas he would be caught and he did not wish to surrender his honour, his religion. Others then lined up behind him with a similar wish.[26] The story of the collective suicide at the well provides a fitting denouement to this account of heroism and community pride.

A retired military man from the neighbouring village of Thamali, who has been collecting information from survivors (and from priests in various centres of pilgrimage who maintain a genealogical family record over generations) to write a history of all that happened in the region, was the only person I talked to who spoke of any Sikh conversions to Islam from his own village.[27] There was *one* family of Sikhs in Thamali who became Muslims and stayed on, he said to me. Everyone else I met from Thamali had repeated the common account that not a single Sikh gave up his or her *dharma*. But the exception in the military man's statement served only to reinforce the larger narrative of valour and undefeated pride, in Thamali as in Thoa Khalsa and all the surrounding villages: 'Our women fought too, and kept fighting . . . (many of them in male attire). They fought with great courage. Everyone fought . . . They recited their prayers (*shabad parhte rahe*) and stayed awake (and fought). They had no fear . . . and showed great bravery . . . ' On the 12 March, he notes, came the attack on Thoa Khalsa. 'They were very courageous Sikhs too. Their resistance was great. Fifty to a hundred girls [women] started jumping into a well . . . At this they [the Muslim attackers] left that village, out of fear . . . then they turned towards Thamali . . . '[28]

[25] See ch. 4 above.

[26] The motif of different individuals offering themselves for sacrifice before all others is a common one in survivors' recollections of the time; see, for example, Kirpal Singh, comp., *Shaheedian*, pp. 104, 105, and Menon and Bhasin, *Borders and Boundaries*.

[27] Interview with Gurbachan Singh Oberoi (Bhogal, 29 January 1995).

[28] Gurbachan Singh Talib's comment on Thoa Khalsa is at one with these remarks: here, on 12 March 1947, 'after long and heroic resistance, 200 Sikhs were killed. The women were asked to embrace Islam, but 93 of them, old and young, decided to escape dishonour by drowning themselves in a well . . . The Muslim invaders, aghast at this tragedy, fled from the place', Talib, comp., *Muslim League Attack on Sikhs and Hindus*, p. 83.

Like other interviewees, the military man denied that any woman or girl (the word generally employed is *ladki*, literally, girl) had been abducted from his village in the course of this terrible battle and killing.

If [at all] they managed to take any girls from our village [*sic*], we got them back. Not a girl of ours was taken away. No such mistake [*galt kaam*, literally, bad deed] occurred... People *were* killed. But they were extraordinarily brave. No one was afraid of... [the] Musalmans, our women too were not in the least bit afraid... The girls/women were all killed earlier... the young women [and girls] were not surrendered... They lost their lives, killed by their own kinsfolk – or by the enemy... [29]

Commentators with some knowledge of Punjab noted that the heavily outnumbered Sikhs of the remote north-western districts of the province, who were the chief targets of the March 1947 attacks, were mainly of the commercial classes, quite different from the Jat peasants of the districts further south and east who were enthusiastically recruited into the British Indian army.[30] However, this did not deter Sikh (and Hindu) spokespersons – then or subsequently – from painting the resistance and sufferings of the Sikhs and Hindus of Rawalpindi, Multan and other affected districts as the sufferings of a homogenised, militaristic and manly people.

Escaping – 'somehow, anyhow'

It goes without saying that a sense of rupture and radical change – and the fact of radical change itself – had shaken people and contributed to a sense of breakdown and the need for reconstruction. However, the way in which the reconstruction is articulated in these accounts is through a denial of change and an assertion of the continued existence of the community. This happens even as the signs of breakdown of earlier community are clearly indicated: in other words, in a simultaneous assertion and denial of change. It is in this ambiguous space that notes of dissonance surface.

Times of extreme physical and psychological danger produce diverse responses, not all of which are consciously, or first and foremost, related to the question of preserving community honour. We come across many accounts of the March 1947 events that speak of the panic and the chaos, the difficulty of knowing what was happening in different parts of the same *haveli* (mansion) and its compound, let alone in other parts of the village (or town, which is what many of these villages resembled in size); the irrelevance of the question of choice at a moment such as this, and the

---

[29] Interview (29 January 1995). This respondent was away from Thamali at the time of the attacks. His account is based upon enquiries he has made from survivors of the attacks on Thamali and neighbouring villages. In that sense, it assumes even more the character of collective testimony.

[30] Cf. Moon, *Divide and Quit*, p. 78n.

desperate efforts to survive however one could. For, apart from the fact that some clear-cut notion of the community's honour was not necessarily uppermost in everyone's minds at such a time, the preservation of Sikhi (the *dharma* and the community) might still conceivably be accomplished by means other than suicide.

Let us return for a moment to the celebratory account of the Thoa Khalsa incident provided to Butalia and Vaid by Bir Bahadur Singh, which I have cited earlier. It is necessary to note that this account comes from a man of some political ambition, a long-time member of the Shiromani Gurdwara Prabandhak Committee (SGPC) and now an enthusiastic supporter of the Bharatiya Janata Party (BJP), who led two Sikh *jathas* to Ayodhya in 1990 and 1992 to bring down the Babri Masjid, someone who is naturally concerned to maintain his position and leadership within the particular Partition-affected Sikh community of Delhi of which he is a part. Every year on 13 March, which is observed as '*shahidi divas*' (martyrs' day) by the community, this informant makes a major speech, recounting the sacrifices of the Sikhs of Rawalpindi (and especially of Kahuta *tehsil* or subdivision), and promises to write a history that will bring these sacrifices to the notice of the world and earn his people their rightful place amongst 'the greatest of India's freedom-fighters'.[31] The truly exceptional, and constructed, character of his account becomes even clearer when we realise that the woman he refers to in the last sentence of the extract quoted in chapter 4, in the third person and with some suggestion of doubt as to whether she is still alive – 'Till today I think she is alive' – is his own mother. How much might one not read into that expression of doubt, fifty years after Partition, about the very survival of his mother as a real, living being.[32]

To underscore the irony of this account, let me move on at once to the recollection of the same event by the very much alive, eighty-six-year-old mother. A woman of remarkable energy and spirit, even at this age, she tells of the day-to-day struggle waged by her family to recover something of their lost status and make something of their lives: of their refusal to beg, and their willingness to do whatever work was necessary for a living. 'We washed dishes', 'we washed clothes' and 'always maintained our dignity and self-respect'. When she is ready for the (formal) interview, and has made her invocation to the Guru to say that everything she recounts will be the truth as she knows it, she launches into her narrative

---

[31] These details come from interviews with Bir Bahadur Singh in March 1995 and 1996, and my attendance at the commemoration service in Bhogal on 13 March 1996.

[32] See Butalia, *Other Side of Silence*, p. 161, for an interpretation of this ambivalence. Butalia leaves out the phrase 'I think' from the Sikh politico's account as cited in her book (cf. her 'Community, State and Gender', p. WS-14), but Bir Bahadur's ambivalence is still evident.

of events from 'the ninth (*nau tareekh ke din*)', without pausing to explain that this 'ninth' refers to 9 March 1947, and almost without waiting for the interviewer's questions. (I say 'almost' because I, as interviewer, had of course already explained why I was there, what my antecedents and my interests were and what I wanted her to talk about.) Hers is a polished narrative of a great battle and a great sacrifice, and she fills it with remarkable detail of who was killed by whom within the Sikh community of the village, what different people said as the martyrdoms began, the names of the martyrs, those who jumped into the well, in what order and so on.

We must bear in mind that such tales of unprecedented sacrifice – unlike other stories, involving the forcible conversion or abduction of a family member, for instance – are usually not being recounted for the first time. They will have been told many times before: initially to relatives, friends, neighbours and other sympathisers, later sometimes to children and grandchildren, perhaps even at local public gatherings for festivals, marriages, commemorations, and again to investigators like ourselves. The very telling and retelling will have tended to fix the form and the main points of the account.[33] Yet neither family, community and nation, nor time and the procedures of collective 'memory', are enough to wipe out all signs of dissonance and homogenise all recollections of the past. We have other recollections, therefore, that speak of the tension and ambiguity, the grave uncertainty and the desperation of the time.

The following account from another survivor of Thoa Khalsa, then a girl of twelve or thirteen studying in the girls' primary school there, provides a striking example.[34] 'Whoever could – escaped', she said simply. 'However we could... wherever we could.' 'Many women and children went out and sat down at the well, to pray and... they called out to us too. But it was a question of where desire [fate?] took you that day... My cousin held my hand and said, "Don't move." He stood in my way. But I slipped under his arms and ran down the stairs after my elder brother, who was saying, "Run as fast as you can. Run wherever..." A servant who was among the attackers blocked my path. "Where are you going? You'll go nowhere," he said, and grabbed my *chunni*. But I escaped, leaving my *chunni* in his hands.' The *chunni*, a long scarf worn over the shoulders and upper body, and used to cover the head as well, is a sign of a girl/woman's modesty – a symbol of honour, here having to be left behind

---

[33] On the way in which the local, collective narrative comes to be fixed very early on, sometimes within days of an event, see my 'In Defense of the Fragment: Writing About Hindu-Muslim Riots in India Today', *Representations* (Winter 1992).

[34] Interview (Delhi, 4 March 1995). I have withheld the interviewee's name at her request.

temporarily in a struggle to escape from greater dishonour, and to preserve life 'somehow, anyhow'.[35]

The girl's mother was with her, as were three of her brothers and two or three other girls, and the respondent names some other women who managed to flee. In recalling the desperate moments of that escape from death, she mentions other incidents that go against the generalised, homogenised account of Sikh heroism, but are no less moving and heroic for that. 'I was like one dead. I had high fever. My brother had said to my mother, "Shall we save ourselves or try to save her . . . Her condition is very bad." My mother said simply, "She will be killed, how can I leave her here?" They acted with great courage and brought me along. To protect my little brother, they opened out his hair, and combed and platted it, so that he would be mistaken for a girl.' 'Girls were only being converted, and taken away', she states poignantly – as if, somehow, the disguise would have saved her brother from death, had they been discovered.

The more celebratory accounts too contain traces of these other dimensions of a besieged Hindu, Muslim or Sikh population's immediate concerns in the face of violence in 1947. While they differ considerably in detail, many of them underline the confusions of the moment, the uncertainty and fear felt by the victims and the frequent need for coercion before they agreed to become 'martyrs'. One more example is all I can give here. It comes from an SGPC report compiled on the basis of the statements of Sikh survivors from village Chakkari Dheri in the Campbellpur *tehsil* of Campbellpur district. Here, Muslim attackers had, under threat of dire consequences, persuaded a number of Sikhs to accept Islam. They then marched with these 'converts' to the house of Sardar Jaswant Singh and called upon him and his family to follow their example, only to be met with a blank refusal. When they began to break down the roof of the house, however, Jaswant Singh's wife, cradling her four-month-old baby in her lap, appealed to the men of the house to agree to what the other Sikhs had already accepted. She was told to keep quiet, but persisted with her plea, at which Jaswant Singh's elder brother reportedly shouted in anger: 'I am prepared to sacrifice my grown son, and you are bothered about your four-month-old? [*sic*]' On her continued refusal to see his point, the report says, Sant Singh drew his sword from its sheath and 'martyred' his sister-in-law and her son at the same time.[36]

The SGPC document implicitly celebrates the 'martyrdom' (and the murder), but neglects to address the question of choice – of alternative possibilities and hopes of preserving life and honour. Yet, if one cares to

[35] Veena Das, 'Composition of the Personal Voice: Violence and Migration', *Studies in History*, 7, 1, n.s. (1991), p. 69.

[36] SGPC report, extracted in Kirpal Singh, comp., *Shaheedian*, pp. 103–4.

look, these surface again and again. The logic of unanimity has its limits,
even in the local historical reconstruction of community at the time of
crisis. In his statement recorded in the 1950s, Gulab Singh speaks with
some shame of the Sikh headmaster of the Thoa Khalsa village school
hiding in a Muslim servant's house, where his wife, hiding with him,
cooked the evening meal wearing 'Muslim League clothes'. The military man from Thamali, quoted above, acknowledges that 'one family
of Sikhs' accepted Islam and stayed on in the village. Alongside Gulab
Singh's challenging recollection that even the tyrannical Aurangzeb and
Farrukhsiyar had been unable to destroy the Sikhs, we have another survivor's simple report that 'whoever could – escaped, however we could,
wherever we could'. Alongside the Thamali military man's assertion that
'not a girl of ours was taken away; not a single Sikh gave up his (her)
religion', we have Satnam Kaur's matter-of-fact statement that, faced
with the choice between converting to Islam and being butchered, 'all
the Sikhs [in her village] yielded'. Other accounts indicate more, that numerous families – on both sides of the border – were willing to sacrifice a
young woman (or women) of the family to buy the family's security.[37]

The ambiguous community

In nearly all the recollections quoted in this chapter, everyone who is part
of the narrator's community appears in the position of a victim. In the
reflections of the Sikhs of Gharuan, 'attacks' are almost always represented as 'defence' or, when the respondents are being more forthright,
as 'counter-attacks'. I do not wish to suggest, however, that this is the
only kind of story that is ever recounted, or that every tale of remembered violence is equally coy about acknowledging a part in aggressive
actions.

Clearly there are numerous examples of the gleeful reporting of violence in the contemporary records and in survivors' accounts. Witness
Khosla's general finding in his 1949 survey of Partition violence: 'There
are many who boast that the total number of Muslims killed [in East Pun-
jab] was more than the number of Hindus and Sikhs who perished in West
Punjab . . .', he wrote.[38] Or Ram Chandra Thapar's pride in the good
work of the Hindus in the 'Calcutta Killings' of August 1946: 'Calcutta
has taught . . . [the Muslims] a lesson which they'll remember long. Their
loss in lives amounted to about 7000 against about 1000 Hindus. They
did play havoc on the first two days but on the third and fourth the Hindus,

---

[37] Cf. Svati Joshi, 'Torn Up by the Roots', p. 14. Other examples are found in Kirpal Singh's
Shaheedian, and indeed in the oral accounts of survivors from Rawalpindi.
[38] Khosla, *Stern Reckoning*, p. 290.

seeing that the Police and Military were not coming to help, retaliated and relentlessly.'[39] Or Dehlavi's report of the crowds at Lahore station, waiting to settle scores in the presence of refugees whose train had been attacked on its way from India, stopping a refugee special going the other way, and paying back the killers on the other side – as they said – 'with interest'.[40]

Not surprisingly, one also finds recollections that openly celebrate the narrator's own part in the aggressive actions of the time. The account of a captain in the army of the erstwhile Alwar state, recorded by Shail Mayaram in 1993, provides an excellent illustration. The captain speaks of his army's 'operations' against the local Muslims in 1947, and it is worthwhile quoting him at some length:

I was the ADC to HH Tej Singh [the ruler of Alwar]...It had been decided to clear the state of Muslims. The orders came from Sardar Patel. He spoke to HH on the hot line. The killings of Hindus at Noakhali and Punjab had to be avenged. All the Meos from Firozpur Jhirka down were to be cleared and sent to Pakistan, their lands taken over. [Because] the refugees from Pakistan were coming in. They told us all sorts of stories of what had been done to them. We did whatever was happening there, like parading women naked on the streets in Tijara and Naugaonwa after their families had been killed...

In Tijara, after a battle that lasted eighteen hours against a force he describes as consisting of 10,000 Meo Muslims, the captain and his troops managed to take the town. 'We killed every man, all of them.' And again, speaking of other sites where the Meos were reported to have gathered in large numbers:

The women – if they were of marriageable age, were all taken. They were *shuddh* [pure] after drinking *ganga jal* [water from the sacred river Ganges] and could be taken...Not a single Muslim was left in Alwar. Alwar was the first state to clear all the Muslims. Bharatpur followed...[41]

One may gather similar stories of the aggressive assertion of 'us' against 'them' even in Gharuan and other villages and communities where there is a general proposition of 'peacefulness' and 'harmony' within the locality. Indeed I suspect this would apply to virtually any village or town in eastern (now Indian) Punjab, from where the Muslims were largely, if not entirely, driven out in 1947: and I have little doubt that the same would be true of western (now Pakistani) Punjab where the violence and the refugees flowed the other way.

---

[39] (Imperial War Museum, London), Major H. H. L. Smith collection, 88/28/3, letter from Thapar (8/9 October 1946).
[40] Dehlavi, *Dilli*, pp. 176–7.
[41] Mayaram, *Resisting Regimes*, pp. 179–81.

If such accounts seem to fit all too well with the saga of sacrifice and war that is the stuff of so much nationalist history, and especially with the gory popular 'histories' produced by militant right-wing states and movements, the note of defensiveness that is so often present in them still calls for explanation. The survivors' stories recounted above frequently become statements, not only of pride in how successfully the aggressive actions were carried out, but also of the *necessity* of this obliteration and eviction: 'It was war, wasn't it?' 'They were doing the same thing to our people on that side.' 'Who began it all?' Indeed, the idea of *revenge* has a great deal to do with the ongoing cycle of violence in 1947 and the years before and after.

Two aspects of these stories of revenge and aggression require further discussion, however. The relevance of the first is obvious enough. We need to ask questions about how the 'us' and 'them' are constituted – or, as I am suggesting, reconstituted – in and by these accounts. But, secondly, we might also ask: how is it that so many of these accounts, in which what is being described is something like a state of war, and where the 'enemy' has in many instances been completely wiped out, contain within them a note not just of celebration, but of apology and shame as well? This shame too is related in part to the effort to reconstitute community – to rethink the 'us' of the story in the fragile moment when a new idea of community collides with the breakdown of earlier senses. Statements of *revenge* are already statements of *defensiveness*; and the idea of revenge depends on that of 'betrayal' – and hence of 'community'.

No doubt, the greater or lesser 'defensiveness' of different recollections stems in part from the divergent circumstances of different field interviews. This includes the question of the degree of trust established between interviewer and interviewee, and the particular physical and social setting of an interview. It depends to an extent on the personal circumstances and careers of the respondents: their military or professional training, the extent of their involvement in 'public' debate, or of their non-involvement. It has to do also with political context: the time and place in which accounts are collected; the extent of political militancy at the time, among specific groups and classes, in specific regions; the readiness, consequent on some of the above, to propound radical (in the India of the 1980s and 1990s, exclusivist, right-wing) solutions, or, on the contrary, the disillusionment that sometimes creeps in when goals that once seemed laudable fail to produce the benefits they were meant to produce.

However, there seems to be another factor at work here too. What is perhaps being relived in tales of violence constructed in a frankly assertive way is the actual or anticipated disappearance of particular senses

of community and the emergence of others. Frequently, one sees 'our people' and 'theirs' being redescribed – different senses of 'us' and 'them' in
contention, new notions of the community struggling to be born – in the
course of the very same narrative. Particular understandings of the local
community come at a particular historical conjuncture to have much reduced value. This may be seen as much in Rahi Masoom Raza's 'divided-
village' called Gangauli, as in the Mewat, Punjab or Alwar of 1947. In
Raza's telling phrase, 'for some time now, in Gangauli, the number of the
people of Gangauli has been declining, and the numbers of Sunnis, Shias
and Hindus have been increasing'.[42] At the time of the general elections
in undivided India in 1945–6, according to one intelligence report, 'Punjabis ceased to be Punjabis and became Muslims, Hindus and Sikhs.'[43]
Or as Intizar Husain has it in his 'Unwritten Epic', this was a time when
even zamindars stopped being zamindars and 'start[ed] being Hindus
and Muslims'.[44]

What appear to count more and more in the context of Partition are
'believers' and 'non-believers', 'Hindus' and 'Muslims' and 'Sikhs', and
even the usually remote 'India' and 'Pakistan'. Violence – indeed, excessive, unforgiving violence – is sometimes thought to have been indispens-
able in the struggle to establish these new – 'pure', 'real' – communities
on secure foundations: and it is no shame to declare it. It is just this kind
of drive for the reconstitution of community that appears to be at work
in the Alwar account. Those who were suspect in the slightest, those who
were only nominally Muslim as well as those Muslims who did not wish
to go to Pakistan, had to go. 'The Meos were not Muslims', says the captain, 'they were half-Hindu. In their marriages they had both *pheras* and
the *nikaah* [Hindu and Muslim rites respectively]. They were not with
the Muslim League. They did not want to go to Pakistan. But we had
orders to clear them.' Hence, 'Not a single Muslim was left in Alwar.'[45]

However, the 'reinvention' of community is not always easily accomplished, for history – and everyday social life – has an uncanny knack of
messing things up. Even in the Alwar region, from where the captain's
bombastic account comes, other Hindu inhabitants who took part in the
looting and killing of 1947 will, in the presence of Muslim neighbours,
often deny that anything happened in their villages, and go to the extent of asserting that the local mosque which lies in a shattered state
before the visitor's eyes was not in fact destroyed by human hands, but

---

[42] Rahi Masoom Raza, *Aadha gaon* (Delhi, 1966), p. 13 (translation mine).
[43] Rees papers, PBF bundles, Secret 'Log' of 4 August 1947.
[44] Intizar Husain, 'An Unwritten Epic', in Memon, ed., *An Epic Unwritten*, p. 168.
[45] Mayaram, *Resisting Regimes*, p. 181.

'came down in a storm'.[46] There are, one might say, two different notions of community in contention here. The Gharuan case that I have discussed in detail above is another example of this kind of simultaneous loyalty to what we would see as two (or more) different 'communities'. So is Dehlavi's Delhi 'which had now become . . . a witch', but 'still remained a mother'.

'Nothing happened in our community.' It was 'outsiders', 'criminals', 'politicians', 'madmen', the demented and the temporarily crazed who were responsible for the 'storm'. Two interestingly different resolutions are encountered here. Gharuan changed, but Gharuan lived on (with some of its Muslim inhabitants staying on too). Alternatively, 'Delhi still exists: but where is that Delhi now . . . ? *(Dilli ab bhi baqi hai, lekin ab woh Dilli kahan . . . ?)*'

Where is 'home' now?

Where is the Delhi we knew? In asking the question, Ebadat Barelvi, the professor of Delhi College who managed to escape to Lucknow in September 1947 and later wrote of the miracle Gandhi's martyrdom brought (when 'the world . . . changed' and it seemed as if 'strife had never occurred'), and who returned to his teaching duties in Delhi in April 1948, encouraged by Abul Kalam Azad, Zakir Husain and others as part of their effort to restore normalcy, reflected his own sense of loss and bitterness in his memoirs published forty years later. Delhi had become a veritable 'refugee-istan', he recalls.[47] The Delhi College was soon full of Hindu and Sikh students and professors from Sindh and Punjab – 'good human beings', but of a culture far different from that the college was used to (135, 151). After Jinnah's death and the Indian government's take-over of Hyderabad in September 1948, Hyderabad became another scene of mass killing of Muslims and the mass rape of Muslim women, he writes. 'Our eyes shed tears of blood (*Aankhen khoon bahati rahin)*' (131).

Ultimately, after much deliberation and misgiving, Ebadat Barelvi left Delhi at the end of 1948. His migration to Lahore appeared to him, in retrospect, as the moment of real liberation. 'Tears welled up at the thought that I was now in Pakistan. I had spent the year or eighteen months prior

---

[46] I cite this particular example from the village of Tilpat, south of Delhi, which I visited with my colleague from Delhi University, Nayanjot Lahiri. Cf. her 'Archaeological Landscapes and Textual Images: a Study of the Sacred Geography of Late Medieval Ballabhgarh', *World Archaeology*, 28, 2 (1996), photograph on p. 254.

[47] Barelvi, *Azadi*, p. 150. Page references for the quotations that follow are provided in the text.

to my arrival here in great mental anguish and vexation' (159). Once his family had also safely crossed the border, he writes further, he breathed even more freely: 'Now we would all live in Lahore, without any fear, and . . . pass our days in this pure and holy land in accordance with our beliefs and customs . . . ' (172). He dwells on the 'treasure of peace and security' that he found in Lahore, that 'wealth of respect and honour', the desire for which had been eating into his soul for a long time (177). And he writes of the beauty of Lahore, the 'city of lights' and 'grace' and 'bounty' and 'romance', which now 'appeared to us like the land of fairies' (164). 'Delhi', that magical city, was indeed very far away now. Lahore had become the new 'Delhi'.

Delhi still exists, but where is the Delhi of yesteryears – the Delhi of the poets Ghalib and Zauq, and of the nationalist leaders, Mukhtar Ahmad Ansari and Hakim Ajmal Khan? It is a question that Gandhi had raised, too. What would happen to Delhi, he had asked, if the 'Great Mosque' – the Jama Masjid built in the time of Shah Jahan – was removed from the city?[48] What has happened to India after 1992, we might ask, when a small unused mosque in Ayodhya, built in 1528 during the days of Babur, the first Mughal ruler of northern India, was torn down amidst the glare of television cameras and reporters of the world's press, by a huge gathering of Hindu militants – yelling 'victory' to their gods and their nation as they attacked this sixteenth-century 'symbol of slavery' and urged vengeance on their twentieth-century Muslim co-citizens?[49]

What happens to the plural, 'exceptional' character of India in the face of this kind of militant 'nationalist' assault? What happens to the dreams of democracy, and participatory development, and secular tolerance, that constituted the ground for a century of anti-imperialist struggle? What sense of 'home' – and of 'India' – do the 'minorities' have now? Some of the best Muslim writers of the subcontinent asked this question in the wake of Partition: and I invoke two of them – an Indian and a Pakistani – to conclude these scattered reflections on violence and civilisation, nationhood and history.

In their remarkable writings on the period, Rahi Masoom Raza and Intizar Husain initiate a subtle, but direct, challenge to the claims of nationalism and nationalist historiography, as they think through the twin themes of the breakdown, and the possibility, of community. Raza subverts the rules of the writing of novels, and of nationalist thought, through an 'introduction' that appears towards the end of his novel, *Aadha gaon* – literally, '*Half a Village*'. This is the life-story of the Muslim half of his

---

[48] *CWMG*, vol. LXXXIX, pp. 176, 179–81, and 201.
[49] Cf. Kapoor, *Resources Against Communalism*.

home village, Gangauli, in Ghazipur district, on the eastern border of
Uttar Pradesh. It is a 'half' that is itself divided in half by the Pakistan
movement – even though the village is located hundreds of miles away
from the borders of both East and West Pakistan (now Bangladesh and
Pakistan respectively).

'You must be wondering why there is an introduction in the middle
of the story', Raza writes in this interlude which appears between the
second last and third last chapters of the book. 'At this moment', he goes
on, 'the story of half the village has reached a very delicate point... The
fact is that now our story has come to a place where one age ends and
another begins. And doesn't every new age demand an introduction?'
He then sets out the consequences of Partition for families that were
split up:

I am not hurt because Safir-va became a Saiyid[50] in Pakistan. He must have done
so. And who can say that there was no blood of some purest of the pure Zaidi
Saiyid in his veins? But I am concerned about Sallo and her daughter Shahida
whom Tannu left here and whom Rabban-bi continually curses. Hearing Rabban-
bi's curses, Sallo beats Shahida – and the question is, what sort of mother will
Shahida be when she grows up? The question is, when Saddam has married
again in Pakistan, what will become of the Hakim Sahib's litter of grandchildren
here... There are other questions of this nature too...

Finally, the writer asserts his right as a native of Gangauli to stay –
where he belongs:

The Jan Sangh [the leading right-wing Hindu political party of the 1950s and
1960s, and a predecessor of today's Bharatiya Janata Party] says that Muslims are
outsiders. How can I presume to say they're lying? But I must say that I belong to
Ghazipur. My bonds with Gangauli are unbreakable. It's not just a village, it's my
home. Home. This word exists in every language and dialect. And that is why I
repeat my statement – because Gangauli's not just a village, it's my home as well.
'Because' – what a strong word this is. And there are thousands of 'becauses' like
it, and no sword is sharp enough to cut this 'because'... And I give no one the
right to say to me, 'Rahi! You don't belong to Gangauli, and so get out and go,
say, to Rae Bareli.' Why should I go, sahib? I will not go.[51]

'This introduction', writes Raza, 'was necessary to carry the story forward.' The following pages of the novel describe the 'loneliness' of the first
Muharram after Partition. It was not only over the death of the departed
martyrs, Imam Hasan and Imam Husain, that the mourners now wept,
but over the departure of many living loved ones – and the consequences

---

[50] That is to say, a Muslim claiming noble descent.
[51] *Aadha gaon*, pp. 303–5. Here I have used the translation found in Rahi Masoom Raza,
Feuding Families of Village Gangauli, tr. Gillian Wright, (New Delhi, 1995), pp. 290–1.

of their being far away, in Pakistan. 'One moment had produced a bound-
less emptiness . . . the universe began to echo, as if there was no one . . . for
a vast distance . . . In short with independence several kinds of loneliness
had been born . . . '[52]

Intizar Husain's '*Bin likhi razmiya*' ('An Unwritten Epic') is in some
ways an even more searing tale. It is the story of a story (an 'epic') that
cannot be written, yet gets itself written, immediately after Partition –
even as the author celebrates Pakistan as a great historic moment, the
moment of *hijrat*.[53] It is the story of a Muslim village called Qadirpur,
again left on the wrong side of the border when Partition occurred: for
Muslims at the time, that was the Indian side. Pichwa is the central character of this epic. He is an unlikely hero, since he was simply a local tough,
a body-builder, master in the art of club-fighting and head of what might
be called the village gymnasium. But (says the author) he possessed 'a
certain dignity and greatness', and this was after all to be an epic of the
common people (*Jumhurnama*).[54]

Intizar Husain leaves for Pakistan and there begins to write the story of
his native Qadirpur, with Pichwa as his hero. But, following another round
of violence and killing in the village, Pichwa himself arrives in Pakistan –
thus ruining the basis of the story. While he was still in Qadirpur, the
writer could picture him as he wished. That possibility was now ended.
The 'epic', however, gets written – on different dates.

On 12 April 1950, several months after the writer had begun writing
his story, his diary entry reads: 'When I met Pichwa this morning, he
said, "Miyan, get me some kind of work. . . . if I can't get any work, at
least have a house allotted for me." I was greatly astonished when I heard
these words from Pichwa's mouth. He was never worried about daily
necessities in Qadirpur . . . but now that he's come to Pakistan and wants
a place to put his feet and something to fill his belly, all the height and
grandeur of his character are destroyed . . . '

On 22 April 1950, he wrote: 'How can I write the Mahabharata of
Qadirpur? The Arjuna of this Mahabharata[55] is now the picture of failure
and he wanders the streets and lanes of Pakistan looking for a house
and a job . . . ' On 6 May 1950: 'My creative desire continues to cool, and
whatever magic there was in the fictional potential of Pichwa's personality

---

[52] *Ibid.*, p. 292.
[53] *Hijrat* means 'migration', and in Muslim usage usually carries the sacred associations
of the Prophet's migration from Mecca to Medina. (I am deeply indebted to Sudhir
Chandra for discussions on Intizar Husain's work, his sensitive reading of '*Bin likhi
razmiya*', and his insistence that I engage with it in this book.)
[54] Intizar Husain, 'An Unwritten Epic', in Memon, ed., *An Epic Unwritten*, p. 165. The
following quotations are all taken from Memon's excellent translation.
[55] A reference to the classical Hindu epic and one of its foremost heroes.

ebbs away. He no longer seems like a person at all; he seems more like a
chess piece . . .'

Then Pichwa leaves for India, by an order of the Pakistani government
because Pakistan cannot accommodate any more refugees; but whether
he ever reaches or not, no one knows. A letter of enquiry sent by the
writer to Qadirpur produces the following response from a respectable
elder who had stayed behind: 'Your letter arrived late, but I am thankful
it came . . . Qadirpur is no longer Qadirpur. Now its new residents call it
Jatunagar[56] . . . Where is Qadirpur now?'

Soon after, the author learns of Pichwa's death, but his proposed novel
still does not come to life. On 27 May 1950, he writes: 'I have definitely
decided not to write my novel. But how long can I just sit at home and
do nothing?'

At this point, through the good offices of an associate from Qadirpur,
the novelist is allotted a flour mill. And the world veritably changes. He
writes on 29 May 1950: 'As the owner of a flour mill, I see a strange kind
of change in myself. As long as I was stuck in the web of literature, I felt
cut off from my nation . . . Now, however, I consider myself a responsible
citizen – a dutiful member of a rising nation.' A new kind of community
is establishing itself.

There are different kinds of community at stake in the stories I have
quoted – some made by literature and poetry, and human dignity, others
by flour mills and the demands of the state.[57] The 'small voice' of literature – like the 'small voice of history'[58] – is now in greater danger than ever
before of being swept away by the forces of nationalism, of globalisation
and of the attendant 'disciplines'.

A final word

The relatively small-scale, 'face-to-face' communities of the past have
given way more and more to the relatively large-scale, bureaucratised
communities of the present. These are *lived in*, but perhaps not *lived* as
they once used to be. At the same time, they are inadequately recognised

---

[56] Qadirpur means 'the home, or habitation, of Qadir' (a Muslim inhabitant or ancestor);
Jatunagar, 'the home (or town) of the Jats' (a Hindu caste group). '*Nagar*' is also a more
Sanskritised suffix than '*pur*'.

[57] Glover, *Humanity*, p. 51, reports the statement of a Soviet soldier who fought in
Afghanistan: 'Before I went into the army it was Dostoevsky and Tolstoy who taught
me how I ought to live life. In the army it was sergeants.' In the post-colonial states of
the 'Third World', one is tempted to say, it is local licensing and rationing officers.

[58] Cf. Ranajit Guha: 'If the small voice of history gets a hearing at all . . . it will do so only by
interrupting the telling in the dominant version, breaking up its storyline and making a
mess of its plot', 'The Small Voice of History', in *Subaltern Studies*, vol. IX (Delhi, 1996),
p. 12.

as *political* constructs – products of human interaction and the human imagination, working in particular, constrained historical circumstances. The large-scale, bureaucratised, modern community tends both to homogenise its constituent elements and to atomise them. It structures them politically as a mass of individuals who have erected over themselves – for purposes of efficiency and efficacy in the modern world – a supreme authority or state (or rather, several such supreme authorities across the globe).[59] However, to gain the backing of this mass of individuals to the greatest possible extent, to maximise and obtain the full benefits of their labour, energy and resources (and at times their very physical being), ruling classes and their ideologies have widely represented the modern, bureaucratised community as predestined, if not primordial, and the modern nation-state as the 'natural' condition for the good society. This move towards the bureaucratisation, homogenisation and freezing of cultures, facilitated and ensured by a state power existing above the multitude of atomic individuals – who, in their turn, paradoxically, constitute the natural, moral communities to be defended – is perhaps the most important hallmark of political history and political endeavour over the last two centuries. And it is this, together with the phenomenal technological advances of the era, that has allowed genocidal murder and violence on an unprecedented scale.[60]

This book has dealt with one instance of genocidal violence, and with what the renditions of that violence tell us about existing communities. Throughout this study, I have been concerned with the question of how communities are constructed and how national as well as local traditions are reconstructed, through the language of violence. In its course, we have observed that the reconstruction of community, and of local sociality, depends upon particular reconstructions of the past, and sought to emphasise the instability of new subject positions.

Perhaps it still needs to be said that the 'communities' that have provided the theme of this enquiry are not the objectified, frozen and enumerated communities of a positivist sociology or political science – entities already out there, awaiting identification by the internal or external observer. Rather they are solidary collectivities that come into being through the very narratives that invoke them. What we find in a great many of the non-disciplinary accounts of 1947 considered in this and preceding chapters are senses of community that remain significantly malleable, fuzzy,

---

[59] For arguments that parallel the above to some extent, see Adorno's early and somewhat schematic comments on 'secondary communities' and 'intermediary objectified social processes' in Theodor W. Adorno, *The Stars Down to Earth and Other Essays on the Irrational in Culture* (London, 1994), p. 36 and *passim*.

[60] Cf. Zygmunt Bauman's now classic *Modernity and the Holocaust* (Ithaca, N.Y., 1989).

contextual – might one say, 'historical'?[61] To take account of this lived, and changeable, community is to understand how the community – the subject of history – is forged in the very construction of the past, in the course, one might say, of a historical discourse.

At the beginning of the twenty-first century, it is perhaps time to expressly recognise the modern nation and the nation-state (and its history) also as alterable, malleable, historical constructions of this kind. We might then ask whether it is possible to recover a different kind of 'national' past, recalling not suicide and murder ('sacrifice' and 'war') and the eternally fixed collective subject, but labour and creativity, and varied, internally differentiated communities, made up of thinking, acting, changing and fallible human beings. And on that basis struggle to build other kinds of political community in the future, more self-consciously historical and more self-consciously accommodating.

Are there other histories that we might conjure up in the hope of conjuring up these other kinds of less self-righteous, less exclusive and more elective, political community? What would it mean to think of England, for example, not as an 'ancient nation' that broke away from the Roman Catholic Church and built a worldwide ascendancy on the basis of a much advertised common sense and stiff upper lip, but as a historical community of old and new migrants, men and women, white and black, contributing different elements to the common culture, and struggling in diverse ways to expand the arena of social and political rights?[62] What would it mean to imagine India as a society in which the Muslim does not figure as a 'minority', but as Bengali or Malayali, labourer or professional, literate or non-literate, young or old, man or woman?[63] The politics, and history, of the coming decades could provide an answer.

---

[61] For the 'enumerated' and the 'fuzzy' community, see Sudipto Kaviraj, 'The Imaginary Institution of India', in *Subaltern Studies*, vol. VII (Delhi, 1992). I also make an argument about the always malleable, contextualised notion of the local 'community' in my *Construction of Communalism*, ch. 4.

[62] It will be clear that I differ from Adrian Hastings' fascinating account of the early origins of English nationhood, in his *Construction of Nationhood*, on account of my emphasis on the modern construction and reconstruction of nations and communities, and the politics of those reconstructions.

[63] Cf. Azad's important argument against thinking of the Indian Muslims as a minority, Syeda Saiyidain Hameed, *India's Maulana. Selected Speeches and Writings of Maulana Abul Kalam Azad* (Delhi, 1990), pp. 158–9.

Select bibliography

CONTEMPORARY WRITINGS, DOCUMENTS, SPEECHES AND MEMOIRS

Abbasi, Jalil, *Kya din the* (Delhi, 1987).

Ambedkar, B. R., *Pakistan, or the Partition of India* (Bombay, 1946).

Azad, Abul Kalam, *India Wins Freedom. The Complete Version* (Madras, 1988).

Aziz, K. K., *The Historical Background of Pakistan, 1857–1947: an Annotated Digest of Source Material* (Karachi, 1970).

Barelvi, Ebadat, *Azadi ke saaye mein* (Lahore, 1988).

Bose, Sarat Chandra, *I Warned My Countrymen. Being the Collected Works 1945–50 of Sarat Chandra Bose* (Calcutta, 1968).

Chaudhuri, Nirad C., *Thy Hand, Great Anarch! India 1921–1952* (London, 1987).

Das, Durga, ed., *Sardar Patel's Correspondence, 1945–50*, vols. IV–V (Ahmedabad, 1972–3).

Dehlavi, Shahid Ahmad, *Dilli ki bipta* (*Naya Daur*, 1948), reprinted in Mumtaz Shirin, ed., *Zulmat-i-nimroz* (Karachi, 1990).

Gandhi, M. K., *Collected Works of Mahatma Gandhi*, various volumes (Delhi).

Hameed, Syeda Saiyidain, *India's Maulana. Selected Speeches and Writings of Maulana Abul Kalam Azad* (Delhi, 1990).

Hasan, Mushirul, ed., *India Partitioned. The Other Face of Freedom* (Delhi, 1995), 2 volumes.

Khosla, G. D., *Memory's Gay Chariot. An Autobiographical Narrative* (Delhi, 1985).

Stern Reckoning. A Survey of the Events Leading up to and Following the Partition of India (1949; reprinted Delhi, 1989).

Moon, Penderel, *Divide and Quit. An Eyewitness Account of the Partition of India* (Delhi, 1998).

Nehru, Jawaharlal, *Glimpses of World History*, vol. II (1934; 2nd edn, Bombay 1961).

Selected Works of Jawaharlal Nehru, 2nd series, vol. I (Delhi, 1984).

Pyarelal, *Mahatma Gandhi. The Last Phase*, vol. II (Ahmedabad, 1958).

Qidwai, Begum Anees, *Azadi ki chhaon mein*, Hindi tr., Nur Nabi Abbasi (Delhi, 1990).

Sherwani, Latif Ahmed, ed., *Pakistan Resolution to Pakistan, 1940–1947. A Selection of Documents Presenting the Case for Pakistan* (Karachi, 1969; reprinted Delhi, 1985).

Singh, Kirpal, comp., *Shaheedian* (Amritsar, 1964?).
Stree Shakti Sanghatana, *'We Were Making History . . .' Life Stories of Women in the Telegana People's Struggle* (Delhi, 1989).
Talib, Gurbachan Singh, comp., *Muslim League Attack on Sikhs and Hindus in the Punjab, 1947* (Amritsar, 1950; reprinted, Delhi, 1991).
Tandon, Prakash, *Punjabi Century. 1857–1947* (Berkeley and Los Angeles, 1968).
Tuker, Francis, *While Memory Serves* (London, 1950).
Zaidi, A. M., ed., *Congress Presidential Addresses. Volume 5: 1940–85* (Delhi, 1989).
    ed., *The Story of the Congress Pilgrimage. Volume 4: 1940–55* (Delhi, 1990).
Zaidi, Z. H., ed., *Quaid-i-Azam Mohammad Ali Jinnah Papers. Prelude to Pakistan. 20 February–2 June 1947*, 1st series, vol. I, part 1 (Islamabad, 1993).

FICTION RELATING TO PARTITION

Ali, Ahmed, *Twilight in Delhi* (1940; Delhi, 1991).
Bhalla, Alok, *Stories on the Partition of India* (Delhi, 1994), 3 volumes.
Francisco, Jason, 'In the Heat of the Fratricide: the Literature of India's Partition Burning Freshly', review article in *Annual of Urdu Studies* (1997).
Hasan, Khalid, tr., *Kingdom's End and Other Stories* (London, 1987).
Manto ke numaindah afsane, comp. Atahar Parvez (Aligarh, 1981).
Memon, Muhammad Umar, ed., *An Epic Unwritten. The Penguin Book of Partition Stories* (Delhi, 1998).
Raza, Rahi Masoom, *Aadha gaon* (Delhi, 1966).
    Feuding Families of Village Gangauli, tr. Gillian Wright (Delhi, 1995).
Sahni, Bhishma, *'Amritsar aa gaya'*, in *Kitne toba Tek Singh. Bharat vibhajan ki das Kahaniyan* (Delhi, 1987).

OTHER SECONDARY WORKS

Adorno, Theodor W., *The Stars Down to Earth and Other Essays on the Irrational in Culture* (London, 1994).
Agamben, Giorgio, *Remnants of Auschwitz. The Witness and the Archive* (New York, 1999).
Alam, Javeed, and Suresh Sharma, 'Remembering Partition', *Seminar*, 461 (January 1998).
Ali, Chowdhury Muhammad, *The Emergence of Pakistan* (New York, 1967).
Amin, Shahid, *Event, Metaphor, Memory. Chauri Chaura 1922–1992* (Berkeley and Los Angeles, 1995).
Ansari, Sarah F. D., *Sufi Saints and State Power: the Pirs of Sind, 1843–1947* (Cambridge, 1992).
Appadurai, Arjun, *Modernity at Large. Cultural Dimensions of Globalization* (Minneapolis, 1996).
Asad, Talal, ed., *Anthropology and the Colonial Encounter* (London, 1973).
    'Are there Histories of Peoples without Europe? A Review Article', *Comparative Studies in Society and History*, 29, 3 (1987).
Basu, Aparna, *Mridula Sarabhai: Rebel with a Cause* (Delhi, 1996).

Bauman, Zygmunt, *Modernity and the Holocaust* (Ithaca, N.Y., 1989).
Berger, Stefan, Mark Donovan and Kevin Passmore, eds., *Writing National Histories. Western Europe since 1800* (London, 1999).
Bhabha, Homi K., *The Location of Culture* (London, 1994).
Bhalla, Alok, 'Memory, History and Fictional Representations of the Partition' (forthcoming).
Billig, Michael, *Banal Nationalism* (London, 1995).
Burke, S. M., and Salim al-Din Quraishi, *The British Raj in India. An Historical Review* (Karachi, 1995).
Butalia, Urvashi, 'Community, State and Gender: on Women's Agency During Partition', *Economic and Political Weekly*, 'Review of Women's Studies' (24 April 1993).
  The Other Side of Silence: Voices from the Partition of India (Delhi, 1998).
Cesaire, Aime, *Discourse on Colonialism* (1955; English edn, New York, 1972).
Chakrabarty, Dipesh, 'Postcoloniality and the Artifice of History: Who Speaks for "Indian" Pasts?', *Representations*, 37 (Winter 1992).
  'Remembered Villages. Representation of Hindu-Bengali Memories in the Aftermath of the Partition', *Economic and Political Weekly* (10 August 1996).
Chakravarthy, Renu, *Communists in Indian Women's Movement, 1940–1950* (Delhi, 1980).
Chananana, Karuna, 'Partition and Family Strategies: Gender-Education Linkages among Punjabi Women in Delhi', *Economic and Political Weekly*, 'Review of Women's Studies' (24 April 1993).
Chatterjee, Partha, *The Nation and its Fragments. Colonial and Postcolonial Histories* (Princeton, N.J., 1994).
Chatterji, Joya, *Bengal Divided. Hindu Communalism and Partition, 1932–1947* (Cambridge, 1995).
Daniel, E. Valentine, *Charred Lullabies. Chapters in an Anthropography of Violence* (Princeton, N.J., 1996).
Das, Suranjan, *Communal Riots in Bengal, 1905–1947* (Delhi, 1991).
Das, Veena, *Critical Events: an Anthropological Perspective on Contemporary India* (Delhi, 1995).
  'Official Narratives, Rumour, and the Social Production of Hate', *Social Identities*, 4, 1 (1998).
Das, Veena and Arthur Kleinman, eds., *Violence and Subjectivity* (Berkeley and Los Angeles, 2000).
Diner, Dan, 'Historical Understanding and Counterrationality: the Judenrat as Epistemological Vantage', in Saul Friedlander, ed., *Probing the Limits of Representation. Nazism and the 'Final Solution'* (Cambridge, Mass., 1992).
Dumont, L., *Religion/Politics and History in India* (Paris, 1970).
Elias, Norbert, *The Civilizing Process. Sociogenetic and Psychogenetic Investigations*, revised edn (Oxford, 2000).
Fanon, Frantz, *Black Skin White Masks* (New York, 1967).
  The Wretched of the Earth. Offenses against the Person (London, 1963).
Furet, Francois, *Interpreting the French Revolution* (1978; Cambridge, 1981).
Gilmartin, David, *Empire and Islam: Punjab and the Making of Pakistan* (London, 1988).

'Partition, Pakistan, and South Asian History: in Search of a Narrative', *Journal of Asian Studies*, 57, 4 (November 1998).

'Religious Leadership and the Pakistan Movement in the Punjab', *Modern Asian Studies*, 13, 3 (1979).

Girard, Rene, *Violence and the Sacred* (Baltimore, 1972).

Guha, Ranajit, *Dominance without Hegemony. History and Power in Colonial India* (Cambridge, Mass., 1997).

Elementary Aspects of Peasant Insurgency in Colonial India (Delhi, 1983).

'The Prose of Counter-insurgency', in Ranajit Guha, ed., *Subaltern Studies*, vol. II (Delhi, 1983).

'The Small Voice of History', in Shahid Amin and Dipesh Chakrabarty, eds., *Subaltern Studies*, vol. IX (Delhi, 1996).

Habermas, Jurgen, 'The European Nation-State: on the Past and Future of Sovereignty and Citizenship', *Public Culture*, 10, 2 (1998).

Halbwachs, Maurice, *The Collective Memory* (New York, 1980).

Hasan, Mushirul, ed., *India's Partition. Process, Strategy and Mobilization* (Delhi, 1993).

Legacy of a Divided Nation. India's Muslims since Independence (London, 1997).

Hastings, Adrian, *The Construction of Nationhood. Ethnicity, Religion and Nationalism* (Cambridge, 1997).

Hegel, G. W. F., *Reason in History. A General Introduction to the Philosophy of History*, tr. Robert S. Hartman (Indianopolis, 1953).

Hodson, H. V., *The Great Divide: Britain, India and Pakistan* (London, 1969).

Hunt, Lynn, *Politics, Culture, and Class in the French Revolution* (Berkeley and Los Angeles, 1984).

Jalal, Ayesha, 'Nation, Reason and Religion. Punjab's Role in the Partition of India', *Economic and Political Weekly* (8 August 1998).

'Secularists, Subalterns and the Stigma of "Communalism": Partition Historiography Revisited', *Indian Economic and Social History Review*, 33, 1 (January–March 1996).

The Sole Spokesman: Jinnah, the Muslim League, and the Demand for Pakistan (Cambridge, 1985).

Jeffrey, Robin, 'Grappling with History: Sikh Politicians and the Past', *Pacific Affairs*, 60, 1 (Spring 1987).

Jeganathan, Pradeep, 'After a Riot: Anthropological Locations of Violence in an Urban Sri Lankan Community' (Ph.D. dissertation, University of Chicago, 1997).

Kamal, Ahmed, 'A Land of Eternal Eid – Independence, People, and Politics in East Bengal', *Dhaka University Studies*, part A, 46, 1 (June 1989).

Kapur, Rajiv A., *Sikh Separatism: the Politics of Faith* (London, 1986).

Kaviraj, Sudipto, 'The Imaginary Institution of India', in Partha Chatterjee and Gyanendra Pandey, eds., *Subaltern Studies*, vol. VII (Delhi, 1992).

Khan, Nighat Said, *et al.*, eds., *Locating the Self. Perspectives on Women and Multiple Identities* (Lahore, 1994).

Khan, Shafiq Ali, *The Demand for Pakistan and the CPI* (Karachi, 1986).

Knowlton, James, and Truett Cates, trs., *Forever in the Shadow of Hitler? Original Documents of the Historikerstreit, the Controversy concerning the Singularity of the Holocaust* (Atlantic Highlands, N.J., 1993).

Koselleck, Reinhart, *Futures Past. On the Semantics of Historical Time* (Cambridge, Mass., 1985).

Kuwajima, Sho, *Post-war Upsurge of Freedom Movement and 1946 Provincial Elections in India* (Osaka, 1992).

Langer, Lawrence, *Holocaust Testimonies. The Ruins of Memory* (New Haven, 1991).

Lefebvre, Georges, *The Great Fear* (London, 1973).

Maier, Charles, 'A Surfeit of Memory? Reflections on History, Melancholy and Denial', *History and Memory*, 5 (1993).

Major, Andrew J., '"The Chief Sufferers": Abduction of Women during the Partition of Punjab', *South Asia*, 18 (1995).

Mayaram, Shail, *Resisting Regimes. Myth, Memory and the Shaping of a Muslim Identity* (Delhi, 1997).

Menon, Ritu and Kamla Bhasin, *Borders and Boundaries: Women in India's Partition* (Delhi, 1998).

'Recovery, Rupture, Resistance. Indian State and Abduction of Women during Partition', *Economic and Political Weekly*, 'Review of Women's Studies' (24 April 1993).

Murshid, Tazeen M., *The Sacred and the Secular: Bengal Muslim Discourses, 1871–1977* (Calcutta, 1995).

Nandy, Ashish, *At the Edge of Psychology. Essays in Politics and Culture* (Delhi, 1980).

Nora, Pierre, 'Between Memory and History: Les Lieux de Memoire', *Representations*, 26 (Spring 1989).

Rethinking the French Past. Realms of Memory. Volume I: Conflicts and Divisions, English edn (New York, 1996).

Novick, Peter, *The Holocaust in American Life* (Boston and New York, 1999).

Page, David, *Prelude to Partition. Indian Muslims and the Imperial System of Control, 1920–1932* (Delhi, 1982).

Pakistan Historical Society, *A History of the Freedom Movement in Pakistan* (1970; reprinted, Delhi, 1984), 4 volumes.

Pandey, Gyanendra, 'Can a Muslim be an Indian?', *Comparative Studies in Society and History*, 41, 4 (1999).

'Community and Violence', *Economic and Political Weekly* (9 August 1997).

Memory, History and the Question of Violence. Reflections on the Reconstruction of Partition (Calcutta, 1999).

'Partition and Independence in Delhi, 1947–48', *Economic and Political Weekly* (6 September 1997).

The Construction of Communalism in Colonial North India (Delhi, 1990).

'The Prose of Otherness', in David Hardiman and David Arnold, eds., *Subaltern Studies*, VIII (Delhi, 1994).

Philips, C. H., and M. D. Wainright, eds., *The Partition of India. Policies and Perspectives, 1935–1947* (London, 1970).

Qureshi, I. H., *The Muslim Community of the Indo-Pakistan Subcontinent, 610–1947: a Brief Historical Analysis* (The Hague, 1962).

Rai, Satya M., *Partition of the Punjab* (London, 1965).

Ricouer, Paul, *Time and Narrative*, vol. III, tr. Kathleen Blamey and David Pellauer (Chicago, 1985).

Roy, Asim, 'The High Politics of India's Partition', review article, *Modern Asian Studies*, 24, 2 (1990).

Said, Edward, *Orientalism* (New York, 1979).

Sarkar, Sumit, *A Critique of Colonial India* (Calcutta, 1985).

Modern India, 1885–1947 (Delhi, 1983).

Sayeed, Khalid bin, *Pakistan: the Formative Phase, 1857–1948*, 2nd edn (London, 1968).

Seminar, 'Partition' number (August 1994).

Shaikh, Farzana, *Community and Consensus in Islam: Muslim Representation in Colonial India, 1860–1947* (Cambridge, 1989).

Singh, Anita Inder, *The Origins of the Partition of India* (Delhi, 1987).

Singh, Harbans, *The Heritage of the Sikhs*, revised edn (Delhi, 1994).

South Asia, 18, Special Issue on 'North India: Partition and Independence' (1995).

Stephens, Ian, *Pakistan* (New York, 1963).

Symonds, Richard, *The Making of Pakistan* (London, 1950).

Talbot, Ian, *Freedom's Cry. The Popular Dimension in the Pakistan Movement and Partition Experience in North-West India* (Karachi, 1996).

Provincial Politics and the Pakistan Movement: the Growth of the Muslim League in North-West and North-East India, 1937–47 (Karachi, 1988).

Waseem, Mohammad, 'Partition, Migration and Assimilation: a Comparative Study of Pakistani Punjab', in Ian Talbot and Gurharpal Singh, eds., *Region and Partition. Bengal, Punjab and the Partition of the Subcontinent* (Karachi, 1999).

Williams, Brackette F., 'A Class Act: Anthropology and the Race to Nation across Ethnic Terrain', *Annual Review of Anthropology*, 18 (1989).

Wolpert, Stanley, *Jinnah of Pakistan* (New York, 1984).

Yong, Tan Tai, 'Prelude to Partition: Sikh Responses to the Demand for Pakistan, 1940–47', *International Journal of Punjab Studies*, 1, 2 (1994).

Young, James E., *Writing and Rewriting the Holocaust. Narrative and the Consequences of Interpretation* (Bloomington, 1988).

Ziegler, Philip, *Mountbatten* (New York, 1985).

Zurcher, Eric-Jan, and W. van Schendel, eds., *Opting Out of the Nation. Identity Politics in Central, South and West Asia* (London, 1999).

Index

abduction, *see* women, abducted
Abdullah, Sheikh, 143, 155
adivasis, 28
Africa, 1n, 18, 56, 61
Agra, 35, 133, 136
Ajmal Khan, Hakim, 200
Ajmer, 35
Akali Dal, 32, 33
Alam, Javeed, 58–60, 61, 62, 65
Algu Rai Shastri, 102
Ali, Ahmed, 135, 185–6
Ali, Athar, 53
Ali, Maulana Mohamed, 155
Aligarh, 27, 43
    Muslim University, 29, 42, 43
Alwar State, 38, 39, 144–5, 165, 196,
    198
    refugees in Delhi, 122–3
Ambala, 38
Amin, Shahid, 94
Amrit Kaur, Rajkumari, 38
Amritsar, 23, 35, 36, 38, 149, 151,
    178
Anglo-Indians, 20, 156–7, 158, 159,
    169–70
Ansari, Mukhtar Ahmad, 155, 200
Anthony, Frank, 159
Arabia, 7, 157, 158
Asad, Muhammad, 119
Asad, Talal, 12
Assam, 37, 111
Attlee, Clement, 40
Aurangzeb (Mughal emperor), 53, 195
Australia, 63, 157, 168, 177
Ayodhya, 177, 200
    see also Babri Masjid
Azad, Abul Kalam, 29, 123, 128, 143,
    155, 172, 199

Babri Masjid, 59, 192, 200
Bahawalpur, 39, 89, 90
Baldev Singh, Sardar, 33, 40

Balkanisation, 1n, 48
Baluchistan, 183
Banaras, 55
Bangladesh, 6, 13, 14, 16, 20, 43, 53,
    61, 133, 151, 201
Barelvi, Ebadat, 128, 135, 136–7, 138,
    148, 185, 187, 199–200
Basu, Aparna, 117–18
Baynes, F.W.W., 71, 110
Beas, 149
Bengal, 37, 42, 111, 186
    division of, 31–5, 42
    Muslim League, 30
    and Partition, 14, 18, 40, 169
    see also East Bengal
Bengali *bhadralok*, 31, 186
Bhalla, Alok, 62, 63
Bharatiya Janata Party, 201
Bharatpur, 39, 144–5, 196
Bhasin, Kamla, 68, 89
Bhopal, 32, 93
Bihar, 14, 23, 24, 25, 29, 32, 37, 71,
    92, 95, 98, 102, 103, 107, 111,
    113–14, 115, 131, 132, 162
Billig, Michael, 176
Bir Bahadur Singh, 84, 85, 192
Bombay, 23, 25, 37, 92, 125, 157
Bose, Subhas Chandra, 97
Bosnia, 63, 121
Braudel, Fernand, 12
Buddhists, 156, 158, 177
Burke, S.M., 115
Butalia, Urvashi, 68, 84, 89, 192

Cabinet Mission plan, 22, 26, 33, 40
Calcutta, 23, 24, 25, 52, 90, 92, 95, 98,
    103, 131, 180
    Calcutta killings and Garhmukhteshwar,
    92, 95, 98, 102, 103
    and Gandhi, 142
capitalism, 7, 8, 12–13, 27–8, 51, 93,
    119, 135

Cariappa, Major-General K.M., 161
caste, 19, 55, 64, 156, 157, 160, 165,
    186, 187
    see also Dalits, 'untouchables'
Caveeshar, Sardar Singh, 32
Central Provinces, 37
    see also Madhya Pradesh
Chakmas, 20, 43
Chakrabarty, Dipesh, 13, 119
Chakravarthy, Renu, 118
Chandigarh, 178
Chatterjee, Partha, 13
Chatterji, Joya, 31, 59
Chaudhuri, Nirad, 56–7
Chauri Chaura, 94
children, 65, 111, 173
China, 7, 176n
Chittagong Hill Tracts, 43
Christians, 17, 60, 61, 152, 156, 158,
    180, 205
    see also Roman Catholics
citizenship, conditions of, 17, 20,
    158–9, 160, 164
civil disobedience campaigns, 23
Civil and Military Gazette, 153
'civilisation'
    and Europe, 7
    in Indian history, 54–6
    and violence, 6, 52–6, 70, 177
Cold War, 1
colonialism, 1n, 12, 63–4, 71
    and capitalism, 135
    colonial account of Garhmukhteshwar
        violence, 108–14
    colonialist historiography, 48, 61–2,
        81
    decolonisation, 1, 48
    and the 'local', 120
    and right-wing politics, 104
communalism, 48, 53, 163, 187
Communist Party, 29, 98, 99, 118
community, 1, 7, 43, 66, 139–42, 152,
    156, 160, Ch. 8 passim
    and capitalism, 8, 13
    relationship with violence, 3–4, 175,
        188–91
Congress, 14, 21, 22, 23, 27–8, 32, 40,
    51, 141
    account of Garhmukhteshwar, 96–7,
        101–4, 105, 107, 109–10, 115
    and secularism, 6, 115, 142
    see also Gandhi; Nehru; Patel
Constituent Assembly, 159, 163, 164,
    166, 170
    of Pakistan, 41, 153

Croce, Benedetto, 4 & n
Cyprus, 1

Daily Mail, 36
Dalits, 17, 20, 64, 140, 150, 185
Das, Veena, 68
Das, Durga, 161
Das, Suranjan, 52, 59
Dawn, 28, 99, 107–8
decolonisation, 1, 48
Dehlavi, Shahid Admad, 128, 132,
    135–6, 142, 146–50, 149–50,
    185, 186–7, 196, 199
Dehradun, 37
Delhi, 14, 35, 111, 120, 121–51,
    132–9, 142–51, 184–7,
    199–200
    Partition violence in, 24, 56–7,
        128–32, 136–8, 183–7
    refugee camps in, 123, 124, 131–2,
        137, 138, 139–42, 148, 149, 185
    refugees in, 38, 122–3, 122–4, 126,
        131, 143, 186–7
democracy, 6, 8, 17, 19, 28–9, 53, 63,
    135, 142, 153, 200, 205
    see also majorities; minorities
difference, 17, 61, 64, 127, 132, 139,
    205
    in the construction of nationhood, 17,
        20, Ch. 7 passim
    and the needs of a modern state,
        160–4
    see also minorities; women
Dumont, Louis, 53

East Bengal, 23, 42, 102, 103, 108, 170
    see also Noakhali
East Pakistan, 43, 201
    see also East Bengal
East Punjab, 32, 33, 37, 41, 72, 90, 104,
    111, 139, 154, 165, 174, 178, 195
    see also Gharuan
Egypt, 61
Elias, Norbert, 54
England, 157, 168, 205
Europe, 7, 12, 58, 119

Falklands War, 177
Fazl-ul-Haq, 155
Ferozepur, 36
feudalism, 7
France, 10, 12, 47
French Revolution, 47, 49–50, 52,
    68, 70
Furet, François, 49–50, 52

Gandhi, Mohandas Karamchand
(Mahatma), 21, 25, 27, 29, 72, 101,
126, 127, 134, 140–1, 142–6,
148–9, 176, 199, 200
assassination of, 142, 144–6, 159
and the return of abducted women, 165,
174
Gangauli (Ghazipur district), 198, 201
Garhmukhteshwar, 23, 69, 70–1, Ch. 5
passim, 131
genocide, 1, 5, 45, 59, 67, 204
Germany, 59, 59–60, 63, 121, 177
nationalism in, 46, 47
Ghalib, 200
Ghanzanfar Ali Khan, 100–1, 105, 106
Gharuan (Patiala State), 177–83, 184,
185, 186, 195, 196, 199
Ghazipur district, 198, 201
Gilmartin, David, 59
globalisation, 12, 203
Glover, Jonathan, 184
Gobind Singh, Guru, 24
Godse, Nathuram, 161
Gramsci, Antonio, 4
Guha, Ranajit, 13, 68, 69–70, 79, 81
Gujarat, 25
Gulab Singh, Sant, 85, 190, 195
Gulf War, 177
Gurdaspur, 43, 164
Gurgaon, 114, 131

Habermas, Jürgen, 46n, 47n, 59–60
Halbwachs, Maurice, 8, 9
Hapur, 95, 96, 101, 102
Haq, Fazlul, 30
Hardwar, 37
Hasan, Mushirul, 51, 59
Hashim, Abul, 30, 40
Hazaribagh, 169, 170
Hegel, G.W.F., 9–10, 11, 54–5
Hindu Mahasabha, 29, 31, 34, 35n, 81,
144
Hindu nationalism, 133, 154–6, 163–4
see also Hindu Mahasabha; nationalism;
right-wing politics
Hindus, 2, 14, 16, 20, 23, 26, 27–8, 31,
34, 50, 51–2, 59, 61, 68–9, 133,
151, 159–60, 164–5, 166, 167–8,
191, 198–96
and the assassination of Gandhi, 144–5,
159
at Garhmukhteshwar, 94–5, 98–9, 101,
102, 103–4, 105, 115, 117
at Thoa Khalsa, 84–8
in Delhi, 130, 131, 134, 185–6

in the Punjab, 25, 75–6, 81–2
refugees, 38–9
at Amritsar, 149
in Delhi, 124, 127, 128, 137, 139,
140, 143–4, 186–7
and Indian Muslims, 163
right-wing, 6, 61, 64, 96, 104, 144–5
Hindustan Times, 71, 97, 103, 161
Hindustani, see Urdu
Hissar district, 98, 114
historiography, 1, 3, 4–13, 15–16, 18–19,
Ch. 3 passim
history, 4–13, 15–17, 175–7, 205
evidence in, 11, 66, Ch. 4 passim
and memory, 6, 7–12, 175–7
and testimony, 67, 69, 71, 88, 91
see also historiography; memory
Holocaust, 3, 7, 8, 15, 45, 46, 59–60, 67,
188
Hunter, W.W., 55–6
Husain, Intizar, 43, 198, 200, 202–3
Husain, Zakir, 131–2, 155, 199
Hyderabad, 32, 43, 133, 199

Independence, 1, 6, 13–15, 18–20, 25–31,
26, 31–44, 33, 40, 48, 124–7,
153–4, 168–74, 176, 198
Independent (London), 119
Indian Mutiny, 113, 114, 136
Indian National Army, 97, 109
Indian National Congress, see Congress
Iran, 157, 158
Ireland, 1
Iskandar Mirza, 107
Israel, 61
Italy, 4
Izzard, Ralph, 36

Jains, 156, 158
Jalal, Ayesha, 30–1, 51, 59
Jalandhar, 72, 149, 173
Jan Sangh, 201
Japan, 7, 60, 98, 157, 176n
Jats, 24–5, 98–9, 101, 103, 108–9, 110,
114, 191
Jews, 46, 61, 119, 152
Jhelum district, 34
Jinnah, Mohammed Ali, 21–2, 26, 27, 28,
29, 30, 31, 41, 51, 82, 107, 110,
153, 155, 170, 199
Josh Malihabadi, 133, 171

Kalka, 38
Kampuchea, 63
Kapurthala state, 72

Karachi, 36, 128, 129
Kartar Singh, Giani, 33, 40n
Kashmir, 19, 38, 43, 166
Khaliquzzaman, Choudhry, 170
Khalistan, movement for, 17
Khan Sahib, Dr, 83
Khan, Shah Nawaz, 97, 98, 101, 103–4
Khan, Ustad Bade Ghulam Ali, 170
Khizr Hayat Khan, 23, 83
Khosla, G.D., 83, 89, 116, 127, 134,
    139, 195
Korea, 1
Koselleck, Reinhart, 50
Kripalani, J.B., 102–3

Lahore, 14, 23, 35, 36, 39, 125, 133,
    151, 178, 196, 199–200
Langer, Lawrence, 67
Lari, Z.H., 170
Lefebvre, Georges, 68, 70
left-wing politics, 51
    see also Communist Party; socialism
Liaqat Ali Khan, 30
local, as against national and global, 46,
    62, 63, Ch. 5 passim
Lohia, Dr Ram Manohar, 161
Lucknow, 107, 133, 136, 138, 171
Ludhiana, 113, 149–50

Macaulay, 113
Madhya Pradesh, 37, 40
Madras, 25, 37
Mahmudabad, Raja of, 162
majorities, notion of, 26–35, 152,
    159–60, 164, 168–9
Malabar, 32, 132
Malda, 43
Manto, Sa'adat Hasan, 43
Mapillas, 132
Marmas, 43
martyrdom, 24, 83, 84–8, 190, 192–5,
    201
    of Gandhi, 143, 145
Mayaram, Shail, 196
Meerut, 37, 95, 96, 97–8, 99, 101, 102,
    117, 149
memoirs, 135–9, 146–51, 184–7
memory, 6, 7–12, 16, 17, 65, 96, 111,
    175–200
Menon, Ritu, 68, 89
mentalities, 16, 65
Meos, 36, 39, 122, 132, 196, 198
Messervy, Frank, 81
Mewat, 36, 39, 198
Mexico, 157

migration, 1n, 14–15, 35–9, 189, 199,
    202 and n, 205
    see also refugees
Mill, James, 55
minorities, 17, 20, 28, 32, 41–2, 64, 115,
    151, 152–73, 205
modernity, 13, 57
Modinagar, 103
Momins, 132
Montgomery, 36
Moon, Penderel, 38, 40, 52, 89–90
Moore, Arthur, 143–4
Moors, 61
Moradabad, 172
Mountbatten, Louis, 1st Earl Mountbatten
    of Burma, 30, 39–40, 89, 139
Mudie, Sir Francis, 90
Mughal Empire, 53, 56, 57, 58, 200
Multan, 23–4, 126, 191
Muslim League, 41, 51, 169
    and the division of Punjab and Bengal,
        31–2, 35
    and the establishment of Pakistan, 21–2,
        23, 25–31, 82
    and the Garhmukhteshwar violence, 96,
        99–101, 104–8, 109–10, 115,
        117
Muslim nationalism, 154, 155–6
    see also Muslim League; Nationalist
        Muslims; Pakistan
Muslims, 2, 14, 16, 17, 20, 24, 34–5,
    50–2, 59, 61, 68–9, 84–8, 94–5, 96,
    99, 100–1, 103–4, 105–7, 110–11,
    115, 117, 121, 151, 153–4, 166–8,
    170–3, 198–9
    at Gharuan, 178, 179, 180–2
    in Delhi, 32, 127, 128–32, 134, 135–9,
        142–51, 184–7, 187
    in refugee camps, 139–42
    returning refugees, 150
    and Indian nationalism, 154–5, 157–9,
        161–3, 169
    in the Punjab, 25, 40, 74–9, 80, 82–4
    refugees, 36, 37–8, 39
    from Delhi, 122–4, 128–9
    violence against, 72
    in Spain and North Africa, 61
    see also Meos; Muslim League; Muslim
        nationalism; Nationalist Muslims
Musselmann, 67
Mussoorie, 127
Muzaffarnagar, 149

Nabha, 40
Nanak, Guru, 85, 142

nation-states, 4, 8, 9, 19, 177, 205
  emergence of, 1, 5–6, 17, 18, 153–4
national, as against local, 93–4, 119–20
nationalism, 6–7, 9, 11–12, 18, 29, 53,
  135, 152, 152–3, 154–6, 160,
  163–4, 168, 169–70, 176–7, 203
  British, 168–9
  French, 47
  German, 46, 47
  see also Hindu nationalism; Muslim
  nationalism
Nationalist Muslims, 22, 29, 107, 154,
  155–6
Nazis, 57, 59–60, 63, 121, 161, 177
Nehru, Jawaharlal, 6, 22, 25, 35–6, 37,
  41, 56, 116–17, 126, 130,
  134, 143–4, 155, 166, 171
Nehru, Rameshwari, 87–8, 168, 172,
  173
New Delhi, 129, 130
  see also Delhi
New World, 1n, 56, 63
New Yorker, 11
Nizami, Khwaja Hasan, 136
Noakhali, 25, 92, 95, 98, 100, 104, 107,
  131, 196
  see also East Bengal
nomenclature, 1, 13–15, 189
Nora, Pierre, 8, 10, 11
North West Frontier Province, 22, 23,
  32, 37, 83, 131
Novick, Peter, 8

oral history, 65, 91
  see also history; memory
Orientalism, 1
Orissa, 111

Pakistan, 2, 13–14, 16, 17, 18, 20, 23,
  35, 36, 42, 42–3, 50, 51, 82, 140,
  145–6, 149–50, 151, 153–4, 158,
  161–2, 164, 167–8, 170–2, 173,
  196, 202–3
  establishment of, 2, 5, 21–3, 25–31, 158
  evacuation of government personnel to,
  128, 129
  movement for, 6, 21–2, 23, 25–31
  non-Muslims in, 61, 151, 170
  splitting up of, 5–6
Pakistan Times, 33, 34–5
Palestine, 1, 61
Parsis, 156, 157, 158, 159
Patel, Vallabhbhai, 38, 162–3, 164, 172
Patiala state, 170
  see also Gharuan

Pathans, 85, 166
Paul Ricouer, 45
peasant struggles, 29, 68, 69, 94, 118
Peshawar, 34
Progressive Writers' Movement, 133, 171
Punjab, 14, 16–17, 18, 23–5, 35–6, 40, 72,
  74–84, 92, 98, 99, 101, 108–9, 114,
  139, 163, 165–6, 174, 196, 198
  division of, 31–5
  estimates of the dead in, 89–90
  and the Muslim League, 22, 26, 28–9,
  30
  refugees, 24, 41–2, 83, 131, 154
Punjabi Suba, 17

Qidwai, Begum Anees, 73, 128, 131,
  138, 139–40, 148, 173
Qidwai, Rafi Ahmed, 100, 109, 123,
  138
Qidwai, Shafi Ahmed, 138
Quraishi, Salim al-Din, 115
Qureshi, Ishtiaq Husain, 128, 133,
  137–8, 148

Rajputs, 88
Rampur, 32
Randhawa, M.S., 38, 144
rape, 2, 15, 35, 59, 61, 62, 68, 69, 73,
  104, 111, 169, 183–4
Rashtriya Svayamsevak Sangh, 98, 99,
  101, 137, 144
Rawalpindi district, 23–4, 25, 34, 74–84,
  82, 84–8, 126, 190–1, 192–4, 195
Raza, Rahi Masoom, 198, 200–2
refugees, 2, 35–9, 41–2, 121–4,
  126, 127, 128, 131, 137, 139, 140,
  143–4, 149, 151, 154, 163, 169,
  186–7
  camps, 24, 37, 82, 123, 124, 131–2,
  137, 138, 139–42, 148, 149, 185
religion
  in Indian historiography, 53–4, 65
  religious and national affiliation, 132–4
right-wing politics, 6, 61, 64, 96, 98,
  99, 102–3, 104, 108, 144–5,
  197, 201
  right wing histories, 62–3
Rohtak, 98, 99, 101, 108–9, 114
Roman Catholics, 130, 205
Rude, George, 68
rumour, 67, 68, 69–74, 79–84, 89, 91,
  96, 111
Rushdie, Salman, 119
Russia, 59
Rwanda, 63, 121

Sahni, Bhishma, 151
Salam. M.A., 162
Sampurnanand, 161
Sarabhai, Mridula, 97, 98, 101, 102,
    104, 117
Sarkar, Jadunath, 58
Sarkar, Sumit, 51–2, 92
secularism, 6, 115, 141, 142, 153,
    155, 161, 163–4
Serbia, 59, 121
Shahjahanpur, 95, 102
Shah Jahan, 122, 185
Sharif al-Mujahid, 115
Sharma, Suresh, 60–2
Sheikhupura, 36
Shimla, 38, 127, 139
Shiromani Gurudwara Prabandhak
    Committee, 86, 192, 194
Sialkot, 39
Sikhs, 2, 6, 14, 16–17, 20, 23, 24–5,
    26, 40, 59, 74–9, 80, 81–2, 84–8,
    128–9, 130, 131, 134, 156,
    164–5, 166, 167–8, 190, 190–1,
    192–5
  and division of Punjab and Bengal,
    31–5
  refugees, 38–9
  at Amritsar, 149
  in Delhi, 124, 127, 128, 137, 139,
    140, 143–4, 186–7
  and Indian Muslims, 163
  right-wing political movements, 6
Sindh, 22, 26, 37, 39, 42, 83, 131
Singh, Master Tara, 32
Singh Sabha movement, 24
Singh, Thakur Phool, 102
Sleeman, W.H., 112, 113
Smith, W.C., 50, 53
Sobti, Krishna, 126, 132
socialism, 28–9, 47, 161
Spain, 60–1
Sri Lanka, 133, 177
state
  history and the state, 9–10, 56
  needs of modern statehood,
    160–4
Statesman, 90, 134, 169
Stephens, Ian, 90
subject positions (in history), 15–16,
    20, 204
Suhrawardy, Hassan, 26
Suhrawardy, Husain, 30, 40, 41–2,
    72
suicides, see martyrdom
Symonds, Richard, 90

Talbot, Ian, 59
Telengana, 118
testimony, as a category of historical
    evidence, 67, 69, 71, 88, 91, 111
Thapar, Premvati, 167
Thapar, Ram Chandra, 195–6
Theresa, Mother, 180
Third World, 11, 65, 203n
Thoa Khalsa (Rawalpindi district), 24,
    82, 84–8, 190, 192–4
Thugs, 112–13
Times of India, 11
Times (London), 11, 25
Toba Tek Singh, 43
Trivedi, Chandulal, 89
Tuker, Sir Francis, 96, 105, 109, 110–12,
    113–14, 114–15
Turkey, 157, 158
Tyabji, Badruddin, 155
Tyagi, Mahavir, 163

United States of America, 7, 157, 177
'untouchables', 28, 64, 156
UP (Uttar Pradesh), 14, 24, 32, 37, 41,
    69, 111, 132, 138, 154, 162,
    170
Urdu, 133, 135–6, 158n, 171, 186

Vaid, Sudesh, 84
Vartman, 156, 157–8
Vietnam, 1, 60, 157
violence, 2, 3, 6, 15, 17–18, 23–5, 35–9,
    52–8, 56–7, 59, 68, 79, 80, 89–91,
    128–32, 136–8, 150–1, 164, 169,
    176, 177–99, 183–4, 190–9
  and civilisation, 52–6, 70, 177
  historians' history of, 45–6, 50–1,
    50–66
  historiography of, 15–16, 52–8, 67–91,
    189
  and refugees, 35–9, 71–2
  relationship with community, 3–4, 175,
    188–91
Vishwa Hindu Parishad, 59

Wah, 81, 82
Waseem, Mohammad, 89
welfare state, 6
West Bengal, 37
  see also Bengal
West Pakistan, 126, 127, 137, 154, 170,
    201
West Punjab, 24–5, 32, 37, 41, 83, 89–90,
    104, 131, 132, 149, 165, 178,
    179

Wolf, Eric, 12
women, 19, 20, 64, 65
  abducted, 24, 68, 72, 73, 75, 99,
    105–6, 178, 179, 181, 182–3
  recovery of, 133, 165–8, 172–4,
    182–3
  and citizenship rights, 17
  and collective suicide, 24, 83, 84–8, 190,
    192–4
  social workers, 73, 87–8

and the Telengana peasant uprising, 118
  violence against, 2, 15, 68–9, 72–7, 103,
    104–7, 110–11, 113, 114, 115, 121,
    183–4
  see also rape
World War II, 21, 60
Wylie, F.V., 69

Zauq, 200
Ziegler, Philip, 89